PIRATES OF THE SLAVE TRADE

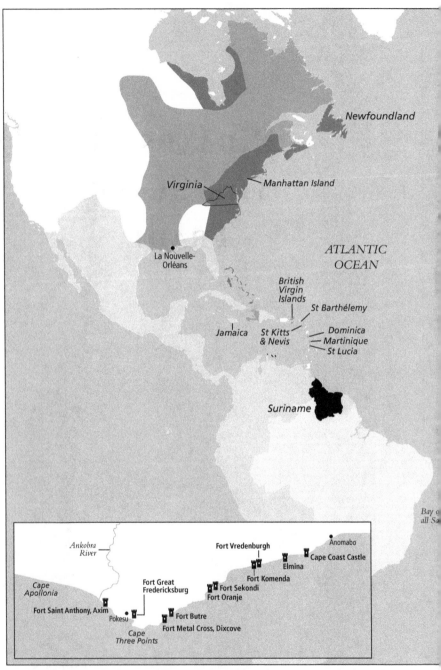

Locations indicated on this map are reflective of the ways in which settlers and human traffickers from European nations wrote about the Atlantic world in 1722. Like most maps depicting the world during this era, this map is a projection of European understanding, desire, and intent. It fails to represent the ways in which people indigenous to Africa and the Americas thought of the world.

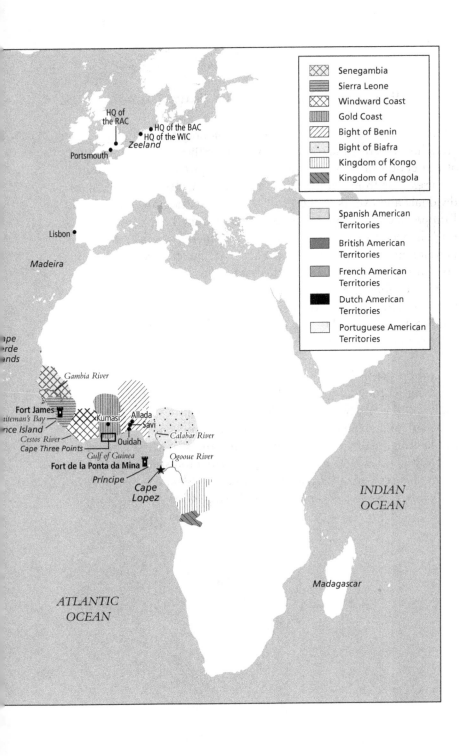

Senegambia
Sierra Leone
Windward Coast
Gold Coast
Bight of Benin
Bight of Biafra
Kingdom of Kongo
Kingdom of Angola

Spanish American Territories
British American Territories
French American Territories
Dutch American Territories
Portuguese American Territories

HQ of the RAC
HQ of the BAC
HQ of the WIC
Zeeland
Portsmouth

Lisbon

Madeira

ape
rde
ands

Gambia River

Fort James
iteman's Bay
nce Island
Cestos River
Cape Three Points

Kumasi
Ouidah

Allada
Savi

Calabar River

Gulf of Guinea
Fort de la Ponta da Mina

Príncipe

Cape
Lopez

Ogooue River

INDIAN
OCEAN

Madagascar

ATLANTIC
OCEAN

PIRATES OF THE SLAVE TRADE

The Battle of Cape Lopez and the Birth of an American Institution

Angela C. Sutton

Prometheus Books

Essex, Connecticut

PB Prometheus Books

An imprint of Globe Pequot, the trade division of
The Rowman & Littlefield Publishing Group, Inc.
4501 Forbes Boulevard, Suite 200, Lanham, Maryland 20706
www.rowman.com

Distributed by NATIONAL BOOK NETWORK

British Library Cataloguing in Publication Information Available

Library of Congress Cataloging-in-Publication Data

Names: Sutton, Angela (Angela Christine), author.
Title: Pirates of the slave trade : The battle of Cape Lopez
  and the birth of an American institution / Angela C. Sutton.
Other titles: Pirate battle of Cape Lopez and the birth of American slavery
Description: Lanham, MD : Prometheus Books, [2023] | Includes
  bibliographical references and index. | Summary: "No one present at the
  Battle of Cape Lopez in 1722 could have known that they were on the edge
  of history. Gentlemen of Fortune is a groundbreaking exploration of the
  figures and events surrounding this lesser-known naval battle, the
  outcome of which signaled a major turning point in the Atlantic slave
  trade and triggered a deep and lasting legacy"— Provided by publisher.
Identifiers: LCCN 2023000737 (print) | LCCN 2023000738 (ebook) | ISBN
  9781633888449 (cloth) | ISBN 9781633888456 (epub)
Subjects: LCSH: Pirates—Africa, West—History—18th century. | Cape Lopez,
  Battle of, Gabon, 1722. | Slave trade—Africa, West—History. | Ogle,
  Chaloner, Sir, 1681?–1750. | Roberts, Bartholomew, 1682?–1722. | Conny,
  John, 165?– | Slave trade—Great Britain—History—18th century. | Slave
  trade—Africa, West—History—18th century. | Royal Fortune (Frigate) |
  Africa, West—History—18th century.
Classification: LCC DT476 .S88 2023 (print) | LCC DT476 (ebook) | DDC
  966/.02—dc23/eng/20230328
LC record available at https://lccn.loc.gov/2023000737
LC ebook record available at https://lccn.loc.gov/2023000738

To Captain Tomba and all the others who resisted.

May you rest in power, and may you live on,
in each of us, through what is to come.

Contents

Acknowledgments

THIS PROJECT SMACKED ME in the face while I was in the middle of my doctoral thesis in Atlantic history, which investigated the mercantile networks and culture of traffickers in seventeenth- and early-eighteenth-century West Africa. I'm grateful to my doctoral adviser, Dr. Jane Landers at Vanderbilt University, for not allowing me to be distracted by the flashy pirates and for convincing me that I needed to carefully track the traders first to explain why the pirates mattered so much. She nurtured my love of collecting the primary sources in the English, Dutch, and Prussian records about John Conny, who is perhaps the most compelling historical figure of this story.

This book was an expensive project. Without the generosity of funders, the costs would have been prohibitive. Thank you to Vanderbilt University and especially the history department and Max Kade Center for the stipends and travel funding to visit forts in Ghana, the British National Archives in London, and the Secret State Archives of Prussian Cultural Heritage in Berlin. Thank you to the Fulbright Foundation and the Netherland-America Foundation for sponsoring a year in the Netherlands at the Dutch National Archives and the Royal Library in the Hague, and the KITLV at the University of Leiden for the wonderful year of affiliation and fellowship while there. Thank you also to the Nederlandse Taalunie for supplementing the costs of the seventeenth-century Dutch reading and paleography courses at Columbia University. I'm deeply appreciative of all the archivists and librarians who hunted through basements, databases, and software to help me find not only what I asked for, but what I didn't know I needed. Finally, the American Council of Learned Societies and the Andrew W. Mellon Foundation's Dissertation Completion Fellowship allowed me some time in Sweden's National Archives, and the extra year of writing to synthesize my ideas and figure out which threads from my dissertation needed to move forward to tell the story of the 1722 Battle of Cape Lopez. It's an embarrassment of riches and all researchers and storytellers should be as privileged.

The number of colleagues, both scholars and professional writers, who have touched this work and helped me think about it in better ways are too numerous to list here. A big thanks goes to Kirsty Logan, whose grasp of techniques helped me transform the necessary facts into fascinating details that support the story and whose twenty-plus years of friendship and encouragement have helped shape my writing in countless ways. Thank you also to my friends at the Association of Caribbean Historians for your thoughtful comments and conversations about my presentations and other topics from the book in Curaçao and Barbados. Your generosity and fellowship remains unrivaled. Thank you to archaeologist Chris de Corse for taking me along with your students on your survey of Fort Great Fredericksburg with Ben Kankpeyengin in Pokesu (Princes Town), Ghana. I learned so much about what the land, architecture, and artifacts can tell us about people who weren't in the position to leave behind documents or whose documents were not valued by colonial record-keeping institutions. Chaz Yingling, I appreciate you and the way you think about the world. Thanks to Colin Nicolson at the University of Stirling, Scotland, who taught me how to use a microfilm reader and is still proud of me after all these years.

I am also grateful to my students who were never afraid to ask the real questions. Thank you especially to the Naval Reserve Officers Training Corps (NROTC) students from Belmont University, Tennessee State University, and Vanderbilt University who learned sea power in history with me, and my students who took my piracy and slavery classes through Vanderbilt's Osher Lifelong Learning Institute (OLLI). You brought a pirate into class who taught us sea chanties and you gifted me a pirate flag and fragrant oranges from your visits to Charleston and Saint Augustine, and these are the interactions good books are made of.

An unpayable intellectual debt goes to the late James Baldwin, whose words always help me get my head on right. Thank you, Marcus Rediker, for writing the books I grew up on that taught me that history consisted of more than dates and the elite and to Kelly Baker Josephs and Roopika Risam for creating the book with the ideas that opened new horizons. Finally, a big thanks goes to the interdisciplinary Black Studies in Digital Humanities working group at Vanderbilt University. It's an honor to learn alongside each of you as we make the interventions that tell the stories that matter. In the publishing world, Erik Hane at Headwater Literary and Jake Bonar at Prometheus Books have spent a lot of time with me, patiently helping me transform my academic research into trade nonfiction. That transition isn't easy or intuitive, and I thank you both for investing in me and in what I hope is the first such story of many.

Final thanks go to Sean Jamal Cardell for not laughing (too hard) at my (many) rants about the audacity and inhumanity of the enslavers whose thoughts I have been working with for far too long. I am grateful to get these thoughts out of my head and into yours, dear reader.

Reader's Note

THE PRACTICE OF "DOUBLE DATING" was common during the transition from the Julian to Gregorian calendar dates. Where manuscripts noted both dates, they were converted to the Gregorian dates. So, for example, January 1, 1718/1719 would be January 1, 1719.

There are many versions of each person and place name used in this book. All names have been Anglicized and/or standardized for an English-reading audience. For example, John Conny was also known as Jan Conny, Jan Konny, Johan Kuny, Johann Cuny, January Konny, Johannes Conrad, John Conni, John Canoe, Nana Konneh, or Nyanyi Kenu, depending on who wrote about him. As far as we know, John Conny himself never wrote his own name (though the gold-headed cane that one of Conny's officers carried had "John Conny" carved on it, according to the account of naval surgeon John Atkins), and most likely used multiple versions of his name depending on who he was speaking with. This was a common practice among West African cultural brokers, or caboceers, at the time. John Cabes, the caboceer from Komenda after whom John Conny styled himself, is often referred to in the sources as John Kabes, as well.

Similarly, to avoid confusion, I use the term "Ashanti" to refer to both the Twi-speaking Ashante/Asante people, as well as the things that are of them and their empire (Ashanti). Most names of fortifications and ships also have been anglicized for the same reason (for example, Fort Groot Friedrichsburg, or Conny's Castle, became Fort Great Fredericksburg, and the Portuguese ship pirated in the Bay of Bahia, the *Sagrada Familia*, became the *Sacred Family*).

Some abbreviations appear in the text and the references, mainly with regard to the European slave trading companies, and the archives in which their documentation appears:

RAC—English Royal Africa Company
WIC—Dutch West India Company
BAC—Prussian Brandenburg African Company
SAC—Swedish Africa Company
BNA—British National Archives, Kew, London, United Kingdom
CO—Colonial Office, London, United Kingdom
NA—National Archives, The Hague, Netherlands
KITLV—Royal Netherlands Institute of Southeast Asian & Caribbean Studies, Leiden, Netherlands
GStA PK—Prussian Secret State Archives, Berlin, Germany
RA—Royal Archives, Stockholm, Sweden

Introduction

Gentlemen of Fortune

IN JANUARY 1722, a fleet more than two hundred pirates strong boldly followed Captain Bartholomew "Black Bart" Roberts's flagship, the *Royal Fortune*, into Ouidah harbor, a neutral African slave-trading port with international presence in what would become coastal Benin. There, the pirates forced the kidnapped musicians onboard to play louder as they rounded up nearly a dozen slave ships anchored in the harbor. The captains of those ships, who were on land negotiating for enslaved captives, watched from the shore with wary eyes as their crews onboard the ships surrendered one by one rather than face death. When the captains rowed to the pirates to negotiate for their ships, the pirates extorted them. The captains could either pay eight pounds of gold apiece to get them back, or they could watch their ships burn right there in the harbor. To show them he meant business, Black Bart ordered his pirates to coat the decks with pitch to ensure a quick and all-consuming flame.

The captains agreed to pay. By this point, Black Bart's fleet of pirates had taken over four hundred ships, assassinated a governor, and caused tens of millions of damage in today's US dollars. As they terrorized the coast of West Africa, they brought the Atlantic slave trade to a standstill. Although eight pounds of gold was an exorbitant amount even for captains in the Atlantic slave trade, it wasn't theirs—it belonged to the companies in Europe that had sent them. Seeing how the pirates had destroyed so many ships already, the

This image of Captain Bartholomew "Black Bart" Roberts standing in front of his two most famous ships, a host of slave ships anchored at Ouidah, and West African canoes, which moved enslaved captives and supplies between ships and forts, comes from an engraving by Benjamin Cole (1695–1766) and was included for publication in the Charles Johnson narrative, *A General History of the Pyrates*. In it, Roberts wears the infamous jewel-studded gold cross designed for the Portuguese royal family, plundered from the treasure fleet anchored in the Bay of Bahia, Brazil. *Rare Book Division, New York Public Library, "Captain Bartho. Roberts with two ships, Viz. the Royal Fortune and Ranger," New York Public Library Digital Collections, 1724.*

captains figured the shareholders of these companies might prefer to lose gold than the time it would take to build replacements.

To avoid accusations of pocketing the sum and to facilitate the insurance reimbursement process, the slave ship captains asked Black Bart on the *Royal Fortune* for a receipt to take back home. The pirate captain joined his crew in a roar of laughter then realized the slave traders were serious. He shrugged and picked up a quill, pressed his tongue into his cheek, and created a note for each shipowner back in Europe to assure them that their captains had indeed been extorted by the "Gentlemen of Fortune."

As soon as the pirates collected the gold, they headed south to Cape Lopez, in modern-day Gabon. The estuaries there were perfect places to refresh their ships, count their winnings, and stay out of the watchful eye of the fanatical British naval captain who had been hunting them for more than a year and a half.

Captain Chaloner Ogle was in charge of two men-o'-war, the *Swallow* and *Weymouth*, and tasked by the king himself to do whatever it took to end this threat to British shipping in Africa. British settlers in the Americas demanded enslaved Africans at far higher rates than British slave traders could traffic them, and settlers of other empires in the Americas echoed these sentiments. The first European nation to solve the pirate problem could emerge as the next global superpower. Both the English and Dutch clamored for this coveted position and each bemoaned that the state of West Africa was keeping them from it.

In 1721 competitive chaos characterized the Atlantic slave trade in Africa. The number of participants in the trade had fostered a culture of competition that rendered it inefficient and financially precarious.[1] Nearly one in three slave ships fell prey to piracy. In addition to that, illness, revolts, and insurrections also could wipe out an entire year's profit margin. Because of this, the coast of West Africa was essentially a free-for-all, with the royal and official trading companies of enslaving European nations complaining greatly about one another as well as about the independent traders and pirates who operated there. Under Black Bart's visionary nihilism and aggressive recruiting, the numbers of pirates on the West African coast had grown exponentially. Slave ship captains lived in fear of attack. Often their ships were looted, damaged, stolen, or burned, and the enslaved onboard freed, murdered, resold, or coerced into piracy to prey on other slave ships. Many, of course, didn't have to be coerced.

The end of the War of the Spanish Succession in 1714 and the new war on piracy had created swaths of jobless former privateers and other maritime laborers who were often impressed into working onboard slave or naval ships of various European empires for pittance. Both were dangerous, violent jobs that few people took on voluntarily. The Atlantic slave trade had created a culture of precarity and danger in West Africa and the waters surrounding it. The steady influx of European slave traders operating with skeleton crews—and the weapons they brought as gifts—transformed the human geography of the coastal states and the surrounding waters. Increasingly, those Africans who refused to work with the Europeans were in danger of being sold into the trade themselves. Wars of conquest by both the emerging Ashanti and Dahomey Empires to the north created large numbers of refugees and captives being marched to the coast. This, in turn, attracted more human traffickers from Europe who introduced further violence.

This stew of desperation helped to create the conditions for the third wave in what historians refer to as the "golden age of piracy." Black Bart and his pirates were no ordinary sea robbers—they were a nihilistic fleet that descended upon the African coast like locusts, consuming every ship within view. As their ranks swelled, they committed unthinkable feats, like utilizing exploding ships filled to the brim with gunpowder as weapons against other ships or even against harbors and fortifications. Until this moment at Ouidah, Black Bart's pirates had evaded the British navy, leaving a trail of burned and scuttled (or partially sunken) ships like a trail of breadcrumbs for them to find. At Cape Lopez, their fortune finally ran out.

On February 10, 1722, Captain Ogle found the pirates at long last and defeated them in battle. He sold the pirates of African origin into the slave trade, and those of European ancestry he subjected to what amounted to a kangaroo court in which the majority were sentenced to death. Back in Europe, the shareholders of the major slave-trading companies cheered on these deaths, optimistic that the slave trade would soon pick up again.

Bartholomew Roberts has been the subject of so many books, almost all of them ending with his death. I wanted to place him into a story where we don't usually find him, and so his death appears in the middle of this book and serves as the beginning of an entirely new story. He belongs to the world of the eighteenth century and its attendant earth-shattering transitions. This century saw a global paradigm shift: the Atlantic world transformed from one full of precarity and possibility toward one in which colonial extraction models calcified and shut down many of those possibilities. The Battle of Cape Lopez becomes a way to see what the Atlantic world looked like before chattel slavery became inevitable and to investigate the legacies of this inevitability.

With the threat of Black Bart's fleet neutralized, Great Britain's slave trade did indeed boom. Safe from pirate attack, traders raced back to the coast to make their fortunes. After the Battle of Cape Lopez, English slavers like Captain William Snelgrave, who had been captured by the pirates in 1719, returned to find the slave trade profitable beyond their wildest dreams. New investors flocked to Britain's slave trade, looking to make a fortune.

With Britain's slave trade now booming in West Africa, the Netherlands were in danger of being cut out of the slave trade almost entirely. With the pirates gone, the largest, most obvious threat to the Dutch West India Company's trade was the Gold Coast king by the name of John Conny. His trading practices at the Prussian-built castle of Fort Great Fredericksburg at Cape Three Points had sustained the pirates that attacked British shipping and had brought the profits of the Dutch slave traders down to 20 percent of what they once were. He entertained anyone willing to trade, and his formidable Prussian fortification, his sizeable army, and his decades of experience dealing with slave traders of both Europe and Africa gave him the upper hand. This allowed him to spark bidding wars and manipulate the trade in his favor and in the favor of his people, the Ahanta. One by one, he poached the customers of the Dutch West India Company and encouraged their competitors. In 1724, the Dutch and British teamed up for their second joint effort to destroy him, with mixed results. The inland trading partners in Ashanti-land avoided the people who had driven away their ally John Conny, and trade routes between the interior and coast reconfigured, once again endangering Dutch shipping while favoring British trade.

With both Black Bart and John Conny defeated, few obstacles remained to West Africa's slave trade. The number of enslaved Africans that were pulled out of the continent increased from roughly forty thousand in 1720 to sixty thousand after 1724. By the 1760s, that number would swell to more than ninety thousand enslaved captives embarking from West Africa each year. These figures formed the start of an exponentially increasing trend that saw the enslavement and transshipment of millions. The Battle of Cape Lopez represents the moment in time when the British slave trade picked up steam and allowed British chattel slavery to proliferate in the Americas.

Prior to the 1722 battle, in the sixteenth, seventeenth, and early eighteenth centuries, many different forms of enslavement existed in the Atlantic world. Most European empires implemented systems of slavery in the Americas that were modeled on that of the Roman Empire. Under this model, enslavement was a state of being and not a permanent identity. People enslaved under models inspired by the Romans still legally were considered persons and remained eligible to claim a more truncated set of human rights while enslaved.

The chattel system, made popular by the British Empire, attempted to strip personhood from the enslaved. Chattel slavery allowed African and Afro-descended people to be considered the legal property of an enslaver. This type of slavery legally rendered enslaved people as objects that could be owned and forced the children born of enslaved women to become objects possessed by the enslavers in the eyes of the law. Chattel slavery created a pernicious system of race and racism from which Americans and the world still struggle to disentangle ourselves.

Prior to the Battle of Cape Lopez, the areas in North America that would become the United States were divided between Roman and chattel models. This created some very important distinctions. People enslaved in the areas colonized by Spain and France (Spanish Florida and Texas, as well as the French Louisiana territory) still were subject to systems inspired by the Roman model. The people who had been enslaved in territories formerly claimed by the Dutch and Swedish in the northeastern parts of the country also had been subject to Roman-derived forms of enslavement. Chattel slavery, on the other hand, was the most common form of enslavement among the British North American colonies. As the British slave trade expanded, so did the British chattel model in the Americas.

For a nation like the United States, with a history of colonial Spanish, Dutch, Swedish, French, and British occupation, this means that incredibly complicated and diverse experiences of enslavement slowly gave way to the overarching model that we know today. Places in what would become part of the United States navigated the chattel system for the first time. Opportunities for the enslaved and their descendants rapidly dwindled as settlers of European descent enshrined their objectification into law.

This book is the story of the Battle of Cape Lopez and how the defeat of the pirates put into motion a series of events that would forever shape the culture of enslavement in what would become the United States. It traces the stories of three prominent men in West Africa—the pirate captain Bartholomew "Black Bart" Roberts, the British naval captain Chaloner Ogle, and the Ahantan king John Conny—plus William Snelgrave, the legacy slave trader to Jamaica and Virginia. Snelgrave wrote vividly horrific descriptions of the slave voyages he piloted before and after the Battle of Cape Lopez, which provide a way to track change over time in the culture of the slave trade in West Africa.

Though the battle happened fifty-four years before the United States claimed its statehood in the Declaration of Independence, it shaped the type of nation we would become. It boosted British involvement and profit in the Atlantic slave trade to create an overseas empire that was a true slave society: a society upon which all politics, religion, economy, labor, and social identities depended on the chattel enslavement of Africans and their descendants.[*]

At Ouidah, the "Gentlemen of Fortune" facetiously referred to themselves as "gentlemen" with tongue-in-check wordplay: Black Bart had named his flagship the *Royal Fortune*, and he and his pirates onboard had also literally extorted the slave traders for a small

---

[*] Historian Ira Berlin wrote about the distinction between a "society with slaves" and a "slave society" in his watershed work, *Many Thousands Gone: The First Two Centuries of Slavery in North America* (Belknap Press: An Imprint of Harvard University Press, 1998, 2000).

fortune. But ultimately, he knew that by doing this, he was going to die and that his men would hang by his side. Together they decided that if they couldn't live on their own terms, then they would die by them instead. "A merry life, but a short one," had been their motto all along, after all.

So then, dear readers, I invite you to read on and with every chapter to ask yourselves: Who were the real gentlemen of fortune here? And what is the legacy of this fortune today?

Part One

THE PIRATE BATTLE OF CAPE LOPEZ

Chapter One

―――――――――――○―――――――――――

How Conny
Became King

THE STORY OF THE PIRATE BATTLE at Cape Lopez begins with the powerful African who sheltered pirates and enabled piracy in early eighteenth-century West Africa: John Conny. Throughout his long and eventful life, the Ahantan king who feasted with pirates, drank from Dutchmen's skulls, and dressed his wives in solid gold—if the European stories were to be believed—went by many names and titles. Each decade of his life was marked by tremendous upheaval, requiring dexterity and flexibility to keep up with the demands put upon his people as the European trade in enslaved captives ramped up. Because he had to reinvent himself regularly, there are many places where the story of John Conny could begin. In 1662, when he was just a teenager, an encounter among his people, the Ahanta, permanently shaped his worldview regarding his place among the Europeans who traded captive Africans on the coast that he called home.

To John Conny, home was among the Ahanta who lived in a town called Pokesu at the top of Manfro Hill. Manfro Hill was covered in palm trees and located next to Cape Three Points on the coast of West Africa in the western region of what today is called Ghana. The people there looked south into the Gulf of Guinea and wider Atlantic Ocean. As a child, Conny had met a few European men, pink faced and soft bellied, who sometimes marched (or, more often, were carried on litters or in hammocks by groups

3

of miserable servants or enslaved captives) into his town to speak with the chief, his distant uncle, in hushed tones behind brightly colored curtains. It sometimes took days for the sour look to leave his uncle's face after their strange visits. Whenever Conny asked about these meetings, he was rebuffed, and an aunt or grandmother would press a sweet treat into his hand or mouth to stop his line of questioning.

That all changed in 1662 when a Prussian ship with billowing white sails and colorful flags sailed into Cape Three Points. The chief of Ahanta had been standing on the shores all morning waiting for the ship to anchor and watching warily as the canoe men he sent collected the White officers and rowed them to shore. Ahanta's chief, who remains unnamed in the documentation, had come from a people whose previous chief had signed a treaty with the Dutch at the neighboring fort at Butre eight years prior in 1656.[1] When the Prussians extended him an offer of alliance, he was uninclined to accommodate them. He claimed the Dutch had not upheld their end of the bargain to protect his people from the African allies of the English slave traders. He was weary, as the Prussians were the third group of Europeans who had tried to get his attention: before his agreement with the Dutch, this chief had signed with the Swedish at Butre in 1650. In a mere dozen years, the Ahanta's history with the English, Swedes, and Dutch made the current chief highly knowledgeable of the desires that European men brought with them to his coast, and his varied disappointments had schooled in him how to extract things like military aid and personal safety from them in return. The chief knew that if he did not at least entertain them, someone else would, and then that same someone else might come for him or his people.

The Prussian Brandenburg African Company (BAC) was an anomaly among the European slave-trading companies that built fortifications and trading posts along the Gold Coast of West Africa. The Prussians promised the chief that they would be fair and adhere to a contract both parties drew up together, unlike their wily Dutch "enemies" at the West India Company (WIC), who generally brought with them to Africa from Europe preprinted form contracts with blank spaces for names and dates and little room for negotiation. After a ceremonial meeting to talk trade, the Prussian ship brought three of the chief's chosen ambassadors, Piegati, Suffoni, and Apani back to the electoral court in Prussia to hammer out a vassalage agreement between the Brandenburgers and the Ahanta.

This happened with some regularity among other Europeans that came to West Africa looking to trade. Many offered to transport African dignitaries and diplomats to Europe to treat directly with their rulers or to establish trust. The 1600s were a strange time, where access to the "new world" in the West rapidly challenged many of the medieval beliefs and customs to which Europeans still clung. When it came to diplomacy, vassalage was a tried-and-true way that Europeans navigated international relations, and many vestiges of these customs were reflected in the contracts between Europeans and West Africans at the time.

In Europe, the three Ahantan representatives came to an agreement and were safely returned from Prussia to wait on the arrival of the first Brandenburg governor to Pokesu, Otto von der Groeben. While they waited, the Dutch, who had caught wind of this brewing agreement, attacked John Conny's town. His family fled, safely taking him north to the interior where they had connections among the Fante people, while the chief and his soldiers stayed to fight. Conny lost his home and much of his family and never again saw the chief.

When von der Groeben arrived at Cape Three Points, ready to work with the three ambassadors and build a Prussian fortification on their land, he found the village laid to waste. Apani was one of the few survivors of the war that claimed the lives of Suffoni, Piegati, and the chief. He explained to the Prussians what the Dutch had done to his people for daring to treat with the Brandenburg Company and he reiterated the importance of building the biggest and strongest fortification upon Manfro Hill—the highest, most naturally fortified spot in the whole region. From this hill, the Brandenburgers and the Ahanta together would be invincible.

Otto von der Groeben drew up a new contract with the survivors of the Dutch massacre. In the new contract, Apani and the new acting rulers of the Pokesu area (Brombire, Ethi, Auffi, Among, Etong, Lessie, Casparo, Eguri, Sacing, Mana, Nache, Assassa, and Eunu) insisted that the Brandenburg fort be large enough to protect all their people against further devastation. They demanded that the Brandenburgers and their ships should side with the Ahanta in every armed conflict. The Prussians agreed to this most inconvenient clause, provided the Ahanta traded with no ships except those with the Brandenburger flag.[2] For the Prussians, trade exclusivity was worth the inconvenience of being dragged into local conflicts, since conflicts with the Dutch and English companies and their African allies and mercenaries were unavoidable, anyway. The Prussians had, in true Prussian fashion, brought a blue-uniformed regiment of their military with them to the Gold Coast in anticipation of trouble, and they were prepared to deploy them when necessary. But on that first night, the military spent their time with the Ahanta celebrating their alliance, alternating African drums with Prussian bugles and West African dances with an assortment of European waltzes. Slowly but surely, refugees from Ahanta, including John Conny, returned to the area to rebuild.

When it was time for von der Groeben to return to Europe, he and his officer debriefed the Prussian king and gave many instructions to the BAC as to how to maintain a good relationship. Johan Nieman pointed out that the people of Pokesu were "great lovers of music, having several instruments for this purpose, including a sort of guitar which they can play fairly well and sing pleasantly to." Captain Benjamin Raule agreed, adding that the next ship sent from Prussia should include musical instruments and musicians to play them. Otto von der Groeben told Raule to tell the king that the instruments the Brandenburgers had with them made the locals at Pokesu deduce that "Your Serene Highness must be a much more powerful master than the Dutch, with whom they had never seen the like."[3] The king took heed and sent Prussian drums and a salaried drummer to play them. Paying close attention to Dutch and English failures allowed the Prussians an in on West Africa's crowded coast.

For years, this contract between the Prussians and the Ahanta held, despite many instances that tested its bonds. Cape Three Points was surrounded by Dutch forts (in Axim, Butre, and Sekondi) and the English (at Fort Metal Cross in Dixcove), each within easy walking distance, which caused much conflict. Due to this proximity, most of the early Prussian ships on the Gold Coast were pirated or privateered by their English and Dutch competitors. The Ahanta became the only reason the BAC could survive in Africa at all, and in turn, the Ahanta thrived under the protection of the heavily armed Prussian military. Because this partnership gave the Ahanta the breathing room needed to regroup from the initial Dutch attack that claimed the lives of Piegati, Suffoni, and the chief, the Prussians became known among locals as European people who adhered to their contracts, unlike the double-crossing Portuguese, Dutch, and English.

Two years later, several other local African groups approached the Brandenburgers to ask for protection. A contract signed February 4, 1685, by refugees of the surrounding regions of Anta and Taccorari indicates that these groups also claimed that their allies, the Dutch and English, had abandoned them. These refugees were caboceers, or African cultural brokers and middlemen who made their living interacting with the Europeans.* The caboceers fled to the Prussians and promised to help finish the construction of Fort Great Fredericksburg without monetary pay, in exchange for Prussian military protection. Brandenburg employees Schnitter and D. G. Reinerman certified at the end of the contract that they had been approached by these groups and had therefore set these more favorable terms.[4] The African Brandenburg alliances reshaped the political map of the western Gold Coast and its hinterlands as Conny grew into a wise young man.

As a result, the English and Dutch had a much harder time securing favorable trading conditions with their West African allies. This panicked the employees of their respective companies, because the 1680s and 1690s were a time of significant change for the interior African powers to the north and along with substantial change in West Africa came trade instability. The interior peoples—including the Ashanti, Denkyira, and Fante—had grown

---

* Caboceer was a term used in coastal West Africa to describe African rulers, administrators, traders, captains, or other appointed persons whose job required that they represent their peoples in dealings with Europeans. It originated from *cabeza* or *cabeça*, the Portuguese/Spanish term for "head," denoting that they were the "head" men, or leaders/chiefs, and that they had strong/wise heads on their shoulders. Caboceers often were multilingual and highly educated and skilled in topics of diplomacy, trade, and warfare.

powerful from access to both the trans-Saharan trade to the north and the coastal European trade to the south. The Ashanti people especially became expansionist at this time and played a large role in the political reorganization of the coast. The African peoples who had signed treaties with the Dutch and English found themselves removed, relocated, divided, or merged with the remnants of smaller groups at a more rapid pace than the ever-revolving cavalcade of uneducated European factors could keep up with.

Even without this complication, John Conny saw how European traders on the coast were already at the mercy of the sporadic arrival of ships full of cargo from Europe or, occasionally, the Americas. The manufactured goods were necessary in upholding the goodwill of African allies and to be allowed to enter a trading relationship. Now the English and Dutch had to curry the favor of both the coastal and the emerging interior peoples, since either had the power to stop all trade in its tracks if they became unhappy with the Europeans. While the Dutch and English tripped over themselves sending extravagant gifts such as fur caps, brandy, pewter jugs with basins, and various dyed fabrics to northern royalty, they also had to take care to avoid distressing their coastal allies by offering them presents of inferior quantity or quality necessary to maintain good trading relationships. Now that the Brandenburger alternative existed, locals took advantage of Dutch and English traders' anxieties to negotiate better deals and treatment. This tighter competition both inland and on the coast exacerbated deep resentments between the Dutch and English, which the more powerful locals were all too eager to exploit. John Conny's young and eager brain soaked up these detailed intricacies like a sponge.

Naturally, the Dutch and English directed these resentments at the Brandenburg company, which, in their eyes, was poaching clients. When the Dutch aggressively asserted their rights to this space in a sternly worded letter to the prince elector of Brandenburg, the Prussians countered with their rights to the land beneath Fort Great Fredericksburg as given to them by the local Ahanta. In response, the Dutch West India Company attempted to stir up the conflict between the Ahanta and the neighboring Adom people who lived further inland.

In a statement concerning Dutch interference with BAC trade on the Gold Coast, Charles LaPetit confessed to the WIC's former factor at Axim, Johannes Verdijck, that from 1686 to 1687, "he had received orders from the Director-General at [Elmina], Sweers, to do the Electoral Brandenburg African Company every conceivable injury," including sending West African allies of the Dutch to occupy roads and stopping all African traders from doing business with the BAC, imprisoning those who persisted.[5] Free African traders suddenly found themselves in the dungeons reserved for captives of the fortifications of their trade partners. They would not forget this indignity.

Had the Brandenburgers not worked hard to maintain the loyalty of the Ahanta in their employ, this type of conflict easily could have ruined them. To protect their newly acquired holding on the Gold Coast, the BAC attempted to expand its sphere of local contracts and collected the signatures of several local rulers and middlemen who represented other peoples who had been wronged by the Dutch and were willing to ally with the Prussians to get revenge and to protect their interests. In this way, the Prussians learned that to maintain access to the most preferable trading routes on the Gold Coast, they had to position themselves as vanquishers of the Dutch and the builders of fortifications large enough to shelter their African allies should the Dutch send a flurry of mercenaries their way. To this day, the Prussian Fort Great Fredericksburg in Pokesu, or Princes Town, is one of the larger, more fortified, and more well-preserved trading forts sitting atop a steep hill overlooking the bay at Cape Three Points to the south and all the western region of the Gold Coast to the north.

Meanwhile, in Europe, the Prussians worked hard to discredit the Dutch West India Company through legal means to keep the wars between their traders in Africa from becoming armed conflicts in Europe. Investors of the BAC argued that the locals enjoyed trading with the BAC and, therefore, the WIC's hindering of their business was "illegitimate." They argued that the West Africans had "their own kings, their own rulerships and preserve their own laws and rights, have engaged in various different wars with one another as well as with European Nations and against the WIC itself, and

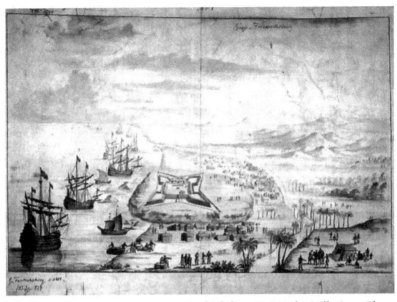

Drawing of the Prussian Fort Great Fredricksburg at Manfro Hill, Cape Three Points, 1684. The image shows the town of Pokesu in the background and Ahantan traders loading smaller boats with supplies for the European ships in the foreground. *The original image has been lost. It and the digital copy are in the public domain.*

continue in such wars to this day."[6] Then the BAC countered that the WIC's treaties with West Africans were the ones that were illegitimate because they were outdated. The successors or descendants of those Africans who signed the initial WIC contracts were not bound by their predecessors' contracts but were free to sign new contracts. Therefore, the BAC's contracts, which were the most recent, were valid whereas those of the WIC were not.

These legal arguments contain painstaking detail about the rapidly evolving state of Gold Coast politics that demonstrates just how far the Prussians went to present themselves as legitimate by appealing to the sovereignty of the Africans with which they traded as powerful, independent, and equal allies. They asked the WIC to produce their contracts from decades prior and then poked legal holes into them. For example, the BAC declared the WIC contract from 1642 with Axim as invalid because only two caboceers had

British map of Western Africa from the early 1700s, with European flags marking the locations of the various fortresses used in human trafficking in West and West Central Africa. Several of the forts on the Gold Coast were within view of one another. *Lionel Pincus and Princess Firyal Map Division, New York Public Library, "A draught of the coast of Africa from the streights mouth to Cape Bona Esprance," New York Public Library Digital Collections, 1702–1707*

signed it, whereas the BAC reconnaissance shows that Axim was divided into the jurisdiction of five caboceers: Jumo, Abupiquen, Cabio, Bocuree, and Axim proper. In no other records from this time are the Dutch or English able to name West African regions or administrators with such accuracy. The implication here was that three of the jurisdictions who hadn't yet signed with the WIC were free to sign contracts with the BAC. The signatures of these three would outweigh the two who allied with the WIC, making the Prussian contract more valid in both the eyes of the Africans who had signed it and the Europeans who had created this form of contractual law between states. Because Axim was only a day's walk from Fort Great Fredericksburg, it mattered a great deal to both the Dutch and the Prussians.

Drawn-out legal battles over slave trade sovereignty show how the BAC took great pains to be aware of the rapidly shifting geopolitical situations on the coast of West Africa. Its repeated appeal to African sovereignty was something that was new among the European powers. Although European powers referred to Asia and the Americas of this time period in colonial terms, Africa and its peoples were, at least on Prussian paper, equivalent to European nation-states in terms of the ability to enter treaties and choose trading partners. The Brandenburgers benefited most from asserting African independence and sovereignty and therefore supported and further instilled that confidence and entitlement to independence and sovereignty in the Ahanta and their other local trading partners. They knew well that this could come back to haunt them later, but it was the only way for this smaller, weaker European state to achieve any foothold in the slave trade.

During the next twenty years, Europe reorganized itself and the face of the world through colonial exploits. The demand for slave labor climbed as the settler population in the American colonies exploded. The Portuguese, French, Danish, Dutch, and English made repeated competing forays to the Gold Coast, building fortresses and signing contracts with various local groups to set up a stable, long-term source of trade in enslaved captives. Competition among the Europeans for African loyalty and trading partners increased exponentially, and many smart locals made their livings playing on these European insecurities and anxieties.

The introduction of the Swedish, Danish, English, French, Dutch, and Prussian challengers on the Gold Coast, though ultimately destructive to the locals, created the political instability and trade scarcity that allowed powerful African individuals to emerge and seize control over their European trading partners. John Conny was the right age and at the right place and time to witness one such man, John Cabes, rise to power over the English and Dutch and bring the European traders to their knees. Naturally, it made quite an impression on Conny's young mind.

This created a radically new and different atmosphere in the culture of the Gold Coast as John Conny grew into a man. Increasingly, Africans like John Cabes successfully played European traders against one another and quickly grew wealthy and influential, while those who chose not to work with European slavers often ended up at the mercy of them. Conny saw how states that agreed to participate in the slave trade grew wealthier and more martial, while those that avoided the trade often ended up conquered by it or forced to vacate the coastal regions. The world of John Conny was radically different—economically, culturally, and linguistically—from the world of his parents and the unnamed chief who first met the Brandenburgers. Now, in addition to the handful of West African languages and Arabic spoken on the Gold Coast, mastery of Dutch and English became part of the skill set of ambitious Africans, and Conny picked up both early in life as he trained to one day take on a leadership role among his people.

CONNY AND CABES

Before John Conny stepped into power in the western region, there was John Cabes of the central region, the most powerful African caboceer on the Gold Coast. Cabes had grown up to the east of Conny in a town called Komenda. Throughout John Conny's youth in the western region, he had heard of the way Cabes and his father navigated the Komenda wars—a conflict between the English and

Dutch who had built fortifications along the coast there less than a stone's throw from one another. Cabes was a powerful leader and caboceer who aligned himself with the English after his father, John Cabessa, was cornered and took his own life in the 1660s to avoid being captured and killed by the Dutch. Cabes inherited his father's relationship with the traders of the English Royal Africa Company (RAC), the national slave-trading company owned by the British Crown, which still depended on the Cabes family to maintain a presence in Komenda. The RAC readily sent home several English employees whom Cabes took a dislike to rather than jeopardize that trading relationship.

As the power of the inland Ashanti Empire grew, so did the coastal empire of Cabes, who eagerly took on the role of middleman, trading with neighboring African groups and mostly the English but sometimes the Dutch and other independent Europeans who came to Komenda or nearby locales as well. His economic importance translated to political clout, so Cabes became the leader of the city, pulling Komenda out of the shadow of Eguafo to function more like its own city-state rather than a dependency. Although the European documents about him at the time treated Cabes with equal amounts of disdain and fear, he set the terms for how Europeans were to interact with him and his people during this period of intense competition in the slave trade.

While the Komenda Wars raged on, John Conny of the Ahanta had been in the north, safe from the Dutch devastation at Pokesu, serving with the military of his allies, the Fante. They wanted to become the middlemen between the Europeans on the coast and the inland Ashanti Empire. The Fante grew stronger because of this conflict, extending the boundaries of their power to the coast and over the trade. This ensured a new precedent for wars fought over slavery and access to captive Africans to enslave. By the end of the seventeenth century onward, Gold Coast wars would be fought on larger scales than ever before, with both European and African participants making use of mercenary troops.[7]

By 1701, the English sent multiple gifts to the Ashanti and to local coastal powers in an attempt to create a lasting alliance between the English company and all the players necessary to facilitate a smooth trade flow from Ashanti to the RAC castle at Komenda. They gifted seven blue perpetuanas (a type of industrial cloth made from wool) and three yards of scarlet cloth to the king of Ashanti's son and additional gifts to the king of Asebu and the fettera of Fetu and ordered more guns and munitions from Europe. They hoped this would suffice to entice the Ashanti traders to keep trade routes open and to give preference to the routes in the central region of the coast (those places including Komenda and Cape Coast Castle) where the English had concentrated their fortifications. At the same time, a Dutch operative at Elmina, the Dutch capital of the Gold Coast trade, wrote to the company's headquarters in the Netherlands that "We thought that the present wars in the interior would rather promote the offer of slaves."[8] The Dutch had assumed that, as in the past, they would be the ones to benefit from the conflicts they stoked, but during the Komenda wars, it turned out that their African allies were the ones who were captured and sold into the English slave trade.

The Komenda wars ended when the English assassinated the Komenda king, who had aligned himself with the Dutch, while John Cabes allied himself with the English. Shortly after, the RAC urged John Cabes to choose a new Komenda king. The English knew that the former king of Komenda was hostile to Cabes's political and economic expansionist agenda. The English hoped that if Cabes were allowed to select a new king more supportive of his ambitions, the Komenda could forgive the RAC for overreaching in African affairs. Murdering a local ruler and giving the position to a weaker puppet figure was a common tactic that the English and Dutch (and all other European colonizing states) had used to attain power around the world. What was different on the Gold Coast was the RAC's deference to John Cabes's decision as to who that puppet would be. They encouraged him to select his own puppet rather than attempt to install one themselves to avoid accountability, and possibly retribution, for the murder.

Cabes claimed all the spoils of war, investing them in maize fields, salt pans, and a fleet of canoes. They were for both fishing and to rent to the Europeans who needed them to ferry people and goods back and forth between Fort Komenda and the English ships anchored at sea. Though the English factors wrote about him as if he were an employee, Cabes controlled access to their every need and charged them a consulting fee for doing so. Without his entrepreneurship, the English employees of the Royal Africa Company in Komenda could not have accessed their own ships, nor any trade goods or captive Africans from the interior to fill them with, nor sufficient food for the voyage to the Americas. Cabes had locked down every business adjacent to the slave trade, ensuring that the English would fail without him. The Dutch, who Cabes had allowed to remain with their fort next to the English one after the wars, served as a constant reminder to the RAC that if Cabes did not get paid, there was another company that would, and often Cabes visited the Dutch fort in daylight and in view of the English fort whenever the English became too demanding or forgot their place with him. It was his way of reminding the English who was in charge.

By 1706, the Dutch WIC, exhausted by this dynamic and now burned by their former instigating tactics, accused the English of unjustly inciting armed conflicts among different African polities in hopes of selling the captives—the very thing the Dutch had hoped to profit from at the start of the Komenda wars. The conflict now over in favor of the English, the Dutch redoubled their efforts in John Conny's territory in the western parts of the coast, where their conflict with the Brandenburgers kept the Dutch from direct access to the Ashanti. If Cabes and the English blocked them from doing it through centrally located Komenda, they would try to do it through Cape Three Points and Axim to the west.

John Conny was among the first to learn about the Dutch encroachment upon the Ahanta at Cape Three Points. In 1708, when Conny was in his forties, he became the chief of the Ahanta while he was working with the Fante. Conny had learned much from the Fante through his military alliance, which he retained in his new life as a coastal chief.

The next year, in 1709, while Conny attempted to keep the Dutch from encroaching on his territory, the Royal Africa Company sought to establish direct trade with the Ashanti. However, the Fante camped out along the routes between the Ashanti capital of Kumasi and the English outposts along the coast. The English wanted the company to fund a dedicated military to flush out these so-called Fante highwaymen from their various locations. Mere months after Conny became the Ahanta chief, top Dutch and English traders from the WIC and RAC learned that when Conny was with the Fante, he had been one such "highwayman" who now had considerable power over a long stretch of coast. They hammered out an agreement at what would be called the Fetu River Convention to permanently dislodge the Fante, who were blocking the trade routes between the coast and the interior. Conny, honor bound to help the Fante allies who had taken him in as a young man when the Dutch raided his town, became a wanted man in the eyes of the English and Dutch.

In 1710, the English overstepped yet again, angering the Fante by threatening to kill the king and enstool a new one who favored the English. When Conny found out, he strategically followed in the previous chief's footsteps, taking on the formal role of caboceer with the Prussian Brandenburg Africa Company at Fort Great Fredericksburg in hopes that working with Europeans on the coast could provide him with a long-term way to maintain the stability of these trade routes to the interior and prevent the English from defanging the Fante as they had the Komenda when they invited John Cabes to choose a new puppet king.

Conny Overhauls Brandenburg

As his forbearers, John Conny had a full understanding of the complexity surrounding the Ahanta's position at this volatile time. He had ambitions for his people that included elaborate plans for using the Brandenburgers' most impressive fort at Pokesu to realize them. He used the model that John Cabes, about fifteen years his senior, employed with the English as a road map for dealing with the Prussians.

By 1710, the Brandenburgers in Africa were in decline. Their Prussian soldiers had wilted in the heat of Cape Three Points, and the conflicts between the Dutch and English and their allies had

significantly disrupted trade from the inland north, where most captives to be sold into the slave trade originated. Brandenburg ships
were few and far between, and employees of the Prussian company
often wasted tremendous resources feeding captives while waiting
for these ships and defending themselves from sieges that came
from both land and sea. Conny appeared with his own military
force, which he had honed to perfection through fighting alongside
the Fante. Both he and the Prussians at Fort Great Fredericksburg
saw the writing on the wall when it came to the threat posed by the
larger and more powerful English and Dutch companies.

Immediately, Conny pushed for the Brandenburgers to abandon "respectable" trade that honored each European company's
mercantile sovereignty. Rather than trading only with the Prussian
ships that came once in a blue moon, Conny believed the BAC in
Fort Great Fredericksburg should trade with any ship that stopped
there, whether those ships were sent from European slave-trading
companies, independent merchants trying their luck in Africa, or
pirates. The demand in the Americas for enslaved Africans and raw
materials of West Africa was evergreen, so he argued that there was
no point in placating the Prussians' European enemies by honoring
Dutch and English insistence that the Brandenburgers trade only
with Prussian ships. Back in Berlin, the shareholders agreed. After
all, the Spanish American province of Tierra Firme (the Spanish
Main that comprised the Caribbean coasts of South and Central
America) was chronically undersupplied and would pay top coin for
any trade ship from Africa. Most likely, they adopted this attitude
from current employees who had formerly worked with the Swedish Africa Company with these aspirations before going defunct in
1663, leaving this market wide open.[9] These forty years had made
Tierra Firme even more desperate to trade. Colonists of many other
locations in the Americas shared this viewpoint: although European
countries wanted to keep trade highly regulated, settlers in the
Americas wanted free trade and welcomed most "illegal" ships.

As predicted, the Brandenburg African Company's new alliance
with Conny and its willingness to trade indiscriminately, undercut-
ting Dutch and English prices, infuriated the competition. Sitting
atop of Manfro Hill at Cape Three Points, Fort Great Fredericks-

burg was the westernmost fortification on the Gold Coast aside from the smaller Dutch fort at Axim. This meant that it was the first large fortification next to a protected cape that ships coming from Europe encountered after a long stretch of dangerous coast with high swell and few places to drop anchor safely. Once it was known that all ships were welcomed at what Europeans and Africans alike began referring to as "Conny's Castle," the Dutch and English ships joined the pirate ships in anchoring there, giving the Brandenburgers first pick of European trade goods and valuable information in exchange for refreshing their water and food supplies.

The Dutch and English slave traders at the forts nearby used Conny's allegiance with the Fante as an excuse to attempt to damage this emerging Prussian competition at Cape Three Points. Fortunately for Conny and the Prussians, the deep-seated distrust between the employees of the Dutch West India Company and the English Royal Africa Company weakened their joint attack on Conny and the Prussians. At the same time, Conny's personal military joined and drilled with the Prussian troops, creating an elite joint fighting force. The Prussians at the fort soon realized that they remained there and grew wealthy by the grace of John Conny, and no one else.

Conny Builds His Empire

After the failure of the combined English and Dutch Fetu River Convention, John Conny was free to turn his attention to building his own empire. The English and Dutch, still determined to squash the Brandenburgers and seize access to the westernmost trade route to the Ashanti Empire, rewarded any African allies who challenged Conny's rise to power. The first challenger was the caboceer Appre at Dutch Fort Axim, about twelve miles to the west of Cape Three Points. In 1711, he enslaved Adjoba, a woman Conny claimed as a blood relative. Appre knew that any coastal African ruler who could not prevent his family from falling prey to the European slave trade would lose respect and standing among his peers. He most likely hoped that the challenge to Conny's power would come from within, and then Appre could appeal to the English and Dutch to help him strike the killing blow. Appre knew that it unsettled both the English and Dutch how swiftly Conny had amassed power in the region. He was certain he could count on them both to send soldiers to help him once he gave them just cause to attack.

As Appre had predicted, this just cause came by way of Conny's forces swooping in to Adjoba's rescue. She sheltered with Conny's family at Fort Great Fredericksburg while Appre, with the help of his European allies, attacked Conny's forces to reclaim her. They failed miserably, and in an act of vengeance, Conny went east instead of west. With his military, he marched to the English fort at Dixcove, whose residents had helped Appre. On New Year's Eve 1712, Conny's forces arrived at Fort Metal Cross in Dixcove. The Royal Africa Company factors had no choice but to allow more than three hundred African civilians and allies to seek refuge inside of the fort while they fought back Conny's forces. The Ahanta easily decimated the English and their allies at Dixcove, and Conny took the refugees back to Fort Great Fredericksburg as captives, incorporating the fighters into his own military. Rumors swirled that Conny would continue marching his way down the coast, avenging himself on the Dutch and English.

The employees working at the forts held by the WIC and RAC grew terrified of this brash display of power and teamed up yet again to try to prevent Conny from becoming the next John Cabes. They would do this, ironically, by leaning upon the actual aging John Cabes and his private Komenda military. They sent letters to Europe for permission, supplies, and support. By September, the English and Dutch buried the hatchet with a joint goal of raising a proper army to defeat Conny. The WIC and RAC sent African and European soldiers from all the Dutch and English forts on the Gold Coast, and John Cabes, in a costly display of allegiance with the English, amassed a large independent contingent of African soldiers to march upon Conny's home of Pokesu.

The employees of the two European companies, however, had taken no time to coordinate their efforts, train the soldiers to fight as one unit, or establish a chain of command between and among the European, Eurafrican, and African soldiers. They had intended to muscle their way through this conflict by brute force, throwing everything they had at Conny, but they significantly underestimated both the size and the discipline of Conny's military. Conny employed nine hundred soldiers who had been trained and drilled by both the Ahanta and the Prussian military. They were proficient in using both firearms and spears, as well as martial tactics, and strategies of both Europe and Africa. The Dutch and English didn't know that Conny personally had seen to it that his mixed-force military had been drilling together since he became chief of Ahanta in 1708. The ragtag assembled forces of the English and Dutch could not hope to offer any real challenge. When Cabes saw the size and efficacy of Conny's forces, he recognized the no-win situation for what it was and bowed out of the fight. He took his soldiers with him, leaving the English and Dutch to fend for themselves. It must have been a moment of great pride for Conny, who had looked up to John Cabes all his life.

Still, this conflict dragged out more than six months. Conny's forces were supplemented by those of his allies to the north: Buo Kofi sent his Wasa military and Nyakoba sent Ashanti reinforcements. The Ashanti had long preferred the western trading routes that led to Cape Three Points and wanted to keep Conny, a man who visibly controlled the Prussians, in power at Fort Great Fredericksburg. If they did that, they could avoid dealing with the loyalist John Cabes and his less predictable English and Dutch allies to access the coastal trade in the central region. Meanwhile, the Dutch and English bribed the remaining coastal states for help, or at least to keep them from joining Conny's side. They went through considerable amounts of valuable Dutch inventory, gifting presents to leaders of various groups to no avail.

When the English and Dutch finally gave up, they admitted that the war had been "fought at great expense and a considerable loss."[10] The Dutch and the English gave the Prussians an earful about the Prussians' failure to maintain control in their Gold Coast holdings and in allowing John Conny to take over. The Prussians, however, were hardly in a position to exert power over Conny, but that didn't stop one particularly foolish factor from attempting to do so.

JOHN CONNY VERSUS NICHOLAS DUBOIS

In 1712, the Brandenburg Africa Company sent Nicholas Dubois to the Gold Coast as the new factor who would broker peace. He promised to provide powder and muskets in the event of a hostile invasion of the Ahanta if Conny would consider a peace treaty with the Dutch and the English and if his soldiers would provide labor and materials to repair the damages Fort Great Fredericksburg had sustained. The latter was no problem—Conny wanted to ensure this fortification on Ahanta soil, which his peoples depended on for protection, was at its strongest.

The former, however, failed to tempt Conny. He was utterly uninterested in the Dutch and English employees in West Africa. The foolhardy Dubois represented Conny in negotiations because Conny refused to attend. Dubois told the English and Dutch that Conny would pay them to purchase peace and that he would return the enslaved whom he had captured during the conflict from the pens and dungeon at the English Fort Metal Cross in Dixcove. In turn, the Dutch and English agreed to restrain their African allies from attacking Ahanta. All three European powers agreed that the elders of Appre's people in Axim and Conny's people in Pokesu/ Ahantaland would settle the initial disagreement between the two caboceers.

Naturally, Conny did not feel beholden to this European ar-rangement. Like Cabes, Conny became the executive director of his peoples, exerting power over the king and the Europeans alike. Now that he had captured many of the soldiers who fought against him during the Fetu River Convention and converted them into his personal fighting force, his military was the largest of any on the coast and that meant that he would disrupt any trade he deemed unnecessary.

However, that factors from all three European companies felt they could join in concert to muzzle Conny after having spent years at war with and flagrantly undermining one another was a stark warning to Africans everywhere. Until this point in 1712, Gold Coast Africans had been used to exploiting European competition in order to gain the upper hand in all matters of commerce and politics. Would the tactic of dividing and conquering the Europeans continue to work?

Within a few months of Dubois's brokerages, the Gold Coast aligned itself along two axes. Virtually all the peoples found themselves aligned with one of these two groups. Much to the chagrin of the English, who had incurred considerable expenses fighting the Fante, they were joined together with Conny's other inland allies to the north (the Ashanti and Wasa) on one side against a confederation led by the Denkyira, also of the interior, on the other. Most of the land on which the English had built fortifications along the coast was now in territory ruled by people who had allied themselves with the Fante and, by extension, Conny's people. The tension on the Gold Coast grew, and the English and Dutch felt pressured to take sides to safeguard their ability to remain at their posts and obtain enslaved captives from the north.

The Prussians, however, felt no such compunction, since the new elector of Brandenburg back home in Prussia, Frederick William I (father-to-be of Frederick the Great), announced a new set of priorities that did not include trade in Africa. Immediately, the English and Dutch companies fell back into their old competitive habits, scheming ways to gain control of Brandenburg's holdings at Cape Three Points. This western region, which historically had been less important to the two companies, was now prime real estate since it now provided the Ashanti and Wasa direct coastal access with little interference.

This rekindling of the Anglo-Dutch rivalry proved advantageous for John Conny. Both the WIC and the RAC instructed their employees to gain control of the Cape Three Points region at any cost. Whereas before factors from the two companies tried to extinguish Conny's seat of power, they now vied with one another for his allegiance. Conny leaned back in his seat and crossed his arms, unimpressed with their disingenuous groveling.

A murder at the Dutch fort in Boutry in 1714 tested these newly emergent dynamics between Conny and the Europeans. The caboceer Oben, a friend and ally of John Conny, was killed by an African ally of the Dutch while negotiating at the fort during what appeared to be a trade disagreement. This, in Conny's eyes, made the crime the fault of the Dutch, since European factors were responsible for guaranteeing the safety of Africans when they came to European forts to trade. Immediately, Conny threatened the Dutch West India Company with war, and the Dutch backed down. They arrested the guilty parties and forced them to compensate Oben's family for his death, as was custom. The Dutch then forgave all of Oben's debts with the company and volunteered to broker a peace treaty between the Ahanta and the persons responsible for the murder. This was a far cry from the actions of a company that just two years prior had sunk hundreds of guilders into a war to unseat Conny and that expected Conny to be bound to a treaty he did not sign and pay a handsome sum to secure a peace he did not seek.

A year later, in 1715, it happened again. Two of Conny's servants, Bosom and Kra, escaped to Ankobra near the Dutch fort at Axim, hoping that the past animosity between Conny and this region back when they enslaved Adjoba would prevent their being returned to Conny's service. To escape the wrath of Conny, the caboceer at Ankobra handed Bosom and Kra over to the Dutch governor at the fort at Axim. The Dutch governor, a foolish man brand new to the region and unwise in the ways of the Gold Coast, held Bosom and Kra ransom to coerce Conny into paying the restitution that Nicholas Dubois had brokered in exchange for peace back in 1712. He was most likely hoping to take a generous cut of the profit for himself.

This was an insult to the Ahantan chief. Rather than pay, Conny took eight hostages from the Dutch fort at Elmina, which was no small feat, considering the fortifications of the Portuguese-built Dutch capital of Gold Coast trade. Then he laid siege to the Dutch fort at Axim, parading his armed soldiers around the fortification each day, letting no one in or out. As his soldiers grew bored, Conny created a large bounty for the head of the Dutch governor of the fort and the caboceer who had handed the servants over to him. His allies to the north, the Wasa, sealed off all trade to the interior, ending the supply of food to the town around Axim. The young men of the city of Axim rebelled and made it clear to the Dutch that they would not be part of any war with Conny's intimidating forces.

There was nothing the Dutch could offer them that would warrant starving to death or being killed in war with John Conny.

The Wasa had helped Conny at their own expense. By refusing to trade with Axim while Conny besieged them, they had taken a financial hit. The Dutch realized that the Wasa were conflicted and hoped to exploit this friction between Conny and his interior allies, but the Ashanti, emboldened by their new expanding empire to the north of Cape Three Points and Axim, came down to the coast to intervene. They prized Conny's willingness to trade with pirates and every other ship that passed Cape Three Points on the way to the Dutch and English forts and factories further down the coast, since that gave Conny first pick of goods from Europe and the Americas. Conny passed on to the Ashanti these superior goods, which were often better and fresher than what the English and Dutch offered. As Conny valued his alliance with the inland states, he often reserved the best of the best for them, including arms and munitions that they requested to fight their wars of expansion to the north. These also had the side effect of creating a steady supply of captives marching south into European ships. This was why the Ashanti preferred to journey to the coast via Cape Three Points instead of using the more eastern paths by Komenda. Though the documentary record becomes sparse during this time, it is safe to assume that the Dutch never got that money from Conny that the fool Nicholas Dubois of the BAC promised them.

The conflict came to its end when Conny's scribe, Bosman, a man with a European father and African mother, attempted to kill Dubois by enlisting a surgeon to poison him. They failed, and Conny and Dubois agreed it was time to part ways. Conny imprisoned his scribe and the surgeon until Dubois could get himself to safety on a ship bound for Europe and then took control over the Prussian fort. The detailed journal of the Brandenburgers' last years at Great Fredericksburg ends on Saturday, January 23, 1717. Nicholas Dubois wrote the entry and many before it, detailing how heavily he depended on Conny, who oversaw much of the fort's operations. He said that he felt confident leaving the fortification in Conny's capable hands. Though the Prussians sent a factor to replace Dubois, a few months later, they recalled all their European operatives, leaving Conny in charge.[11]

Conny's first order of business was to inform the Dutch and English, who were both desperate for control over Cape Three Points, that he intended to sell Fort Great Fredericksburg to the French. This likely was a tactic on Conny's part to attempt to extort more money from them, to find out how serious they were about obtaining control over his region, or to learn how much bargaining power they had with their companies back in Europe. Plus, it kept them too busy competing with each other to interfere with his affairs. While they negotiated with Conny, a Portuguese man-o'-war from Brazil dropped anchor outside Conny's Castle. They, too, wanted the opportunity to trade from Cape Three Points. It looked as if Conny was going to sell off the precious access to the Ashanti's trade to yet another European competitor. In a panic, the Dutch shareholders in Amsterdam reached out to the prince elector of Brandenburg in Prussia and forged an agreement behind Conny's back. The Dutch agreed to pay top price to Prussia for the forts on the Gold Coast, and the remaining Dutch copy of this contract concerning this transfer suggests that the WIC would inherit the friendly trading relationships the BAC enjoyed with Conny and his people.[12]

John Conny, tired of not being consulted, had better plans, however.

LONG LIVE KING CONNY

With his army at its mightiest due to annexations of the armies that had unsuccessfully defended the English and Dutch forts at Dixcove, Axim, and Butre, John Conny secured Fort Great Fredericksburg before the Dutch could move in and ran it as his own. When the Dutch arrived to collect their prize, their records indicate that Conny refused the Dutch entry.[13] He told them the deal his people had made with the BAC was between the two parties alone and was nontransferable. According to the West African legal customs that everyone adhered to, the land upon which Fort Great Fredericksburg sat belonged to Conny and the Ahanta, who had generously allowed renting European tenants to build on it, and now that they had abandoned the structure, Conny would make use of it.

The Dutch attempted to raise an army on the Gold Coast to charge the castle on Manfro Hill, but they could not find Africans willing to fight against Conny. The soldiers at Axim in particular balked at this request, still raw from the months that Conny's military besieged them. This meant an attack on Fort Great Fredericksburg from the West India Company would have to come by sea. The Dutch sent three ships full of cannons, mortars, and armed soldiers from the Netherlands. They planned to send an initial wave of soldiers to set fire to the town of Pokesu to burn the soldiers' family homes. When Conny's soldiers spilled from the fort to put out the fires, the Dutch would take advantage of the chaos by storming and securing the fort for the West India Company.

Of course, the Dutch military hadn't considered that Conny had been in conflict with the Dutch in some capacity for all of his life, and before that, his people had been in conflict with them. Conny anticipated this very type of lowly sneak attack. When he caught sight of the Dutch tricolor flags approaching the cape, he ordered a regiment to hide among the houses facing the sea, waiting for the Dutch to advance. Conny's regiment promptly caught, beheaded, and dismembered this first Dutch wave of fire starters. The Dutch ships retreated in alarm, leaving behind thirty-six of their dead. Conny promptly ordered their bodies put on display as a warning to the company and any other Europeans who would try to commit such cruelty against the Ahanta. Europeans quickly spread exaggerated rumors of Conny's savagery, which he did nothing to dissuade. Soon, every European factor knew of the African king who drank out of a chalice made of a Dutchman's skull.

The Dutch council of the West India Company's fort at Elmina noted that along with John Cabes, John Conny of Pokesu was "virtually master" of the entire western Gold Coast.[14] They realized that there was no way to win an attack on Conny's Castle without local soldiers, so they begged the Netherlands to send ships full of the highest quality manufactured goods to help pay mercenaries to dislodge Conny. Tired of sending fine merchandise and getting few results in turn, the Dutch shareholders suggested they try to buy out Conny instead. In their eyes, it was worth paying for the properties twice to finally access that interior trade with the Ashanti.

For seven years, John Conny refused to entertain any offers from the Dutch and controlled Fort Great Fredericksburg as a free port, entertaining all the pirates and other freebooters who sailed along the Gulf of Guinea. While Conny built his empire with pirate booty and illicit trade, his army looted wrecked ships and used their cannons and other supplies to further fortify Fort Great Fredericksburg. They built a strong wall around most of the town of Pokesu to minimize the damage from attacks by sea. Conny operated the fort arguably more efficiently than the Prussians of the BAC had done, simultaneously fending off Dutch attacks of the fort while enslaving and transporting war captives from the Ashanti hinterland and selling them to any ship—company based, independent, or pirate—with goods of interest to trade.

Soon every European seaman who had spent time in West Africa knew that Conny could obtain for them everything they needed. Merchants with no affiliation to any European company tried their luck in the trade, competing with pirates for Conny's allegiance. The bigger slave-trading companies, like the WIC and RAC, grew increasingly nervous as Conny's indiscriminate trading practices attracted even more competition for them. Employees of the RAC and WIC even caught their own official company ships stopped by Conny's Castle! Though these Dutch and English captains could be reprimanded for stopping at Conny's Castle, they much preferred trading with Conny rather than with their company representatives, as Europe's mercantilism laws required them to take on cargo they didn't want at prices that didn't suit them. Representatives from the national companies sent panicked letters home, certain they could never compete with Conny's free-trade policies. Conny, naturally, was keen to fragment European power while he consolidated his own. In the eyes of most West Africans, these freebooters that Conny traded with presented yet another power that the West African caboceers could leverage against the conniving employees of the bigger European slaving companies.

From his position at Fort Great Fredericksburg at Cape Three Points, Conny saw every ship that passed by on its way to the Gold Coast strongholds of Dutch Elmina and English Komenda and Cape Coast Castle. The patterns of trade and the flags on the ships didn't miss the sharp eyes of the astute man. Every ship that stopped at his castle had valuable information from Europe or from other forts on the Gold Coast. His intel was arguably the best, since he could openly welcome all ships with and without flags. Pirates and company employees sat in uncomfortable detente together in the courtyard at the fort while Conny and his large family entertained them. Conny was wise enough to know what their latest information was worth and when his silence was worth more.

Conny had played the long con. His actions indicate he believed it was absurd that Europeans should have so much power on the Gold Coast. There was no reason in his mind why European factors should be the only ones to sit in their fortified castles, growing wealthy by pulling African people and resources out of the continent. He had waited out the Prussians, outmaneuvered the English, and rebuffed the Dutch. Anyone else who wanted his castle would have to come and get it, facing his private army up a steep hill or from the sea. Until then, Conny and his family would sup with sailors and pirates alike as the atmosphere along the Gold Coast grew increasingly violent and foreboding.

Chapter Two

———————————○———————————

William Snelgrave
and the Pirates

BEFORE JOHN CONNY SEIZED Fort Great Fredericksburg as his own in 1717, he had already convinced the Prussian traders of the Brandenburg African Company to abandon their principled aims and adopt the West African model of free trade, prioritizing the best deals and relationships over European trade restrictions. Still, many ship captains remained cautious about being seen visiting Fort Great Fredericksburg, fearing that interacting with Conny and the pirates would anger the European slave traders who trafficked from castles and factories along the Gold Coast. After all, the employees of state-run slave-trading companies like the English Royal Africa Company and the Dutch West India Company were extensions of their governments, and some of them held sway back home in Europe.

Once the Prussians left West Africa, however, Conny climbed Manfro Hill once more and lowered the Brandenburg flag. With that, Pokesu in Cape Three Points became an Ahantan free port city, geographically poised to facilitate the best deals between European traders and West Africa's Ashanti Empire inland. Conny's Castle, the new Fort Great Fredericksburg, attracted every type of illicit behavior that the European companies had spent so much money to try to suppress. West Africa, already lousy with people who plundered, smuggled, conned, lied, and murdered their way to wealth on the backs of enslaved Africans, now became a place where predator often became prey. A messy yet vivid portrayal of how this dynamic, which John Conny inadvertently helped create, changed the atmosphere in West Africa is found in the writings of well-to-do English slave trader William Snelgrave, who trafficked Africans to Virginia and Jamaica and survived a pirate attack off the coast of Sierra Leone in 1719. His account of this story, published fifteen years later, was a widely read and best-selling narrative dedicated to other European slave traders, and it highlights some stark ideological and social realities of piracy and the slave trade.

All traders from Europe who made their way to the Gold Coast had to pass by the coast of Sierra Leone. By 1719, Sierra Leone had become an outlaw hotspot due to a lucrative trade in a geographically advantageous area with no law enforcement at a time when vast swaths of seafaring men struggled to find employment. Getting there wasn't exactly the easiest of feats. It was impossible for a large slave ship to land safely along most of the coast in this region. The surf broke all along the coast at a great height, and Snelgrave hadn't yet figured out how to maneuver a larger ship close enough. Due to this, there were only two ways to transport people and items from coastal Sierra Leone onto the large European ships. The first required the knowledge and assistance of locals who navigated their smaller, more responsive canoes through the swell with careful timing, transporting passengers and cargo between ship and shore. The second required sailing through Whiteman's Bay and up the Sierra Leone River to Bunce Island.

Though the current was pleasant enough, sailing up the river was a treacherous proposition. Places for idling ships were well-hidden by sharp bends and forks in the river and thick vegetation that played tricks on the eyes. A dense wall of mangrove trees that might have seemed impenetrable to Snelgrave's eyes was perfectly navigable by someone who knew what gaps to look for. And by 1719, plenty of pirates had learned from the locals how to look.

A few miles up the river was Bunce Island, a place where the Royal Africa Company had set up Fort St. James with a handful of employees to manage the trade.* This was as far as a larger slave ship could proceed safely upriver. As Snelgrave's crew made their

---

* Bunce Island was usually spelled "Bense" or "Bence" on maps of this time period.

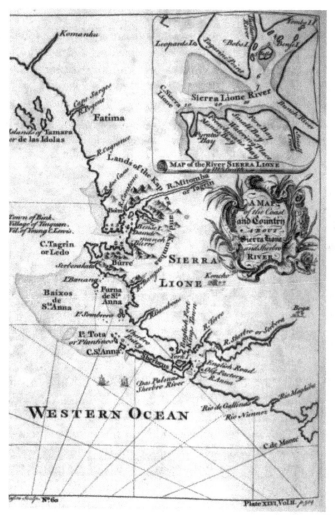

The coast of Sierra Leone. Locals often referred to the entire inset area as "Tagrin Bay," named after Tagarine point. It was also referred to as "White-man's Bay," as many independent European human traffickers, such as John "Captain Crackers" Leadstone made it their home. Bunce Island (#4 in the top-right inset) was where Howell Davis and his pirates sacked the English Royal Africa Company's Fort James. *Rare Book Division, New York Public Library, "A map of the coast and country about Sierra Lione and Sherbro [or Serbera] River; Map of the River Sierra Lione," New York Public Library Digital Collections, 1745–1747*

way there, they passed several trading posts they called "factories" of the Royal Africa Company. The Industrial Revolution in England wouldn't happen for another forty years, so these factories were little more than thatched huts where the lowest-paid Royal Africa Company employees sat unprotected, forever waiting on locals to bring them elephant tusks, dyewoods, gold, and enslaved captives for trade. These factors, as they were called, were employed by the Royal Africa Company, but had no real way of protecting themselves from the locals and pirates. Only those who could navigate this divided loyalty with finesse lived long enough to move on to a more lucrative, secure job in a fortified location like St. James.

Just out of sight of the river were a number of compounds set up by independent operators. Most of them were Europeans, or had some European parentage, and had formerly worked for one of the companies—usually the British or French—and now preferred the free-trade life. They were often more experienced and responsive than company employees, and as they became more powerful, the independent operators lost their fear of European laws and reprisals. By 1719, they also assisted pirates who sacked the nearby trading posts and ambushed ships from behind heavily vegetated bends in the river.

Captain Crackers was the most infamous of the private European free agents living on the water in this area, hidden from view of the coast among the mangrove trees. Two cannons flanked the entrance of his home, and several local hired women, called *gromettas*, managed his compound and attended to his every need. Surrounding his home were several sturdy wooden cages, some empty and others filled with enslaved captives for trade. He had been on the West African scene much longer than most and had the most checkered of pasts.

Captain Crackers shows up in various sources beginning in the early 1700s, when the Royal Africa Company foolishly employed him as a factor on the very same slave-trading post at Bunce Island in the Sierra Leone River. At the turn of the century, the French, who were averse to the fighting along the Gold Coast, had set up most of their forts and factories here instead. Crackers was just John Leadstone then, one of several contemptible employees of the RAC unqualified to navigate the slave trade, piracy, and local African politics with success. Most of his colleagues had very short lifespans and high attrition, though the few leathery men who survived their first year tended to stick around. Leadstone saw how everyone except the enslaved seemed to have it better than him in West Africa, and so when the opportunity presented itself to him, he took it.

He stole a large quantity of iron that he was supposed to hold for trade to the English, then sided with the French when they sacked the RAC factory. Then, like a pirate, he went into business for himself. His name pops up next in the Portuguese records, where slave traders at Cacheo in the Gambia hired him. He stole the cargo and murdered the Portuguese trader who attempted to stop him. After stealing a small ship, he began pirating and coastal raiding in earnest, attacking smaller French vessels as well as the coastline, kidnapping people from any and all unprotected African settlements, then turning back around to sell them to the French traders. He definitely wasn't the only one doing this: whenever unknown ships approached the coast in Sierra Leone, ship captains reported that the locals left their fires burning and ran into the interior for cover, anticipating such actions.

Every pirate who ever found themselves in Sierra Leone interacted with Leadstone, whom they dubbed "Old Crackers," or "Captain Crackers," after he retired from his exploits and set up his stationary compound in Whiteman's Bay, near modern-day Freetown. In his old age, he "kept open-house for all pirates, buccaneers, and privateersmen," as well as to any passing ships in need of anything.[1] Old Captain Crackers and his employees tended a supply of food, water, brandy, and African raw materials for trading to supplement the income they made from human trafficking. Most seafarers in Sierra Leone relied on Captain Crackers in some way.[2] It was possible that Snelgrave would have even tried to trade with him if the RAC fort St. James didn't have any enslaved people for sale. Although Snelgrave prided himself on being an upstanding individual, it behooved him to fill his hold as quickly as possible rather than linger on the coast waiting for more captives to be marched down to his ship. Every additional day spent in West Africa increased the chance that something bad would happen to his ship or crew.

Unfortunately for William Snelgrave's ship, the seafarers who relied on Captain Crackers the most were the large group of pirates living it up with him at his compound. They had eaten their way through Crackers's livestock and had been living from prize to prize when they spotted Snelgrave's slave ship, the *Bird Galley*, snaking its way up the river toward the fort on Bunce Island, which they had sacked weeks earlier. Slave ships didn't necessarily make the best prizes, but they often had plenty of supplies onboard.

Piracy was a menace to both the independent merchants and the various royal slave-trading companies. In England several royal interventions were put into place in an attempt to eradicate the problem. Back in 1687 King James II commissioned the ship *Mary* to "seize and destroy all such pyratts freebooters and sea rovers."[3] This failed to do much good, so in 1700 he authorized the court of assistants of the Royal Africa Company to pass a resolution that pirates were to be tried directly on the West African coast if it was "to be done upon reasonable terms" to expedite their eradication.[4] The naval power sent by Britain to exterminate the piracy that had been plaguing their slave-trading company since its inception succeeded in stemming the flow of pirates for only a decade before the post-Spanish-succession period, in which vast swathes of unemployed sailors turned to triangular-trade piracy for their living. The golden age of piracy was well in swing by the time the pirates of Sierra Leone caught up to the *Bird Galley*.[†]

There's a good chance that at least some of the pirates knew that the *Bird Galley* did not belong to the English Royal Africa Company, but to the private slave trader, Humphry Morice. Morice was a merchant, investor, member of Parliament, governor of the Bank of England, and embezzler extraordinaire who had been im-

---

† The golden age of piracy is defined in various ways in the historiography to refer to different time periods and locations. Here I am using Markus Rediker's parameters of the post-Spanish-succession period of 1716 to 1726, wherein history's most colorful and infamous pirates—such as "Black Sam" Bellamy, Stede Bonnet, Edward Teach (more commonly known as Blackbeard), Calico Jack Rackham (who sailed with the world's most infamous woman pirates, Anne Bonny and Mary Read), and "Black Bart" Roberts, among others—enjoyed their heyday in the Atlantic world. See Markus Rediker, *Villains of All Nations: Atlantic Pirates in the Golden Age* (Boston: Beacon Press, 2004).

plicated in the rug pull of the South Sea Company's investment bubble a few years earlier. Above all, he prized profit and keeping shareholders happy. His ships were known as "ten percenters," or ships whose captains paid a ten-percent affiliation fee for the privilege of trading with the Royal Africa Company's agents in Africa. Rather than having the naval backing that the ships of the RAC had, ten percenters carried insurance.[5] It was lucrative enough, though many of the captains and crew onboard knew of the heightened peril of piloting a private merchant vessel. In fact, Snelgrave reinforced in his narrative that pirates favored such independent merchants.[6] The pirates who had attacked his own ten percenter ship had also taken many of the Bristol ships.[‡] He was only a little worried. After all, he had brought many guns, ready for a potential fight.

SLAVE SHIP PIRATES

What Snelgrave hadn't counted on was being attacked by not one pirate, but a confederation of pirates. One ship, or perhaps two, the *Bird Galley* could withstand. But three ships with the combined crews of the ten that they had previously plundered onboard? With each of the pirates armed with cannons, pistols, muskets, assorted slashing weapons, knives, and makeshift bludgeoning devices? Those odds didn't strike him as favorable in the least.

The pirate crew was about eighty strong, versus Snelgrave's crew, which was less than half of that. Each of the three ships

---

‡ "Bristol ships" were slave ships equipped on the Avon in Bristol by members of the Society of Merchant Adventurers, a group of investors who pushed for the RAC to lose its monopoly in 1698. They, too, were ten percenters. A handful of coastal cities in Great Britain had large investments in the slave trade, and those that weren't folded into the Royal Africa Company became independent merchants. If they paid their ten percent, the British considered them legal, and if they did not, their trade was deemed illicit. For more information on this phenomenon in various British port cities, see David Richardson, *Bristol, Africa and the Eighteenth-Century Slave Trade to America*, vols. 1–3 (Bristol: Bristol Record Society, 1987), Suzanne Schwartz, *Slave Captain: The Career of James Irving in the Liverpool Slave Trade* (Liverpool: Liverpool University Press, 2008), Matthew David Mitchell, *The Prince of Slavers: Humphry Morice and the Transformation of Britain's Transatlantic Slave Trade, 1698–1732* (London: Palgrave MacMillan, 2020), and Rafael Ocasio, *A Bristol, Rhode Island, and Matanzas, Cuba, Slavery Connection: The Diary of George Howe* (Lanham, MD: Lexington Books, 2019).

was led by a pirate captain: Howell Davis, the flamboyant Welsh
captain his crew called a gentleman, the English Thomas Cocklyn, who, along with his crew, Snelgrave described as the "basest
and most cruel villains that ever were," and Oliver Levasseur, the
Frenchman known as La Bouche, or "the mouth," for his quick
wit and eagerness to humorously point out the errors of others as
a means of maintaining power.[7] This witty tactic was particularly
respected and powerful among the sailors turned pirates, and they
chose La Bouche as the fleet's commander.

Even if the numerical odds were more balanced, Snelgrave
couldn't have won, for he failed to account for another very important factor: betrayal by an insider among his crew. The pirates
had been hiding in the mangrove behind a bend in the river, and
when darkness fell, they rowed to Snelgrave's ship and boarded it.
Snelgrave later said that the pirates had "depended on the same
good fortune as in other ships they had taken; having met with no
resistance: for the people were generally glad of an opportunity of
entering with them."[8] Essentially, the pirates knew the slave-trading
crew onboard wouldn't put up much of a fight, and they were right.

Snelgrave ordered his crew to fight back, but curiously they
claimed they could not find the chest in which they kept the arms.
The pirates threw a few grenades to create smoke, noise, and confusion, and then one of Cocklyn's pirates homed in on the captain.
The shot he fired missed, so he pistol-whipped Snelgrave, claiming
that no quarter was to be given to any captain who defended his
ship. One of Davis's pirates stepped in and saved Snelgrave's life,
warning the captain that he would indeed forfeit his life if any of
his crew later claimed abuse at his hands.

What followed was a display of power and disdain. The pirate
quartermaster asked Snelgrave what time it was by his watch,
which the captain understood to be a polite way of robbing him of
it. Snelgrave handed it over, telling the quartermaster that "it was a
very good going Gold watch." The quartermaster "held it up by the
chain, and presently laid it down on the deck, giving it a kick with
his foot saying it was a pretty football."[9] Snelgrave mentioned in his
recounting of the pirate attack that he relayed this quip to show
"the humors and temper of these sort of people."[10]

The so-called humors and temper likely came from their nihilistic outlook and lack of career prospects. In a few years, they
devolved from celebrated hero privateers who bolstered the Royal
Navy's mission to reviled pirate scum who had been coerced into
the deeply unpleasant work of staffing the ever-increasing numbers
of slave ships. They were among the large swathes of people denied
the implicit promises of imperial riches and American opportunities. Many committed to seafaring lives with the hopes of becoming
naval heroes, captains, merchants, ship owners, or amassing enough
money to build a tavern or brothel in their favorite port, only to find
that their tattoos and other markings from a hard life at sea made
them targets for impressment and abuse for minimal or no wages
onboard naval or slave ships. As maritime wages stagnated, the
slave trade drastically ramped up, and opportunities for self-made
men shrank at that same rate. In short, it was nearly impossible to
earn an honest living, and so they stole their living.

Later, Snelgrave discovered that the ship's chest of arms had
been deliberately locked and hidden below deck by Simon Jones,
the very first of Snelgrave's crew to volunteer to join the pirates.
Snelgrave blamed this betrayal on poor circumstances at home and
a wife Jones could not love; anything to avoid addressing the coercion that was inherent in this job, which had made first his father
and now himself a well-to-do man. Jones ultimately persuaded
others in Snelgrave's crew to jump ship, too. One of the men who
remained loyal to Snelgrave reported that Jones had admitted that
he had volunteered for night watch so that he could be the first to
meet with the pirates when they came.

When another ship, the *Dispatch*, piloted by Captain Wilson
of the Royal Africa Company, appeared at the mouth of the Sierra
Leone River, Simon Jones, the man who had betrayed Snelgrave's
crew, pointed it out as a ship on which he was "unjustly used" and
requested that he and his newfound pirate crew take revenge. A
"witty brisk fellow" named John Stubbs intervened, saying that he
knew that ship—it was one of the oldest, most worm-eaten ships of
the company and had only a small cargo of redwood and malagueta
pepper seasoning onboard. Stubbs told Jones that if the pirates
burned the ship, the slave-trading company would "be highly

obliged to you for destroying her." This was because of the insurance money that the company would reap from the ship's destruction and nearly two years of the crew's unpaid wages that it would retain in such an arson. Stubbs was certain the sailors' wages were three times the value of the vessel and her "trifling cargo."[11] This convinced the pirates; although bloodthirsty and eager for revenge, they wanted sailors to be compensated for labor and companies and the captains to suffer for exploiting them. That Snelgrave paid close attention to this nascent labor rights movement and wrote about it in detail, even penning the men's dialogue, is telling of his motivations in publishing his pirate adventure.

So far, Snelgrave's pirate narrative overemphasizes how humane he himself was toward his crew. It was this factor that saved Snelgrave's life when pirates overran his ship and his crew spoke out favorably about his treatment of them, something that was rare at this time, when abusive behavior by captains and officers toward the crew was the accepted norm. However, his actions after that underscore that he was, above all else, a calculating and callow man, viewing the humane treatment of crew as a necessary tool to safeguard his own place in the slave trade and social hierarchy. The story emphasizes that it was the treatment of slave ship sailors that endangered the trade in captive Africans; treating sailors humanely first and foremost would bring order and stability to the trade. It also drove a wedge between sailors and the captives, ensuring that sailors didn't identify with their living "cargo," the enslaved, who were often mistreated in similar ways on board.

In both Snelgrave's narrative and among the pirates he quotes, there existed a high level of understanding of working conditions, the failure of the economy to serve the sailors, and mechanisms by which the colonial ruling classes were able to profit from slave voyages regardless of their outcome, placing all the risks of failed voyages onto sailors, who essentially were working in what modern people might refer to as the "gig economy."§ Snelgrave's work, a nar-

---

§ The gig economy shares a lot of the defining features of coerced labor. It isn't a coincidence that readers will spot many continuities between maritime labor in the eighteenth century and abuses of the workforce in the twenty-first. For a fuller exploration of the ways these coercive mechanisms fall into place today, see Erin Hatton, *Coerced: Work under Threat of Punishment* (Oakland: University of California Press, 2020).

rative dedicated to European slave traders in West Africa, serves in some places as a cautionary tale.

The next day, the pirates threw overboard "between three and four thousand pounds worth of the cargo" that had been in Snelgrave's hold. He had hoped to trade it for enslaved captives to take to the Americas. He watched in dismay as the pirates wasted cases of India goods, bales of woolen goods, and other manufactured items. The pirates were after only money, gold, and what they referred to as "necessaries": provisions, alcohol, and munitions.

Fortunately for Snelgrave, a handful of locals who witnessed the attack informed their trading partner, the Royal Africa Company governor, Captain Henry Glynn. Glynn knew Snelgrave from his previous slave voyages. He had supplied Snelgrave with captives before and held an uneasy truce with the independent traders at Whiteman's Bay and along the river. He used his social capital with Davis and La Bouche to try to save Snelgrave's life, for he knew that most of the men onboard those ships had been used and abused by sea captains in the slave trade and would be itching to take it out on his snooty business partner with the golden watch and powdered wigs.

Captain Davis, the pirate his men called a gentleman, agreed to help Glynn. He gathered the pirates and Snelgrave's stragglers together and addressed the crew saying that "they should remember their reasons for going a pirating were to revenge themselves on base merchants, and cruel commanders of ships." As Snelgrave's crew hadn't accused their captain of being either, they couldn't in good conscience murder him. Snelgrave dryly and without self-awareness mused that this speech "was by no means relished by this pack of miscreants; for in their hearts they hated Captain Davis, because he kept his ship's company in good order. . . . [B]eing a brave generous man, they dreaded his refinement."[12] To quell their grumbles, Davis saw to it that the crew was allowed to drink through the *Bird Galley*'s supply of brandy and claret while the pirate captains and their most trusted officers retired to the captain's quarters to make plans for Snelgrave.

The pirates' plan for Snelgrave had two complex parts: one in West Africa and another in the Caribbean. They proposed that

Snelgrave and his remaining crew be put into the service of pirates. First, they wanted to consolidate all the remaining cargo from the dozen or so ships they had recently pirated into one of the older, slower ships. This they would give to Snelgrave to captain. He would then sail down to the Gold Coast, stopping where he could exchange the cargo for gold and enslaved Africans. This part of the plan indicates certain knowledge about the workings in coastal West Africa. Sierra Leone was where enslaved captives and ivory could be obtained, and those were usually traded for manufactured goods and munitions from Europe. But the Gold Coast, so named for the alluvial gold that flecked the soil after rains and made the coast gleam, was where gold was exchanged. However, it would be suspicious for a European slave-trading captain to arrive at the forts asking only for gold, so Snelgrave would also trade for what he thought of as living cargo: captive Africans.

The pirates proposed that while Snelgrave sailed down to the Gold Coast, they would accompany him in the faster ships and plunder some French and Portuguese slave ships en route. This served multiple purposes: in promising to plunder only French and Portuguese ships, the pirates were promising to spare Snelgrave's English colleagues. They were also promising to behave like a security force, defending Snelgrave's ship from the French pirates that operated in West Africa. Next, the pirates' plan took on a new level of sophistication. The pirates would then have Snelgrave transport the African captives to the Caribbean Island of Saint Thomas, the Danish free port, and sell both them and the ship. The money would be split between Snelgrave and his crew, and those loyal to him could return to London. Snelgrave mused that "this proposal was unanimously approved of by them: but it struck me with a sudden damp, apprehending it would be fatal to me."[13]

FALSE FLAGS, PRUSSIAN PASSPORTS, AND THE FRESHWATER CON

This plan the pirates had made for Snelgrave was one that illustrates the many ways in which the economic and social factors rearranged the Atlantic slave trade after the turn of the century. John Conny, like most West Africans along the coast, saw that European insistence on monopolies was impractical. He used his international knowledge base and wide-ranging contacts in West Africa to act on this understanding. Even before the Prussians left West Africa, he had helped them craft what essentially became an Ahantan free port on the Gold Coast to support the Ashanti's desire for competitive pricing and first-choice access to European manufactured goods. The side effect was that his actions created a niche for independent merchants and pirates in the slave trade. It gave them a place to trade and spend coin and an excuse to linger on the Gold Coast. These freebooters developed a handful of deceptive practices that the pirates who took William Snelgrave's ship drew on when they created their plan for him. In this way, Conny's actions contributed to the creation of places like Saint Thomas, which functioned as sites of illicit resale and distribution in the Americas.

To appreciate the ingenuity of the pirate plan that gave William Snelgrave his damp apprehending feeling, it helps to have context for how swiftly free trade became the norm in Atlantic Africa and the Americas despite the European laws forbidding it. Most of the European slave-trading companies attempted to require monopolies with their African trading partners and their American colonies. This economic system was based on the ideology of mercantilism, and it was utterly infeasible. Mercantilism ignored the realities of coordinating supply and demand across the globe in the age of sail, when significant political, social, or environmental upheaval could change the supply chain before a ship could make it from one continent to the next. Europe's trading partners around the world lacked motivation to adhere to an infeasible system that would have rendered trade with Europe nearly useless, and no European nation had sufficient sea power to both police the seas for trade infractions and to fend off attacks on the disparate parts of their empires.

Over a relatively brief period, this situation led to conditions under which the alternate, illicit economy became the main economy. In essence, by 1719, free trade was the main type of international trade, and those who paid close attention while in port always were aware of the best places to buy and sell any commodity at all, whether that was cargo or enslaved captives.⁣ But often, finding the best place to conduct illicit business wasn't necessary if one could provide the appearance of legality through plausible deniability and a handful of thinly veiled cons. By 1719, the most common of these were false flags, the Prussian passport, and the freshwater con.

False flags were the oldest of complaints regarding interimperial trade and smuggling to come from company employees on the Gold Coast. Slave traders employed by the WIC and RAC at the nearby forts had observed many of the ships that stopped at Conny's Castle at Cape Three Points raising and lowering various national flags as they approached and departed Fort Great Fredericksburg. Dutch factors at nearby Axim complained that Dutch ships sent by their shared employer, the West India Company, swapped out the Dutch tricolor for the French as they sailed past the fort at Axim on their way to trade with the Brandenburgers, whose business relationship with John Conny offered a larger selection of wares and of enslaved captives. The factors at Axim couldn't believe that the Dutch ships, which had a contractual obligation to trade with the Dutch fort at Axim, would blatantly sail past to make better deals with the Prussians. Or rather, they believed it—and may have even wished that they were in the position to do the same—but expressed disbelief to the West India Company when explaining why their profits had dropped so drastically.

Each time this happened, goods of the WIC as well as people the Dutch had enslaved didn't get picked up at Axim. More importantly, the ships from Europe didn't drop off new things for the employees at Axim to trade with and gift to the WIC's African

---

⁣ In addition to the trade in enslaved Africans, there existed a robust illicit trade in enslaved Indigenous people across the globe, which ran concurrent with the trade in enslaved Africans. This trade was ubiquitous, and enslavers often didn't make distinctions between enslaved Africans or Indigenous people, especially in rural, frontier, and borderland locations. This is a relatively young field of study and the estimated numbers vary and are expected to increase as this line of scholarship develops. See Erin Woodruff Stone's *Captives of Conquest: Slavery in the Early Modern Spanish Caribbean* (Philadelphia: University of Pennsylvania Press, 2021), Alan Gallay's *The Indian Slave Trade: The Rise of the English Empire in the American South, 1670–1717* (New Haven, CT: Yale University Press, 2003), and Kevin Waite's *West of Slavery: The Southern Dream of a Transcontinental Empire* (Chapel Hill: University of North Carolina Press, 2021). For the upcoming data of the Indigenous enslaved across the Americas, see the Native Bound Unbound archive, funded by the Andrew W. Mellon Foundation in 2022. Find it at https://linktr.ee/natboundunbound.

partners at these forts.** This in turn fomented ill will locally as
the Africans who had signed treaties with the Dutch watched the
European goods that they had been promised sail past, right into
the pockets of Conny and the Ahanta instead of to them. Since
most European slave traders were still heavily reliant on African
allies at this precolonial time, employees of the company panicked
in their letters home, asserting that angering the locals in this way
was treacherous and that every Dutch ship that passed by opened
the Dutch employees at Axim to abuse and violence from their dis-
gruntled local trading partners. This sometimes resulted in factories
and fortresses being burned and European lives lost in retaliation.

In addition to flying multiple flags when it best suited them,
non-company traders also attempted to secure their place in West
African waters with a Prussian passport. The Brandenburg African
Company was always much smaller than its Dutch or English
equivalents. Occasionally, it allowed ships and captains from other
nations to sail under its flag in exchange for a fee, much like Spain
outsourced its slave trade to other European powers or the Royal
Africa Company allowed ten percenters to operate for a fee. Non-
company merchants who wanted to trade in West Africa could get
this permit from the Prussians and use it as an excuse to be on the
West African coast "legally." The people who did this most often
were Dutch merchants from the south of the Republic in Zeeland
who had been locked out of the slave trade and the Dutch West
India Company and wanted to share in its riches.

The glaring issue[14] with this, of course, was that because of the
prevalence of false flags, there was no way for Dutch employees
on the coast or on WIC ships to know whether a ship's Prussian
passport was legitimate if a ship that was blatantly not of Prussian
design flew the Brandenburgers' flag. However, the numbers of
Prussian flags on the Gold Coast were suspicious in and of them-

** It wasn't only the Dutch slave traders who traded for self-interest at the expense of
their employers. Prussian employees of the Brandenburg Company also traded on their own
behalf instead of for the BAC. Those on the ground at Fort Great Fredericksburg and the two
smaller Prussian trading posts followed the examples that powerful Africans like John Cabes
and John Conny set and traded with anyone who approached their fortresses. See Andrea
Weindl, "The Slave Trade of Northern Germany from the Seventeenth to the Nineteenth
Centuries," in *Extending the Frontiers: Essays on the New Transatlantic Slave Trade Database,*
ed. David Eltis and David Richardson (New Haven, CT: Yale University Press, 2008).

selves, because although the English and Dutch had dozens of trading factories and fortifications on the Gold Coast alone, the Prussians had only Fort Great Fredericksburg and two smaller trading forts nearby. There was no way that the allies of the Prussians were able to march enough African captives through them to fill all the ships flying the red eagle of Prussia. This meant that many of these ships were obtaining captives from elsewhere, which resulted in fewer captives for the national slave-trading companies. Legitimate Prussian passport or no, it was becoming a problem for the Dutch slave traders: the uptick in Prussian flags coincided with an uptick in violent sea robbery and loss for the West India Company.

Once the scheme was in play in West Africa, the Prussians were unable to take control of it. In 1716, the Netherlands and Prussia narrowly avoided an international incident over the Prussian passport due to the actions of the crew onboard the ship named *King of Prussia*. According to the West India Company, this ship appeared to be a respectable Prussian ship headed for Fort Great Fredericksburg, when in reality it was clearly equipped with Dutch goods from the south. When pressed on this matter, the crew of the *King of Prussia* "viciously attacked" and "decimated" a WIC slave ship and so were brought in for questioning. They presented the WIC with a passport that they claimed originated with the prince elector of Prussia, but, when pressed, no one could explain what made the ship Prussian other than a piece of paper. The traders were clearly interlopers in the eyes of the WIC, and on the same level as pirates.[15] Some of these merchants even hired scribes to produce the stacks of various forged documents that captains would need to convince company employees to trade with them: introduction letters, insurance information, and royal missives. This type of forgery alludes to the prevalence of a class of highly knowledgeable, cosmopolitan, multilingual maritime people who kept their fingers firmly on the pulse of the ever-shifting sociopolitical situation of the Atlantic world. They likely did not view themselves as pirates or even smugglers, but as business entities that did what was necessary when they fell out of favor with the governing bodies that bestowed the monopoly on the slave trade onto the West India or Royal Africa Companies.

At this time, the Brandenburg Company was on the verge of shutting down. Its approach to business and allowing John Conny to monopolize access to the Ashanti already had made them unpopular with the Dutch and the English slave traders. These companies' mutual hatred for the Prussians threatened to supersede even the decades of bad blood generated between them through the Anglo-Dutch Wars and the Komenda Wars. Years before, Herr Kuffler, an employee of the BAC, was tasked with creating a thoroughly researched report that considered the state of the Brandenburg Company when it came to these fraudulent smuggling tactics in West Africa. It is through his report that we learn about the beginnings and proliferation of the tactic which the WIC and RAC complained about the most, known as the "Freshwater Con."[16]

Fresh water was the most important thing onboard a ship. Without it, crews and enslaved captives would perish within days. Maritime history is littered with reports of crews who miscalculated water needs, whose water supply was damaged or contaminated, or who were blown off course without access to a place where they could renew water supplies. The deaths were painful and gruesome. Since Europeans first began sailing across the Atlantic, they had a shared understanding that regardless of the relationships between nations, individuals begging for water could not be turned away. Even if the Netherlands and Britain were at war, it was understood that if a Dutch ship peaceably approached an English fort anywhere in the world, the English would allow them to renew their water supply. Naturally this was exploited easily by non-company merchants and pirates.

The captains onboard these ships would slip on their most respectable coats and claim that they were out of potable water in order to be allowed onto land without being fired upon by the fort's cannons. Then the fort's doors would swing open as the acting governor sent out a team of water carriers, usually enslaved. The crews onboard the interloper ships would use the opening to storm the fort and snatch all the other enslaved people imprisoned therein.[17] Of course, African traders like the Ahantan John Conny and, before him, the Komendan John Cabes freely traded with crews that had committed "freshwater cons" at the British and Dutch forts, as their standing armies were powerful enough to repel anyone who tried it with them personally. When Conny and Cabes were questioned about this by employees of the Prussian and British slave-trading companies, they claimed that they could not tell the difference between legitimate and illegitimate traders.[18] It's possible this answer lies somewhere between open belligerence toward their European business partners and honesty, for no groups of Europeans in West Africa could agree on who was "legitimate" and who wasn't, and the criteria changed often, as alliances shifted in Europe, Africa, and the Americas. Most likely African caboceers like John Conny didn't think it was important to keep track because they had their own ideas about the selection of trading partners, which were not in line with those of slave-trading company officials.

Kuffler's BAC report ends with the assertion that these independent merchants trading on the coast led to acts of violence and instability of the royal trades.[19] Beyond that, merchants who engaged in false flags, kidnapping, smuggling, the freshwater con, and acts of piracy had several pronounced effects on the coastal West Africans and on the enslaved captives as well. In some instances, African locals were able to use these unlicensed traders to their advantage, as excuses or to otherwise foment discord and extort a more favorable position with European company employees when it came to trade. In others, they were the victims of these unauthorized slavers and were cheated, robbed, or taken to the Americas in shackles along with the enslaved captives onboard.

These types of behaviors that non-company merchants and pirates used to obtain enslaved captives in Africa created ships full of Africans who couldn't be sold legally in the colonial ports, which were monitored and controlled by the colonial arms of the European companies. Rather, enslaved captives obtained in this way could be sold only in places on the peripheries of empire that were less choosy about the origins of the ships in their ports. In the Atlantic world, different eras had different locations that functioned as clearinghouses where nearly anyone and anything could be bought and sold, with no questions asked and their origins safely obscured. Saint Thomas, in what today is part of the US Virgin Islands, was the worst-kept "secret" clearinghouse, which hosted the largest illicit market of captive Africans of the early eighteenth cen-

tury. It's why the pirates who attacked Snelgrave's ship suggested it
for the second half of their plan.

SMUGGLING, PIRACY, AND PRIVATEERING
AT SAINT THOMAS

The year 1719 was pivotal for Saint Thomas and the illicit American trade in enslaved Africans. Back in 1685, the Prussian Brandenburg African Company had taken over the slave trade to the
Danish Caribbean island of Saint Thomas. The Danes leased half
of the island to the Prussians and received a small percentage of
every import and export price. Their cooperation created one of the
largest Caribbean auctions of enslaved captives of the time.

Although the BAC was pressured by European powers to enforce
monopolies in order to supply this auction of enslaved Africans, it
was most profitable for both Prussian and Dutch inhabitants of the
island of Saint Thomas to accept any and all incoming shipments of
enslaved Africans, regardless of how they were captured, who supplied them, or where those ships came from. At first the Prussian
company considered this contraband trade detrimental, but both the
settlers living on Saint Thomas and the Prussian traders working out
of Fort Great Fredericksburg in Cape Three Points benefited greatly
from this less discriminate trade. Even if the Prussians had made an
earnest attempt to enforce monopoly through their company, they
would have found employees and settlers on both sides of the Atlantic unwilling to comply. All people involved in human trafficking
were determined to turn a profit in a world of unfeasible regulation
designed to benefit only European shareholders.

When John Conny began working with the Brandenburg company in 1710, stepping into the role of caboceer, he pushed it further in the direction of free trade, showing the Prussian employees
in Africa that relaxing their company's mercantilist edicts resulted
in better relationships with the emerging Ashanti powers inland,
which ultimately proved very profitable. For the next five years, the
half of Saint Thomas controlled by the Brandenburg company saw
unparalleled economic growth as a result. Slowly, the enthusiastic

free trade on the island became an open secret, and BAC employees brainstormed how to make the most of their popular slavery market on Saint Thomas. In addition to enslaved Africans, BAC records contain a list of all the things for which people in the Spanish American colonies wanted from the Prussians: paper, spectacles, bells, furs, spice, tobacco, cannonballs, nails, carpentry materials, and buttons from the city of Nuremburg.[20] Employees of the BAC believed they could expect large amounts of ambergris, pearls, turtle shells, saltpeter, salsa pareille, china, copper, indigo, cochineal, Nicaraguan wood, cocoa, wool, emeralds, sapphires, and other precious gems in return for double or triple their price in Europe.[††] The report makes the case that mercantilism could not be honored because the settlers in the Spanish Empire were so desperate to trade and had access to a glut of natural resources yet nowhere to trade them, so settlers and other colonists welcomed the ships of companies like the BAC (and the Dutch WIC) to facilitate this trade that their empire forbade.[21]

Participating in the illicit trade did not render Saint Thomas immune from the attention of others who preyed on the slave trade. As the Brandenburg company increasingly displayed indiscriminate mercantile behavior contrary to the European trade agreements that their Prussian king signed back home in Europe, BAC ships had become the target of privateers. Slave ships in the Caribbean generally were "slow of sail and weary of crew," making them easy prey.[22] And ships returning from a delivery of enslaved Africans were heavy with the valuable coin and goods they had traded for them. In 1714, the governor of Prussian Saint Thomas, Johannes Zeneman, along with the wartime commissioner and the minister of maritime advice, expressed fear to the BAC about sending out the doubloons that they had amassed in their slave trade. Both French and Spanish privateers were circling the island and the route between Saint Thomas and the Dutch clearinghouse of Curaçao,

---

†† I am led to believe from the context that "salsa pareille" is a Prussian misspelling of *salsepareille*—the French name for the medicinal plant *smilax aspera*, which was made into an ointment or tincture and used to cure many common ailments from rheumatism to gout and—most importantly in the age of Atlantic trade and all forms of cross-cultural contact—syphilis.

waiting for heavy ships to pass by.[23] The privateers were aware that Prussian naval power in the Caribbean was negligible.

Despite the dangers, trading in this way was highly profitable. Two years later, in 1716, the BAC's new director of Saint Thomas, Sivert Hoess, wrote to the king of Brandenburg mentioning the illicit sale of enslaved African captives that had been brought to the island via a smuggler's ship. The governor explained that everyone, including the Danish governor, was very interested in this market and profited heavily from the sale.[24] The implication was that in his position he hardly could be expected to forbid this most profitable breach of the BAC's policy and no longer felt the need to disguise it. Flouting mercantilist edicts enriched everyone involved in the trafficking of Africans, and Prussia needed to update its policies.[25] This letter was similar to the letters from the employees working with John Conny out of Fort Great Fredericksburg on West Africa's Gold Coast who valued his connections and trade preferences more than the connections and preferences of the Dutch or English traders.

Alongside employees in West Africa, English and Dutch governors in the Americas also heavily circumvented mercantilist policies for profit in the slave trade. It was an ongoing concern in the records of the trading companies, as employees accused one another of trading on the side to enrich themselves at the expense of empire. As the Prussians had Saint Thomas, the English had Jamaica and Bermuda, and the Dutch had Curaçao and Saint Eustatius.[26] All colonial governors in the Americas considered themselves overworked and underpaid and struggled to maintain power in fledgling colonies, so they turned a blind eye when colonists traveled to these international clearinghouses to meet demands for enslaved African labor. In general, governors in the Americas allowed interimperial trade between their colonists to occur throughout the seventeenth and eighteenth centuries despite laws that made most of it illegal, much like they courted the presence of "friendly" pirates to act as standing navies to protect a colony the empire considered less important. Generally, imperial authorities in Europe condemned the American governors who made the choices that fostered this profitable commerce even though it constructed colonies, made them viable, and helped empires to grow.[27]

Just a year later in 1717, the Brandenburg African Company had recalled all its European employees from the West African Gold Coast and from Saint Thomas back to Prussia and then dissolved. The Prussians focused on internal matters as John Conny claimed control of Fort Great Fredericksburg. Saint Thomas officially became a fully Danish island in name but in essence continued to be ruled by the wealthiest merchants and highest bidders who always had controlled the largest American market in enslaved African captives.

So, by 1719, when the pirates under Captains Howell Davis, Thomas Cocklyn, and La Bouche tried to convince the slave trader William Snelgrave to bring the enslaved to Saint Thomas, they, like the merchants and pirates engaging in false flags, Prussian passports, and freshwater cons, were intentional in their plans to head where free trade occurred and was least likely to result in reprimand. The relative chaos due to the Brandenburgers pulling out of Saint Thomas provided an additional layer of security. This island with the largest markets would continue accepting ships from everywhere, with no questions asked, and if not, the pirates would pivot mid-plan like they always had and find another buyer. The culture of piracy and free trade in West Africa was created by the actions of slave-trading company employees, inland empires like the Fante and Ashanti, independent merchants (both European and African), and pirates like Davis, Cocklyn, and La Bouche. This in turn created black markets in the Americas where captains of slave ships with dubious origins could take a small risk for big rewards.

SLAVE SHIP CAPTAINS, SAILORS, AND CAPTIVES

Since the pirate captains who had plundered William Snelgrave's ship were aware of most of these economic complexities, they couldn't understand why Snelgrave protested their profitable plan, which was foolproof in their eyes. Captain Howell Davis interceded and explained that for a wealthy man like Snelgrave, the broken system, which impoverished most sailors and many colonists, still worked for those in the top tiers. If Snelgrave did what the pirates asked of him, it would ruin his reputation—and make him a pirate, too. Unlike the pirates, who had nothing but their lives to lose, Snelgrave had a family, social capital aplenty, and an estate back in England. Howell Davis convinced the pirates to compromise and give Snelgrave the dregs of what was left of the cargo from his original ship, the *Bird Galley*, and let him go in La Bouche's older, slower brigantine that they were planning to abandon anyway. They no longer needed it after pirating dozens more ships.

The juncture of the Sierra Leone River where the pirates were was effectively a naval chokepoint. While Snelgrave's sailors wearily transferred cargo to the brigantine he had been allocated, they watched helplessly as an unfortunate French ship appeared at the bend in the river. The pirates scrambled after the ship, took it with ease, and hanged the captain until almost dead while Snelgrave watched in horror. When the pirates finally turned to Snelgrave to allow him and a handful of sailors to depart, he breathed a sigh of relief and left. Despite this experience, he elected to stay in the Gulf of Guinea off the coast of West Africa for a while. He felt a responsibility toward the other Humphry Morice ships in the area. As the pirates took more ships, Snelgrave collected information about the pirate attacks. He recorded an encounter he had with another Humphry Morice ship, the *Elizabeth*, which had been pirated by the same crew that had taken his own ship, and this encounter shows the more sinister and calculating side of him.

In the same account in which he regales the English society with his heroic capers when attacked by pirates, he also writes about how he thwarted a slave ship revolt onboard the *Elizabeth*. She had just been pirated and the abusive Captain Thompson and first mate killed. Snelgrave found her anchored off the Gold Coast while the crew attempted to decide how to proceed on their voyage. The crew onboard consisted of those who had survived the pirate attack and elected to not join their attackers. They told Snelgrave that the pirates had left them their cargo of enslaved people and put the second mate, whom the crew had told the pirates was a "generous and good man," in charge.

While anchored on the coast, the crew of the *Elizabeth* began to interact with the captives onboard and took pity on their plight. Many of the crew were first timers onboard a slave ship and were coming to terms with the awful day-to-day reality of such a trade. Snelgrave wanted to take the 120 captives onboard to sell them, and the cooper told him that the sailors and the enslaved had been onboard together for a long time, and so the crew "had great friendship with them and therefore they would keep them." Snelgrave scoffed at this idea and asked if it was his first time sailing onboard a slave ship. It was, and it seemed likely that the nature of the work, combined with long days at sea and perhaps the interaction with the pirates, had made this cooper think differently about loyalty, crew, employment, friendship, and freedom.

The enslaved found out from the crew about Snelgrave's plan to sell them, so that night, while Snelgrave slept in his bed on the old brigantine anchored next to the *Elizabeth*, a handful of the enslaved men attempted an escape. African captives onboard slave ships knew well what awaited them in the Americas and that the men with the powdered wigs were the most dangerous to their well-being. While at this time the majority of captives came from raids in the interior, they had been subject to the warfare and raiding that the slave trade had encouraged for years. Once captured, they had undertaken the arduous march to the coast, where they had time to interact with traders who explained the workings of the transatlantic slave trade to them.[28] After the march, many of the enslaved would wait weeks or even months imprisoned in pens or in the dungeons of European trading forts, where local employees of the slaving companies were in charge of their welfare. Many of the captives saw ships come in and out or pass by and had time to learn how to communicate with one another, pass knowledge, and to plan or attempt escapes.[29]

Snelgrave, in bed on his ship, heard gunshots from the ship anchored next to his and woke his crew to investigate. The unlucky cooper of the *Elizabeth* was in the way of the escapees and had been killed in their attempt, as were several of the captives who jumped into the water and were torn apart by sharks as the crew gasped in horror at the sound of the frenzy and then the smell of their blood in the water. Snelgrave's crew recaptured two of the men by paddling after them in lifeboats, and these captives confessed to killing the cooper so that they could "escape undiscovered by swimming to shore."[30]

At daybreak, Snelgrave took it upon himself to force the crew to bring all the enslaved prisoners on the ship to the deck and forced both crew and captives to watch as he made an example of the freedom fighters who had killed the cooper in their escape attempt. Snelgrave told the captives that he knew it was customary in his country for murderers to pay a sum of money as restitution to the victims, but "it was not so with us; and he should find that I had no regard to my profit in this respect."

Then, in an act of gross brutality that would echo the lynchings of enslaved Africans and their descendants in Virginia and throughout the US South, he had one of the would-be escapees hoisted onto the yardarm of the *Elizabeth* and slowly shot to death. Finally, he beheaded the corpse and threw it overboard, writing, "This last part was done, to let our negroes see, that all who offended thus, should be served in the same manner." This was a symbolic act of corpse mutilation. Snelgrave wrote about the ways in which he (incorrectly) interpreted the religious beliefs of the enslaved and how he spiritually tortured the escapee by beheading his body, therefore preventing or interrupting access to an afterlife: "For many of the Blacks believe, that if they are put to death and not dismembered, they shall return again to their own country after they are thrown overboard." He then had a translator from among the captives make the other enslaved people swear that they would be obedient during the voyage to the Americas. The tone used in this portion of the text is overwhelmingly self-congratulatory and full of pride: Snelgrave believed that he had cracked the code to keeping the most spirited enslaved prisoners docile and forcing their acceptance of the transition from personhood to chattel.[31]

This incident was all in his own words, published for a tidy sum. Like most of the men in this book, Snelgrave believed himself the hero of his story. He thought that he did what he had to do to maintain order among the crews of the other Humphry Morice slave ships that encountered pirates or others who introduced their crews or enslaved captives to the possibility of flirting with differing conceptions of freedom. He sought to preserve his upper-middle-class lifestyle and supply the Americas with the enslaved African labor that its sugar- and tobacco-planting settlers demanded. To quell what he perceived to be the problems of crews siding with pirates or even with the enslaved, he promoted good treatment of crews onboard slave ships, seeking to eradicate any sympathy that abused crew members might have toward the enslaved, who were usually whipped with the same instruments of torture that captains wielded against sailors. In effect, his narrative is an attempt to bolster the security of the Atlantic slave trade by deliberately driving a wedge between the slave ship sailors and the captive Africans they were tasked with transporting.

These are similar tactics that later would appear in full force in the Americas in attempts to keep poor White people in line and prevent them from siding with the enslaved populations whom they lived and worked alongside. These tactics were perfected in the slave trade and allowed the institution of slavery to flourish, even in places where only a handful of enslavers lived and where the institution of slavery was detrimental to the local White population. Moreover, Snelgrave took advantage of what was legal at the time and bought into the emerging racist depersonalizing rhetoric of the slave trade, justifying in his mind something that other Whites of this time period already knew and acknowledged was wrong. Though many White sailors like the cooper onboard the *Elizabeth* hesitated to treat the enslaved like chattel, both pirates and sailors, captains and crews, already had begun to internalize this rhetoric, which dehumanized the enslaved populations and rendered them, in colonial minds, as objects rather than people.

All of these factors made the interactions between pirates and the enslaved incredibly complex and varied. It is true both that pirates sometimes freed the enslaved and asked them to join their crews, where they would be treated as equals, whereas at other times, pirates attacked slave ships in order to profit from the resale of human cargo. Like the crews of merchant ships and most navies, pirate crews were multiracial. The coastal West Africans, who traded with Europeans, Black, and multiracial pirates, understood well that a wrong move, or twist of fate, or conflict with an unscrupulous person could land them in shackles. At the end of the day, pirates practiced a radical form of egalitarianism among themselves, but they didn't always extend this to enslaved people, who were considered a valuable and expensive commodity in the world pirates and the enslaved shared. Pirates were a force that changed the trajectory of history with their countercultural lives, but even they could not destroy the prevailing culture of the slave societies of the Americas, which had been built and thoroughly shaped by the labor stolen from the enslaved Africans and their descendants.‡‡

Though ship crews were multiracial and multiethnic in the early 1700s, the vast majority of the enslaved people caught up in the Atlantic trade were Black Africans. Historians trace the formation of anti-Black racism to the rise of Atlantic world slavery, though this process was a gradual transition that took place over centuries. The early 1700s were still pregnant with possibilities, though the possibilities for enslaved Africans would dwindle, because in the Americas, their enslaved status associated their skin tones with inferiority among the White ruling classes in an emerging colonized world. The association of Blackness with a consumable commodity would become deeply entrenched over time, and White supremacist thought calcified, justifying centuries of stolen labor and lives.[32]

Perhaps ironically, the independent merchants, smugglers, pirates, and other freebooters unassociated with the royal trading companies hastened this process. Free trade, albeit a fixture of modern life and associated with enlightened societies, was only nascent at the turn of the eighteenth century, and the budding

---

‡‡ The debates raging about the radical nature of pirates and how far one can extend this interpretation of their motives in light of their interactions with enslaved captives (along with women and Indigenous people) make for thought-provoking reading. Start with Markus Rediker's *Outlaws of the Atlantic: Sailors, Pirates and Motley Crews in the Age of Sail* (Boston: Beacon Press, 2014) for an exploration of the most radical examples of racial egalitarianism among maritime laborers and pirates during this time and then work your way to W. Jeffrey Bolster's *Black Jacks: African American Seamen in the Age of Sail* (Boston: Harvard University Press, 2009), Emma Christopher's *Slave Ship Sailors and Their Captive Cargoes 1730–1807* (Cambridge: Cambridge University Press, 2006), and Stephanie Smallwood's *Saltwater Slavery: A Middle Passage from Africa to American Diaspora* (Boston: Harvard University Press, 2008) to find the places where other analytical lenses reveal the limits of that exploration. For a scathing counterbalance that challenges the notion that self-interested pirates had any revolutionary intentions at all, finish with any of Arne Bialuschewski's articles on pirates and piracy during the Golden Age.

philosophy lent itself well to the dehumanizing nature of chattel slavery. In other words, the emergence of capitalism and all forms of exploitation, including slavery, went hand in hand. The illicit slave trade made the Middle Passage more arduous and terrible for the enslaved Africans packed into the hulls of ships. It lengthened the amount of time trafficked people spent in dangerous transit, and each resale or recapture they endured meant yet more time with unpredictable people who had power over the vulnerable enslaved. This in turn increased the demand for workers in the human trafficking business and the number of people who learned to turn a blind eye to the injustice so they could profit from it. This created generations of people like William Snelgrave on both sides of the Atlantic whose finances, self-image, and personal sense of honor were enmeshed in enslaving identities that persisted long after abolition.

After the encounter with the *Elizabeth*, William Snelgrave completed his voyage and sold the enslaved onboard the brigantine in a market in Jamaica. He returned to London and took some time to meet with officials at Humphry Morice and the Royal Africa Company and then to pen his manuscript. For the time being, the Atlantic Ocean was lousy with pirates and Snelgrave would concern himself with using his experiences and connections in England to help restore what he perceived as order on the West African coast. He watched with satisfaction as the Crown agreed to dispatch an unrivaled force from the British navy to West Africa, heavy with seamen and guns and led by the experienced pirate hunter Captain Chaloner Ogle to stamp out the problem once and for all. While Ogle's ships were prepared for the voyage in Portsmouth's naval dockyard, Captain Howell Davis and the other pirates in West Africa pressed on, setting their sights on bolder cons and larger prizes still.

Chapter Three

———————————O———————————

Black Bart,
from Slave Ship Sailor
to Pirate Captain

LIKE ALL LARGER-THAN-LIFE historical figures, before Bartholomew Roberts became the infamous pirate Black Bart, he was just an ordinary man trapped in a dangerous and distasteful yet unextraordinary life. He worked as a navigator for various British slave ships. What he did before that is unclear, but most navigators didn't start out as navigators—they often began working onboard ships in their early teens, doing the menial jobs while trying to avoid abuse from the older members of the crew. Those who had aptitude and luck could work their way into the specialized jobs, like that of navigator, that paid a little more. The extra shillings didn't amount to much when the job was on a slave ship, however, especially in the summer of 1719.

The year aside, being onboard a slave ship was already miserable. Although working the ship wasn't comparable with being enslaved, locked below deck, and treated as human cargo, it was a deeply traumatic and disgusting job even for those fortunate enough to be free. The maritime workforce was in proximity to enslavement, tasked with upholding the mechanism that attempted to rob enslaved Africans of their humanity and render them cargo. Slave ship sailors did this while at the same time being subjected to many of the same types of violence from the captains and shareholders who created this new world dependent on slave labor. The same whips that slave ship sailors used to maintain order among the enslaved were used by captains and officers to discipline the sailors. Sometimes these scarring beatings were the only means of motivating sailors to extreme cruelty toward the enslaved.

Slave ship sailors lived complicated lives. Most crews onboard slave ships were multiracial, with origins from around the world. Free Africans, Afro-Caribbeans, African Americans, and Afro-Latinos were widely represented among slave ship crews, and they saw the ways in which the enslavement of Africans created a racial hierarchy that didn't reflect the hierarchy onboard their ships but shrank their lives and opportunities on land.[1] They understood that little separated them from the Africans locked in the slave ship holds. Black sailors on slave ships were often forbidden from leaving the ship when the ship anchored in American ports because their freedom was infectious.* In addition to this, some slave ship sailors were enslaved themselves. The Brandenburg Company trained enslaved Africans with aptitude how to sail Prussian vessels and had them work onboard.[2] Their colleagues of European origin understood this dynamic and took turns either exploiting it for personal gain or for maintaining solidarity with their Afro-descended colleagues and even the enslaved. These ever shifting and intersecting dynamics made everyone onboard the slave ship, from captain to enslaved, nervous.

This unease permeated everything, and the longer a slave ship spent anchored off the coast of West Africa, the higher the tensions rose. As few natural ports exist in West Africa, most slave ships remained anchored near the coastal trading posts and fortifications while hired African canoe paddlers transported officers, goods, and the enslaved back and forth from ship to coast. Even sailors with more specialized jobs, like Roberts, stayed on the ship, sometimes for weeks at a time while waiting to receive the enslaved Africans who were force-marched in coffles from the interior to the coast. By

---

* The areas that would become part of the United States were notorious for passing laws commonly called "Black codes," which strictly controlled the movement of Black maritime laborers when in American ports to prevent visits to the places where local enslaved and free Blacks congregated. Black sailors and other maritime laborers used port visits to spread detailed news of slave insurrections and rebellions, which taught locals how to increase their own chances of successful revolt. See Julius Scott, *The Common Wind: Afro-American Currents in the Age of the Haitian Revolution* (London: Verso, 2018).

the 1710s, pirate attacks on slave ships had become commonplace, part of the thrum of background anxiety felt onboard slave ships as they approached West Africa. This was because pirate attacks on slave ships were unpredictable. For some of those onboard, enslaved or free, pirate attacks could at least temporarily improve a situation, but for others, the pirate attacks proved fatal.

This anxiety must have been at the forefront of Bartholomew Roberts's mind, as well as the minds of each and every crew member of the slave ship *Princess*, under Captain Abraham Plumb in June 1719. This particular voyage was, like that of Snelgrave, a ten percenter, underwritten by Humphry Morice, making Snelgrave and Plumb colleagues. This meant that though Snelgrave's account wouldn't be published to the wider public for another fifteen years, Captain Plumb and the crew would have been briefed about its details while he registered and made preparations for the voyage back in London.

Bartholomew Roberts was serving as second or possibly third mate on this voyage, and as the ship waited off the coast of Anomabo, the simmering tension came to a slow boil. The *Princess* had encountered what Captain Plumb would consider bad luck on this voyage. Slave ships from Europe or the Americas to Africa always moved from west to east, stopping at each of their country's trading forts along the coast to take on whatever captives were imprisoned there. If the timing was fortuitous for the captains of these ships, they would need to stop only once or twice before the hold was filled and they could cross the Atlantic. But this time, the weather and timing had coincided in such a way that each stop from west to east yielded only a handful of captives. This meant that the journey was lengthened as the *Princess* sailed past John Conny's castle and stopped at each Royal Africa Company (RAC) fortress along the coast, hoping for a larger turnout. When they made it to Cape Coast Castle, the administrative seat of the British company, the factor informed them that a company ship had just left with all of the captives in tow.

Now at Anomabo, they waited in the hopes that more captives would soon arrive. As with Ahanta and Komenda, Anomabo had a long history of Africans exploiting European rivalries. In 1640 the Dutch built a fort there, and in 1653 the Swedish captured it. In 1657 the Danes took it from the Swedes. In 1660 the Dutch wrested control back. For seven years they attempted to curry favor with the local group of Fante, but once the second Anglo-Dutch War ended in 1667, the English gained the right to trade there. The Dutch factors at forts nearby seethed as they watched their work undermined while British ships anchored in the port they considered theirs. In 1674 the English finished building Fort Charles, and by 1698, the ten-percenter ships began favoring this port due to its geography—it was often the very last stop for British slave ships, and most of the RAC ships filled up by the time they reached Cape Coast, so there was no need to continue east to Anomabo. The crumbling outpost wasn't much to look at, with just one story and nine cannons, but Anomabo was generally a place where ten percenters might find some luck at the end of an unproductive voyage in 1719. It wasn't a place that any independent merchant ship of England could afford to overlook.

Ten-percenter slave ships took tens of thousands of Africans out of Anomabo to Barbados, Jamaica, and the wider Caribbean. Even if Anomabo didn't have any enslaved people to traffic to Captain Plumb at this time, the English employees who worked there had a productive relationship with the Fante who supplied the fort with grain and other edible supplies for ships with longer voyages ahead of them. As it was among the last stops that welcomed English ships on the Gold Coast, prices were marked up. The crew of the *Princess* had already made a significant dent in their food stores taking so long to fill their cargo holds. Both captives and sailors would need more food to make it across the Atlantic.

Before Captain Plumb and his crew left Cape Coast Castle for Anomabo, the English factor had warned them to be careful and double-check everything, because con artists and pirates were afoot, and they were getting bolder and more violent in their treatment of slave ships. Slave ships, the sailors knew, were easy prey. They tended to be larger and slower and in poor shape, and they tended to operate with unwilling skeleton crews. Counting the captain, the *Princess* at the time had a crew of just thirty-six, who ran what amounted to a prison ship of 272 African captives who had not consented to being there and were prepared to risk their lives to get back to the coast if they spotted an opening.[3] This had happened to Snelgrave when he stumbled across the recently pirated *Elizabeth*. During that encounter, he mentioned that it hadn't been his first time thwarting an onboard insurrection—his first was during his 1704 voyage (and his next would happen again in 1721–1722).[†] In his accounts of these, Snelgrave mentioned that in addition to the insurrections he had witnessed, he had "heard of several, that have ended in a very tragical manner."[4] Insurrections onboard slave ships were commonplace, and slave ship sailors were keenly aware of how outnumbered they were, should one of them forget to check the shackles or leave a tool unsupervised. They remained on edge for months at a time.

These accounts by a colleague made it clear to the crew of the *Princess* that if their ship were attacked by pirates, there was no way they could defend themselves against two highly motivated groups of adversaries. Every minute they spent sitting like juicy waterfowl on West Africa's coast increased their chances of a pirate attack. Of course, Captain Plumb didn't need to be told this by his colleagues. He had personal experience in the slave trade. By 1719, he had captained at least seven voyages between Africa and the Americas. He was well aware that the great rewards promised by a career in human trafficking came with great risks. When 1719 would come to its end, nearly one in three slave ships would be attacked by pirates in West Africa that year.[5]

---

† In another account that Snelgrave shares, he mentions Captain Messerv of the *Ferrers Galley* of London, who died from blunt force trauma after having his head bashed in with a rice bowl. During this revolt, the first mate panicked and nearly eighty of the captive Africans lost their lives, either by being shot or jumping overboard to avoid being shot. Snelgrave reported that "most of the slaves that remained alive grew so sullen, that several of them were starved to death, obstinately refusing to take any sustenance; and after the ship was arrived at Jamaica, they attempted twice to mutiny, before the sale of them began." Once these three attempts at insurrection were public knowledge, planters in Jamaica refused to bid on the enslaved onboard due to fears about revolt on the plantation, resulting in an unprofitable voyage and attempts to obscure these insurrections. See William Snelgrave, *A New Account of Some Parts of Guinea, and the Slave-Trade: Containing, I. The History of the Late Conquest of the Kingdom of Whidaw by the King of Dahomè . . . II. The Manner How the Negroes Become Slaves . . . III. A Relation of the Author's Being Taken by Pirates, and the Many Dangers He Underwent* (London: P. Knapton, 1734), 185–91.

CAPTURED AT ANOMABO

When it happened to the *Princess*, no one onboard was surprised. Two other English ships were anchored nearby, and neither of them fired a shot in defense of the *Princess* lest the pirates turn on their crews, too. Captain Plumb and the captains of the other two ships were at the fort, and when his ship was spotted in distress, he ordered the factors to fire the fort's cannons. However, the *Princess* was anchored too far away for the shots to do anything except provoke the pirate Captain Howell Davis's ire. The pirates returned fire to the crumbling fort, which ceased fire in the hopes that the pirates wouldn't totally destroy it. Captain Plumb watched in horror from ashore as the pirate ship glided through the mist alongside the *Princess*. Two minutes later, he counted eight of his crew scurrying across the plank to the pirate ship, including his navigator, Bartholomew Roberts.

Like the other two ships anchored nearby, the crew of the *Princess* didn't resist, because they didn't get paid enough to. In addition to an already unsavory job were impossible working conditions. For the past twenty years, wages onboard slave ships had been stagnant as the cost of living rose nearly everywhere. The crew already risked too much for the pittance they were paid, and they certainly weren't going to stick out their necks to preserve someone else's ship or prevent desertion by crew members.

Captain Plumb, along with the captains of the other two ships, took a rowboat out to their ships to confront the pirates. Plumb found Captain Howell Davis's pirate crew plundering the *Princess* for any supplies of value. He almost certainly would have recognized that name from Snelgrave's report. As night fell, the pirate crew celebrated. Although they gave the sailors onboard the three ships the option of staying at Anomabo, they pressed hard to get them to turn pirate. Since Howell Davis's crew now had these additional ships, they needed a larger crew to man them.

Yet again historical accounts get messy due to the nature of the evidence. The most reliable firsthand, primary source available is that of a few of the men who show up later as witnesses and defendants at the High Court of Admiralty. According to these court papers, only one sailor eagerly joined the pirate crew. The rest claimed they were forcibly coerced upon pain of death and eagerly swore so on behalf of their crew members and friends, too.

The problem with these types of records is that by 1719, everyone knew that the penalty for piracy was death. The only pirates who had any hope of being spared this fate were those who could successfully convince the judges that they were coerced and who had witnesses to prove it. Naturally this meant that anyone who was a slave ship sailor at this time knew about the penalty for piracy and had several weeks between leaving Europe and arriving in West Africa to think things through. Even those who wanted to join the pirates and make a living wage would have planned to be seen protesting at least a little by anyone whom they might later meet in court.

Sophisticated and smart pirates like the gentleman Captain Davis would have known to make a public spectacle of the sailors' protests, providing his new crew members with plausible deniability that could save their lives not if, but when they were caught and tried. This delicate public production that the pirates repeated with the crew of every single ship they took would earn the pirate captain the loyalty of his new crew members. Veteran pirates understood: if asked about anyone, claim coercion.[6]

The *Weekly Journal* of October 10, 1719, reported that off Whydah, "the Pirates commit un-heard of Cruelties; they have hang'd Capt. Abraham Plumb of the Prince's Galley [sic]; and just as if they set themselves apart to study Cruelty, have hang'd several of the Negroes by the Legs, and afterwards shot 'em."[7]

But did they? There's no way to be entirely certain about what happened between the pirates, Captain Plumb, and the enslaved Africans onboard the *Princess*, but there is a fair amount of contradictory evidence. Records in the High Court of Admiralty show 228 of the 272 enslaved captives onboard disembarked in the Caribbean. The mortality rate given here (11.9%) is slightly lower than the mortality rate of the enslaved on ships that were not attacked by pirates at this time.‡ And if the pirates hanged Captain Plumb, he

---

‡ This rate is compared to the average rate of other ships that left the Gold Coast at this time (12.2%). Mortality rates of captives onboard slave ships were affected by a wide variety

survived it, because seven years later, the captain was found working again for the same ten-percenter company, Humphry Morice,
delivering a cargo of enslaved captives to Saint Kitts and Barbados,
this time onboard a ship called the *Martha.*[8] What had happened
was that the pirates took the *Princess*, but allowed Plumb and some
of his sailors to board the *Morris*, one of the other two ships they
had plundered. Together with Captain Fenn of the *Morris*, Captain
Plumb sailed back to Cape Coast Castle and bartered the goods
that the pirates had rejected for fifty more enslaved captives to take
to the Caribbean. Because the *Princess* hadn't belonged to Captain
Plumb, he was none the worse for wear, at least financially, after
his pirate encounter. The loss was Humphry Morice's, who had
insured all of his ships.

A GENERAL HISTORY OF THE PYRATES

This pattern of false reporting about the pirates of the slave trade
occurs over and over again in this book. Like most Gold Coast Africans at the time, most of the enslaved, most of the pirates, and
most of the slave ship sailors couldn't read and weren't in a position
to leave behind written evidence. In such cases, most of the men
onboard both the *Princess* and the ships that pirated it ended up
at the bottom of the ocean or hanging from gallows at Cape Coast
Castle without any further documentation. When it comes to primary accounts, we have the words of only the few souls onboard
who eventually found themselves in London for trial. The rest of
it is hearsay or dubious history that originated from the infamous
ubiquitous "Charles Johnson" pirate narrative, *A General History
of Pyrates*, which was marketed as a primary source written by an
anonymous eyewitness under a pseudonym, which has since been

---

of factors, and other than pirate attack or natural disaster, the single largest factor remained
where the enslaved embarked, with voyages from southeast Africa and the Bight of Biafra
consistently ranking the most deadly. See the Slave Voyages database for detailed statistics
from more than thirty-six thousand transatlantic voyages and David Eltis, "Methodology: Im-
puting Numbers of Slaves," in *Trans-Atlantic Slave Trade—Understanding the Database*, 2018,
available online at www.slavevoyages.org/voyage/about#methodology/imputing-numbers
-of-slaves/14/en/.

A GENERAL

HISTORY

OF THE

PYRATES,

FROM

Their firſt RISE and SETTLEMENT in the Iſland of
Providence, to the preſent Time.

With the remarkable Actions and Adventures of the two Female Pyrates

MARY READ and ANNE BONNY;

Contain'd in the following Chapters,

To which is added.

A ſhort ABSTRACT of the Statute and Civil
Law, in Relation to Pyracy.

The ſecond EDITION, with conſiderable ADDITIONS

By Captain CHARLES JOHNSON.

LONDON:
Printed for, and ſold by *T. Warner,* at the *Black-Boy* in *Pater-
Noſter-Row,* 1724.

Cover page of *A General History of the Pyrates* by Captain Charles Johnson, pseudonym of Nathaniel Mist,
1724. *Captain Charles Johnson,* A General History of
the Pyrates, *vol. 1 (London: T. Warner, 1724). Public
domain*

proven not to be.[9] This narrative has been used by historians during the last 150 years to reconstruct the lives of the most notorious pirates of the golden age of piracy, including Howell Davis and Black Bart. Unfortunately, the tales it spawned cannot be relied upon without additional confirming documentation.

Back in the 1700s, historians figured out almost immediately that the narrative's author, pirate captain "Charles Johnson" did not exist, and it was assumed that Johnson was the pseudonym of a lower-ranking pirate or someone adjacent to the pirates, such as a dockworker, innkeeper, or even a chaplain or executioner who heard their final confessions. The book was so wildly popular that multiple editions were released in the 1720s, and a second volume was soon published. The next decades saw translations into Dutch, German, and French. The portraits that accompanied it, including the one of Black Bart on the cover of this book, are still some of the most famous etchings of the golden age pirates in existence today.[10]

By 1932, scholars had assumed that Johnson's narrative was penned by Daniel Defoe, author of the popular novel *Robinson Crusoe*. It wasn't until 2004 that it was discovered that Charles Johnson was none other than eighteenth-century printer and journalist Nathaniel Mist, contemporary and friend of Defoe. Mist never sailed with pirates but had been printing missives about them in his Jacobite newspaper, fleshing out evidence about them with his imagination to move copies and, perhaps, for more sinister reasons: to use these more elaborate tales to draw parallels to the Whig government, something he often did to criticize the government while escaping sedition charges. He couldn't make outright accusations against the government, but he could write about pirates doing these things with certainty that the people who read his newspaper knew what and whom he was talking about.[11]

If Nathaniel Mist had indeed meant these pirate tales to be allegories, then it says a lot that he compared the English government at this time to groups of pirates who hanged the enslaved by their legs and shot at them or, as we explore in chapter 5, burned a ship of enslaved people alive as part of a money-grubbing bluff. That feels significant in terms of the ways in which governmental functioning resulted in the mass exploitation of so many people. The king at the time, George I, and Britain's first prime minister, Robert Walpole, alongside Humphry Morice, the man who had insured both Captains Snelgrave's and Plumb's ten-percenter slave ships, made their fortunes in the collapse of the slave-trading South Sea Company, the joint-stock company they created as a public-private partnership to consolidate Britain's national debt. The South Sea Company had entered a contract, the Asiento de Negros of 1713, with the Spanish Crown to purchase and transport enslaved Africans to the Spanish colonies through the Royal Africa Company. As interest in the slave trade grew, the company's stock inflated to an all-time high before collapsing in 1720, bankrupting its investors and diminishing the British national economy.

The prime minister (as well as Humphry Morice) sold his shares right before the bubble burst, when they were at their highest, making 1,000-percent profit on his investments, and then escaped the insider-trading inquiry in parliament afterward. An estimated thirty-four thousand enslaved people were transported under this contract. This was a type and scale of robbery to which the pirates in this book could never have aspired.

In addition to Nathaniel Mist's outright fabrications, the propaganda war against the pirates was particularly pernicious. Like the Ahantan king John Conny of Cape Three Points, pirates were a serious threat to the economic well-being of empire. All the people who had gained unfathomable wealth from colonial exploits stood to lose it the longer the pirates were allowed to roam the seas. Once the South Sea Company rug-pull occurred, people blamed pirates for the economic devastation. Remember, too, a mere decade later, Richard Snelgrave, the respected English slave trader to Virginia, would boast about performing the same cruel types of public-spectacle violence on the enslaved that Nathaniel Mist had attributed to Black Bart's crew. Therefore, every outside claim about the pirates requires a second or third to verify it. Once verified, there is no choice but to conclude that the *Weekly Journal*'s reporting was active propaganda against the pirates who interfered with Britain's slave exports and made shareholders nervous about their investments in human trafficking. This is the European political

and economic context through which we must understand the pirates of the slave trade.

This is the context in which Bartholomew Roberts found himself after becoming part of the pirate Captain Howell Davis's crew.
At the time, Roberts was taller, older, and more experienced than
most of the sailors onboard slave ships. He had served as Captain
Plumb's second mate and had real navigation skills. Captain Davis,
a Welshman like Roberts, saw something of himself in the sailor
and asked him for advice on their next pirate plan. Roberts, who
knew how unpredictable and rough the South Atlantic could get,
helped Davis adjust the rigging and set the best course for their
next port of call, the Portuguese fort on the West African island of
Príncipe.

SACKING PRÍNCIPE

This island was six hundred miles southeast of Anomabo. Roberts
had been there several times and knew the route and also its layout. Together with Davis, he planned a con to get the pirates in: he
and Davis donned their fanciest stolen white linen outfits, flew an
English naval flag, and began practicing the ruse that would allow
them to bypass the battery of twelve guns protecting the island.
Why storm the island and risk crew members' lives when they could
enter by invitation?

It nearly worked for them. The pirates sailed into the harbor
and a uniformed Portuguese officer in a sloop sailed out to greet
them. Davis convinced him that they were a man-o'-war hunting
down pirates of the slave trade. Because a previous merchant visitor
had shared the news of the pirate attacks off the Gold Coast with
this officer just weeks before, the officer bought their lie. Davis
asked to be allowed into the port to buy provisions for his sailors.
Since he had no money, Davis assured the governor of Príncipe that
England's King George would reimburse him for all expenses.

Had Davis taken the supplies and left, perhaps Captain Black
Bart would have never been created. But knowing how to quit when
ahead was not Davis's strong suit. He and a dozen of his more well-

spoken crew members stayed ashore for two weeks, feasting on the generosity of Governor António Carneiro de Sousa while attempting to befriend him to lure him into a bigger con. Roberts was left in charge of the ship when Davis invited de Sousa for dinner aboard the *Royal Rover*. The plan was to take the governor hostage.§

As it turned out, Governor de Sousa had come from a long line of highly educated Portuguese political leaders and had likely experienced or heard of this type of attempt on his life before. He had guessed Davis's true identity and intentions and, anticipating this very walk to Davis's ship, had hired free Black assassins with guns to hide among the vegetation near the coast and intercept the pirates. From the ship, Roberts and the crew watched in horror as Captain Davis and the other pirates were killed midstride.

Like a phoenix, the great pirate Captain Bartholomew "Black Bart" Roberts "rose out of Davis's ashes."[12] He decided on swift retaliation. He swung the *Royal Rover* out and ordered the gunner to attack the fort with cannon-shot. The Portuguese soldiers ran inland, leaving their battery vulnerable. Walter Kennedy, the Irishman Captain Davis had put in charge of one of the other ships, stormed the island with a force of thirty and set the fort afire while kicking its cannons into the sea below. The pirates then helped Roberts load the smallest and least effective ship in their fleet, a French merchant vessel, with gunpowder, effectively turning her into a floating bomb. They sent her as far inland as they could before she ran aground a sandbank and then they lit the fuse. The explosion rang out over the bay as fire rained down upon the fort.

Soon, the nearby town caught fire. By the time the pirates left to regroup at Cape Lopez in modern Gabon, all of coastal Príncipe was smoldering at their back, avenging the death of Captain Howell Davis, and the more veteran pirates of the crew who survived had seen enough. They were in agreement: Bartholomew Roberts the navigator had what it took to protect their federation of pirates. Roberts became Black Bart and donned Captain Davis's dashing red jacket while making the decisions that would lock his crew into

§ Again, I feel compelled to point out here that the Charles Johnson pirate narrative penned by Nathaniel Mist also mentions that the pirates had planned to sexually assault the governor's wife, Madalena de Lancastre, while they held her husband ransom. I have failed to find evidence of this occurrence in any of the other sources. Unfortunately, until another historian finds out otherwise, there isn't a way to know if this plan was real or came to fruition.

what they called "a merry life, but a short one."[13] Along with Walter Kennedy, one other pirate, Thomas Sutton, was a contender for captain. Both grudgingly became second in command, and Black Bart gave them each their own ship to manage in his fleet.

OUT OF THE ASHES OF HOWELL DAVIS

It might have seemed reckless to return to the Americas, where pirate-hunting activities were at their peak, but Roberts's pirate fleet had swelled so much that it now could outgun a man-o'-war, and he felt secure relying on specific knowledge about how things worked in the Americas from his previous voyages. He had rightly assumed that too many pirates were swarming the seas of West Africa, picking off slave ships left and right, and many more had rounded the horn and tried their luck in Madagascar and the East Indies. The numbers would be in his favor in the Americas. He must have known that in the Americas, most of the antipiracy measures were enforced by European powers protecting only their own colonies. The Caribbean would be dangerous because several islands claimed by Britain, the Netherlands, Denmark, France, and Spain were relatively close together, making the area dense with naval ships. But the Spanish and Portuguese mainland were another thing. Portuguese Brazil, in particular, had the longest coastline of any Atlantic American holding, and the Portuguese navy couldn't protect it all. Portugal extracted more wealth from the Americas than it could protect, making Brazil the ideal target, with many large, poorly guarded prizes and far fewer pirates with whom to share them.

After seeing the way Black Bart behaved in Príncipe, the pirates trusted his judgment where Portuguese holdings were concerned. He had lived at least a decade longer than most of them and had been to more ports and onboard more ships. He was a clear-headed strategic thinker who was hell-bent on retribution for his years of backbreaking, poorly compensated labor. Together the crew navigated through the savage weather of hurricane season and ended up on the Isle of Fernandino, off the coast of Brazil. It was near enough to launch attacks, but not close enough to be spotted from shore. For weeks no ships passed by. If it weren't for the generous supply of alcohol and provisions that they had robbed from several ships en route, the pirates might have revolted. Just as Roberts was second-guessing himself, something almost miraculous happened: the Lisbon fleet arrived at the Bay of All Saints in Bahia.

The Lisbon fleet was an armada from Portugal that sailed from Lisbon, accompanied by a heavily armed naval escort, to transport a year's worth of riches from each Portuguese holding in the Americas. The fleet to Bahia collected all the gold obtained from the region's mines and tobacco and sugar from the plantations, along with commodities like exotic pelts and leathers, wood beams, wild honey, and other highly sought Amazonian goods.[14] Also onboard were a little more than one hundred enslaved people headed for Portugal.[¶] The riches of a year's worth of colonial exploitation were unimaginable, and therefore the Portuguese had made the Bay of All Saints impregnable. The Lisbon fleet was protected by two fortresses and thirty-four well-armed ships, with two men-o'-war among them. In total there were more than a thousand sailors, soldiers, and seamen protecting these goods with five hundred or so cannons among them.

The pirates sighed, resigning themselves to waiting for a safer prize, but Black Bart encouraged them with a pirate tactic he had been saving for the right moment. They went over the plan, which was very similar to plans still in use by pirates today. The crew followed Black Bart's orders exactly by wielding the element of surprise. As if starring in an adventure novel, the pirates lined up each of their ships nose to nose and simultaneously fired every cannon available toward the armada. The blast and kickback rocked the harbor, sending waves spilling over the fort and knocking the seamen onboard the Portuguese vessels off their feet. The

---

¶ Portugal had a sizable population of enslaved and free people of African ancestry some brought by force and others who came voluntarily, brought either straight from West Africa or from West Africa via a stint in Brazil. Some of the enslaved went on to become members of the royal courts, but others lived together in Mocambo, a Black neighborhood in modern-day Santa Catarina, Lisbon. See James Sweet, "The Hidden Histories of African Lisbon," in *The Black Urban Atlantic in the Age of the Slave Trade*, ed. Jorge Cañizares-Esguerra, Matt D. Childs, and James Sidbury (Philadelphia: University of Pennsylvania Press, 2013), 233–47 and Yesenia Barragan, "Uncovering Lisbon's Forgotten History of Slavery," in *Black Perspectives*, June 26, 2017, www.aaihs.org/uncovering-lisbons-forgotten-history-of-slavery/.

pirates sidled up to the last ship in the harbor, the *Sacred Family*, and threw out multiple grappling hooks to pull the ships together. They hastily boarded the Portuguese ship and slashed at the sailors who scrambled to find their footing and fill their cannons. Black Bart's crew locked the men below deck then attached a towline and pulled the ship out of harbor behind them under a volley of returned fire. Though the Portuguese treasure ship heavily weighed them down, they managed to pull her out of the harbor in less than fifteen minutes, and with Black Bart's excellent navigational skills, they caught a favorable wind that allowed them to escape north-west, clean to Suriname, a Dutch colony off the northeastern coast of South America. The Portuguese sailors and soldiers onboard and in the harbor simply weren't paid enough to risk their lives de-fending goods that were being taken out of the Americas to enrich people in Europe.

Such an attack by a single pirate ship on an entire armada was unfathomable. The last time the world had seen anything like it was nearly a full century earlier in 1628, when Dutch Admiral Piet Heyn captured the Spanish treasure fleet heavy with silver in the Bay of Matanzas, Cuba.** Heyn had accomplished it with the sup-port of the Dutch navy at his back. The pirates hardly believed that they managed such a feat on their own with only minor injuries to themselves and both ships. The *Weekly Journal* reported the attack in February 1720 as being perpetrated by a pirate crew of "2,000 or so." Nathaniel Mist might be forgiven for that outsized guess, as anyone who knew anything about the defenses of the Lisbon fleet would have been certain that no less than a force of two thousand could have taken it.[15]

When the pirates took stock of the loot, they were ecstatic. In the hold of the *Sacred Family* was more than they could spend in many lifetimes. Also onboard was the grotesquely outsized jewel-encrusted crucifix crafted for the Portuguese royalty, which Black Bart donned and wore around his neck for the rest of his life. This cross makes an appearance in the most famous rendering of his

---

** This successful raid by the Dutch on the Spanish treasure fleet was what allowed the Dutch to become so prominent in the Atlantic slave trade—it financed the creation of the Dutch West India Company and its fortifications in West Africa.

likeness: Benjamin Cole's 1734 copper engraving reproduced in the infamous Charles Johnson/Nathaniel Mist narrative.

What happened afterward is one of the most infamous and widely reported piracy sprees in history. Black Bart and his crew got their revenge and then some, terrorizing the coastline from Guyana and Suriname in South America, to Newfoundland in what would become Canada, and many more places in between. At every port, the rowdy crew got into drunken brawls then feasted and bedded like kings, tipping sex workers and tavern staff alike with life-changing amounts of coin. Black Bart, who had reached the age of forty by refraining from such a lifestyle, used the time to brew more plans and prepare his ships. He had noticed that the incident with the Lisbon fleet, albeit incredibly lucrative, had also scared a sizeable number of his crew. Once the sailors realized that death was at every turn, they began to sow discontent in the ranks, and Roberts decided to stamp it out.

Unfortunately, his actions were insufficient—while Roberts and his most trusted men were out chasing another prize, Walter Kennedy was left in charge of the *Royal Rover* to guard the Portuguese ship of treasures. He decided to break with Black Bart's confederation and sail back to Ireland to start a new life.[††] Roberts and the pirates on his ship returned to find their hard-won treasure gone. Kennedy had left them with not one barrel of water or weevil-filled biscuits on which to subsist.

By all accounts, Black Bart took the desertion hard. His best, most disciplined crew members were still with him, and, ironically, he had won the respect of Thomas Sutton, the other general in his

---

[††] This new life didn't pan out for Walter Kennedy and those who followed him. He lacked Black Bart's navigation skills and vision, and no one he took with him knew any better. They overshot their course to Ireland, wrecking on Scotland's west coast instead. Their rowdy behavior got most of Kennedy's men locked up and hanged in Edinburgh, though he himself did make it back to Ireland, where he used his share of the prize money to open a brothel. Unfortunately for him, he used the brothel as a base from which to run illegal operations and was turned in by one of the sex workers. His face was memorable, and in Bridewell Work House, he encountered a seaman who had worked on one of the ships Kennedy had pirated. This sailor alerted the authorities, who moved Kennedy to Marshalsea Prison, where he ended up on trial for piracy. Before the authorities hanged him at the infamous Wapping Execution Dock in 1721, he presented them with a list of the other men he knew to be guilty of piracy, including Black Bart. See Marcus Rediker, *Villains of All Nations: Atlantic Pirates in the Golden Age* (Boston: Beacon Press, 2004), 40–41.

fleet who had been angling for the position of captain when Howell Davis was killed in Príncipe. Collectively, they created rules that laid out expected behaviors, rewards, and punishments for everyone left onboard. Though most of the pirates were functionally illiterate, they knew that by creating a paper trail that would almost certainly be used against them in court, they were binding themselves to one another and agreeing that their pirate journey together ended in only one way: death. They could either die by cannon's roar or dangling at the end of a rope. This understanding, Roberts hoped, would prevent any more loathsome displays of disloyalty. The pirates started over, taking a few smaller prizes to build confidence, food stores, and the size of their crew before hitting the Caribbean with full force.

Roberts's crew took ship after ship, but most were smaller merchant vessels with little onboard. They let several of them go when they realized that the paltry crew and worthless trinkets onboard were more trouble than they were worth. Meanwhile, several Caribbean governors dispatched ships to look for these pirate nuisances who interfered with local trade. Black Bart's ranks swelled when his ship attempted to pirate another pirate ship, and he and the French pirate Captain la Palisse of the *Sea King* made an uneasy alliance.

Their ranks swelled again when they stopped at an uninhabited island to air their ships after a brutal disease threatened their progress. Black Bart's crew discovered a group of marooned sailors from an Antiguan ship who eagerly signed Roberts's contract and agreed to a pirate's life over a life of starvation. La Palisse suggested the crew plunder near some of the smaller French islands, such as Martinique, and slowly but surely Black Bart attained the larger, cannon-laden prize ships he favored for his bolder attacks.

Unbeknown to Black Bart and la Palisse, the governor of Barbados had sent pirate hunters after Black Bart on the *Summerset* and the *Philipa*, and on February 26, they clashed in a swift Caribbean battle that mortally wounded twenty pirates. While Black Bart's men lay in the hold bleeding out with only one surgeon to attend to their broken bodies, he raced to Dominica to repair the ship. Before he could get there, he ran into a couple of military sloops that the French governor of Martinique, Florimund Hurault de Montigny, had sent after him. Evading those ships—with hulls taking on water and crew members dying below deck—infuriated Roberts and the remaining crew. By the time they reached Dominica, those twenty injured crew members were dead.

REVENGE

In Dominica, Roberts's crew washed the bloodstains from the ship as they buried their comrades and fixed the *Fortune*'s hull. Revenge was all they could think about. With resentment about the attack brewing as they dug graves for their friends, the crew organized a trial to rid themselves of the members whose cowardly actions had failed the collective. Three men (two White and one Black) were "for defecting sentenced to Death over a Bowl." The bowl in question was a physical bowl, or sometimes a turtle shell or hat, into which each pirate could cast one of two stones—dark colored if they found the person in question guilty and white for innocent. The color most represented decided the pirate's fate. All three were found guilty. The pirates shot two and the third, sailmaker Richard Harris, claimed that he escaped death "only by a fancy Valentine Ashplant (a leading Man among them) took to him."[16] Unfortunately, no more about that relationship is to be found among the documentation, though the casual way it was presented indicates that it wasn't uncommon.

Internal animosities thusly addressed, the pirates focused on revenging themselves against the French governor. They left Dominica, striking hard and often at the unprotected ships and coastal regions further north so that they could trade up to larger and more heavily equipped vessels. In a matter of months, they had a pirate fleet big enough to challenge the French governor at Martinique.

The crew was so serious about this bold decision that they lowered Black Bart's original flag—their captain and the skeletal figure of death facing one another, holding up an hourglass together to signify a lifestyle that ensured it was only a matter of time before the two met—and sewed a new flag to replace it. This one depicted Black Bart facing forward in aggression, brandishing a sword against a black background. Beneath each of his boots was a dead man's skull—one for the governor of Barbados and the other for the governor of Martinique. Its message, though crude, was unmistakable and effective: his carefully selected crew of pirates fully intended to hunt down these men and make examples of them or perish in the attempt. The plan was reckless, ruthless, and rash. It had never been done before, and there was no reason to believe that it could succeed. Then again, Black Bart's pirates had an impressive track record when it came to the impossible.

By September Black Bart's fleet had swelled. The crew had enough ships equipped with all the cannons they believed they needed to make good on their threats. They headed back to the Caribbean, and their first stop was the British island of Saint Kitts. Here, they took advantage of their numbers to blockade the port, forcing all ships trading there to remain. Then they raised their new flag. Black Bart ordered his musicians to play, and the pirates demanded that the governor, Lieutenant General Mathew, face them. When he refused and ordered the fort's guns to blast, Roberts made some decisions.

The most remarkable feature of this stop on Black Bart's revenge tour was that when the governor failed to treat Roberts as an equal and grant him an audience, the pirates burned several of his ships. He was then presented with a letter from the *Royal Fortune*. Black Bart, like most of the pirates of the golden age, wrote few letters, and even fewer of those survived. This one, the lieutenant kept in full, and its contents provide historians with one of the richest insights into the motivations and mindset of the pirate captain in the year before his death. It reads:

> This comes expressly from me to lett you know that had you come off as you ought to a done and drank a glass of wine with me and my company I should not harmed the least vessell in your harbour. Farther it is not your gunns you fired yt. affrighted me or hindred our coming on shore but the wind not proving to our expectation that hindred it. The *Royall Rover* you have already burnt and barbarously used some of our men but we have now a ship as good as her and for revenge you may assure yourselves here and hereafter not to expect anything from our hands but what belongs

to a pirate as farther Gentlemen that poor fellow you now have in prison at Sandy point is entirely ignorant and what he hath was gave him and so pray make conscience for once let me begg you and use that man as an honest man and not as a C[riminal] if we hear any otherwise you may expect not to have quarters to any of your Island yours, *Signed*, Bathll. Roberts.[17]

The letter utilizes every form of persuasion that was available to the pirate captain. In one sentence, he shames the governor for being frightened and blames him for the flaming harm the pirate crew visited on the vessels in the harbor. He also implies that they would have come ashore to collect the governor had the wind been favorable because they had no fear of his cannons. Then the tone switches and Roberts intervenes on behalf of a colleague, calling upon the decency of the governor to free one of his prisoners while reminding him that if he doesn't, the pirates will take the island from him.

Thus satisfied, Roberts's crew plundered the remaining ships and set sail for their next stop: the French islands. At Saint Barthelemy, the governor allowed the pirates to stay for a month while they sold the wares they took from the ships at Saint Kitts. This governor, the island he administered, and all ships in the harbor were spared the Saint Kitts treatment. By all reports, the pirates acted like a security force for the island, keeping away any privateers and other pirates. In October, they left and captured fifteen more ships off the coast of Saint Lucia, and one of the first mates, James Skyrme, became one of Roberts's most trusted crew.‡‡

The ships split up so they could cover more ground and collect more ships and crew while bringing Caribbean trade to a standstill. The new *Royal Fortune*, Roberts's ship, came across a French

---

‡‡ This type of behavior, where pirates became an ad-hoc sea-militia of individual islands, protecting them where European navies failed, was an incredibly common relationship between pirates and Caribbean governors just twenty years prior. This was due to the fact that the navies of the European nations which colonized the islands rarely were well-resourced enough to protect them adequately. Many of the older governors were able to survive in their posts for decades partly because they leveraged this symbiosis between their islands and the pirates. Governors who couldn't navigate this type of relationship tended to leave the settlers on their islands vulnerable and were replaced after only a few years. The War on Pirates and the growth of naval power in the Americas had mostly put a stop to this behavior, but some of the older guard still remembered how it worked and benefitted from it at times.

man-o'-war. Roberts coveted the heavily armed ship and ordered the French tricolor to be raised as they approached. He claimed to be a French merchant with information about the dreaded pirate Black Bart, and the man-o'-war allowed the *Royal Fortune* to approach, believing it to be a friend. Once within range, the pirates fired cannons and muskets as they boarded, taking the warship by surprise. As they looted it and sorted through the crew for new recruits, they found none other than the French governor of Martinique, Florimund Hurault de Montigny, cowering below deck. Roberts's crew roared as they pulled their new flag from its chest. They showed the Martinican governor the skull that represented his own they had sewn onto it and jeered as they waved his future fate in his face.

They unceremoniously hanged the governor by his neck from the yardarm of the ship and sailed onward with the dead governor's body swaying in the sea breeze as the musicians onboard played loud enough to drown out the excited squawks of the seabirds feasting on their gory meal. Most of Roberts's crew were galvanized by this. The very man who had been responsible for the deaths of twenty of their comrades had now joined them in hell. To their minds, Roberts was a just man, and a man true to his word. They knew well that they were headed on a collision course with death, but at least with Roberts, they had a chance to live a short life on their own terms and experience a moment of merriness and justice.

Not everyone agreed, however. One of his captains who had been with Black Bart since the days of Howell Davis was utterly uninterested in the kind of death that would befall the murderers of a governor and deserted soon after. After Kennedy, Roberts, with his crew of nearly one hundred, shrugged it off, no longer interested in being in command of wishy-washy men. For this next final and fatal leg of their journey, he wanted only men who were completely committed on this ride to hell with him. He took his two best lieutenants—the old faithful Thomas Sutton and the promising new upstart James Skyrme—and headed back to West Africa, where it all began.

Chapter Four

———————○———————

"Infested with Pyratts"

SOMEWHERE IN THE MID-ATLANTIC, the body of the Martinican governor swayed in the wind on the yardarm of Black Bart's ship while the crew drank their fill of plundered spirits and took turns dancing to the tunes of the exhausted musicians tooting dented brass instruments.

Back at Portsmouth on the Southern Coast of England, however, the mood onboard the HMS *Swallow* was decidedly less jovial. Captain Chaloner Ogle had been there since daybreak watching stevedores stock the ship with the last of the eight months' worth of provisions and careening gear, each mishap of theirs adding to his impatient ire. Last came the myriad gifts that the Royal Africa Company insisted the navy take with them to their various trading partners in West Africa. When it was finally done, the February air had permeated his wool coat and numbed his hands. On shore, a small crowd assembled to see them off. Ogle ignored them. He examined the seamen standing on the deck of the fourth-rate HMS *Swallow*. Uniforms wouldn't be introduced for a few more decades, so he wasn't looking for anything in particular, except for a reason to make an example of someone to set the tone for the voyage. He marched back and forth, waterlogged wool coat resting heavy on his shoulders in the English sea mist.

81

Anchored next to the *Swallow* at the channel through Spithead was the HMS *Weymouth*, captained by Mungo Herdman. Together, the ships were two of the finest and most heavily armed that the British navy could spare for the suppression of piracy in West Africa. The ships likely were dressed with decorative flags hanging like bunting over the masts and from bowsprit to stern in celebration. And what a celebration it would have been for the captain now in charge of his very own ship were it not for the entire squadron of ships anchored just a short distance ahead.

The ships were all under command of Commodore Thomas Matthews, a man Ogle knew all too well. Commodore Matthews had had a very similar career to Captain Chaloner Ogle. Both came from families that were landed gentry and had begun their careers in the Nine Years' War (1688–1697), had fought pirates in the War of the Spanish Succession (1701–1715), and had spent the past five years helping to secure British shipping by taking prizes in the Mediterranean and Baltic. Though Matthews was five years older, the men had served in the navy for roughly the same time, but Matthews's first assignment was under his uncle, whereas Ogle, from Northumberland, had to work his way up the leadership in what he considered the hard way. Now in 1721, Matthews had become a commodore and had been given a whole squadron with which to hunt pirates in a more lucrative location. Next to Ogle's piddly two ships, it stung.

The Crown had sent them off on the same day in order to fight its war on piracy on two fronts: Africa and India. In Africa, Black Bart had caused millions of pounds of damage roughly equivalent to $30 million in today's money. Meanwhile, "piracy" in India was an entirely different story, and the losses to the British less quantifiable. Those the British called pirates in India weren't the same as those in Black Bart's crew. Matthews had been assigned to suppress the activities of Admiral Kanhoji Angre, the man in charge of the Maratha Empire's navy. The Maratha Empire had existed in India since 1650, before the British had a strong presence there. It had built its navy partly in response to Portuguese traders using sea power to gain unfair advantages over coastal Indian trading ports. The Maratha had naval bases along the entire coast of modern-day Maharashtra, and they obtained cannons and gunpowder through trade with Portugal and hired Portuguese and Dutch mariners to join their navy to gain insight into European tactics and knowledge.[1]

Admiral Angre had adopted the European tactic of building fortifications at every major harbor and river, and his navy forced all ships sailing through the areas to pay a levy. Most importantly, the Maratha navy did not hesitate to take European prisoners ransom, rendering nearly impossible the jobs of factors of the East India Company in Asia, the British counterpart to the Royal Africa Company. Their tactic of firing on European sails with towed cannons and then using smaller vessels to approach these disabled ships head-on to avoid fire from the broadsides allowed them to board and force in-person confrontations that generally didn't go well for the British navy, largely because so many of its seamen had been impressed into service.

Admiral Angre's military force operated similarly to that of the Ahantan ruler John Conny at Cape Three Points; both controlled sizeable forces and used European and native tactics and weaponry together both in defense of their lands and seas and in aspirations of expansion. As with the leadership of John Conny, Admiral Kanhoji Angre's sovereignty was not recognized at times by Europeans specifically because it endangered British shipping and the goals of empire. Therefore, an entire East Asian navy was reduced to "pirates" in the eyes of the Crown. That was strategic, of course: once someone was named a pirate by the English Crown in 1721, they were eligible to suffer a pirate's fate.

The British Crown was exhausted by all the badgering from shareholders, companies, merchants, and the navy. The king, fully intoxicated by the luxury of empire, made no distinction between a local navy asserting its sovereignty and fleets of desperate men committing robbery at sea. He wanted to keep his shareholders and Parliament happy. He hoped that a little ceremony at Portsmouth dispatching not one, but two antipiracy forces on the same day to protect the interests of the Royal Africa Company and the East India Company would satisfy the lobbying, at least temporarily, and put an end to the sinking of British ships and profits. What the king couldn't give Ogle and Matthews in ships and supplies, he gave them in liberal permissions: if they could make the trade nuisance disappear, they had nearly unilateral authority to disregard civil liberties and local laws to do whatever the situation required. Ogle and Matthews left England knowing that they were not leaving to capture "pirates" to stand trial, but to exterminate seafaring people like vermin and pocket whatever riches they could along the way.

Ogle also realized that, unlike Commodore Matthews, he was working against the clock. By 1720, a pattern had emerged among the pirates plaguing Atlantic trade. The vast majority of them had been seafarers for a long time, moving with the demands of the age from working on merchant ships, to being impressed on naval ships, to trying their luck as privateers during wartime, to finding themselves working the most undesirable jobs onboard slavers during more peaceable times before ending up on pirate vessels. They understood the global shifting nature of trade and followed opportunity when they could, which they had been doing for decades. By 1721, the Atlantic world had already experienced two stages of what historians refer to as the golden age of piracy, which was at the peak of its third and final stage.[*] A few notorious and wealthy pirates, about whom all other pirates mythologized in hushed whispers on dark nights, had paved the way for a route from the hellscape of slave and navy ships in the Atlantic world to the riches of the East.[†]

Pirate Captains William Kidd, Edward England, and Henry Every had sailed back and forth multiple times, stealing merchant, naval, and slave ships and refitting them to be sturdy and fast enough

---

[*] Historians generally agree that there were three periods in the golden age of piracy: the first, called the era of buccaneers (1650s–1680s), was characterized by English, French, and Dutch seamen like Henry Morgan and Michiel de Ruyter, who targeted Spanish colonies in the Caribbean. That soon evolved into the second era, the pirate round of the 1690s and early 1700s, in which pirates like William Kidd, Thomas Tew, and Henry Avery/Every from the Atlantic world plundered the East Indies. The final wave began in 1715, after the War of the Spanish Succession, when unemployed Anglo-American sailors and privateers from that war turned their skills of plunder on every viable maritime target from the Americas to the Indian Ocean and West Africa. This period created the most notorious and well-known pirates today. These periods were not three distinct stages, but rather served as a continuous process of criminalized seafaring behaviors that evolved over time with changes in maritime shipping, technology, politics, international relations, and naval responses. See works on piracy by Marcus Rediker, Gabriel Kuhn, Peter Galvin, and David Cordingly for more details.

[†] Indeed, right around this time, the French pirate Captain La Bouche, "the mouth," who had sailed with Howell Davis and helped to rob the slave trader William Snelgrave in the Sierra Leone River in 1719, had stolen a new vessel to try his luck plundering East Indian trade.

to weather the treacherous winds at the Cape of Good Hope and to make it to the Indian Ocean. Although William Kidd had been executed twenty years prior in 1701, Henry Every had never been found, disappearing with his riches in an unheard-of pirate retirement. And Edward England? He was still somewhere out there, preying on the heavy, expensive British East India Company vessels like the *Cassandra*. Edward England had been the one to capture Howell Davis in 1718 and make him a pirate captain. Howell Davis then went on to mentor Black Bart, the pirate fleet Ogle was hunting, which had direct knowledge of how to make a strategic living from East Indian piracy.

Ogle was aware that, in all likelihood, Black Bart's plan involved exploiting West Africa and the chaos of the slave trade to obtain better ships, a bigger crew, and enough supplies to try their luck in the Indian Ocean. If that happened, they would be Commodore Matthews's problems—but also Matthews's promotion. Ogle sneered at his seamen on the deck of the *Swallow* and shouted at them to weigh anchor. They didn't have another moment to waste on ceremonial frippery back in England, when Black Bart already could be halfway to India.

On March 10, *Swallow* and *Weymouth* approached the Spanish Atlantic island of Madeira, off the coast of what is now Morocco. It had taken them longer than planned to get there, because they met with westerly winds off the coast of Portugal that were impossible to sail against. Ogle and Mungo had sat helplessly with their ships for days, crews consuming the victuals that they desperately needed to save for West Africa. By the time they finally had caught a favorable wind, it jettisoned them ahead, and soon they had overtaken Commodore Matthews's ships. They stopped at Madeira briefly to trade. The English sailors offloaded some of their Cheshire cheese and pieces of beef, as well as clothing, household goods, and even secondhand wigs for the island's disease-preventing lemons and limes and the famous wine named for the island, which was heavily prized in the Atlantic world because it didn't go bad in the heat as quickly as most other grape wines.

John Atkins, the naval surgeon onboard the *Swallow* who also served as scribe to Captain Ogle, went out of his way to comment on the diverse racial makeup of the merchants ("the other inhabitants consist of a mixed race: Portuguese Blacks and Mulattoes, who are civil, courteous and equally respected in trade") and the ways in which the Portuguese "nowhere abroad scrupling an Alliance with darker colours," that is, they did not discriminate by race when it came to forging alliances and running empire.[2]

He noted this because he knew that it was an unusual and even "exotic" concept to much of his English readership: middle- to upper-class people who paid good coin to be titillated. It wasn't the notion of Blackness itself that would have been unusual to them; there had been Black people and other people of color living throughout the British Isles since before the Middle Ages, and dark-skinned Africans were heavily represented in the courts of English royalty. Every urban center had visitors and immigrants from Africa, Asia, and the Americas, and most higher institutions of learning had graduated foreign students of color by this time. Rather, it was the idea of Black personhood and some interracial interactions that remained heavily contested among the English in the era of the slave trade, whose anti-Blackness had been cultivated since the Middle Ages.[3] Race, especially the ways in which it signified different things to other, non-English Europeans, was something that Atkins commented on often in his journal of this voyage, and it was something that shaped many of the interactions the British navy had with people, both free and enslaved, in West Africa and the Caribbean.

The Iberians, or the Spanish and Portuguese, had a radically different understanding of race, and therefore enslavement, than did the English at this time. The Dutch and French also followed the Iberian understanding. These nations—as well as the eighteenth-century territories claimed by them—all shared an understanding of slavery and race that echoed that of the historic Roman Empire. For the Iberians, Dutch, and French at this time, skin color was not an automatic indicator of a person's status, and enslavement was a condition and not an identity marker. This means that at this time, in the parts of the Atlantic frequented by the Iberians, Dutch, or French, dark-skinned Africans and their descendants could be found among every rank and occupation. It was understood that enslavement was a temporary situation in which a person could find themself and potentially exit, as well, and many did through a wide variety of means. This racial flexibility, for a multitude of reasons, did not sit well with the English and their aspirations for empire, so they and their agents of empire—in this case Chaloner Ogle and his surgeon John Atkins—often remarked on it and challenged it.[4] The two of them with their English crew knew that they would be coming up against a racially, nationally, and linguistically diverse pirate crew, and they already had made plans for how to address that.

The same gusts that allowed the *Swallow* and *Weymouth* to overtake the commodore's squadron also damaged the masts of Mathews' ships, and Ogle left the commodore's demasted ships at sea in his hurry to get to West Africa. Because time was not on their side, Ogle ordered that the *Swallow* and *Weymouth* split up at Cape Verde to cover more ground. The crew of the *Swallow* spent a few days catching fish to eat and turtles to keep in the hold for later and then headed for Sierra Leone while the *Weymouth* went to the Gambia River. It took the *Swallow* nearly a month to get there, and when they arrived, it was April.

Atkins spent this part of the journey penning a few paragraphs about the physical features of the people of West Africa and what "distinguishes them from the rest of mankind." He made his own contributions to the ideas of the scientific racism prevalent in his community of surgeons, attributing temperament, intelligence, and physicality to skin color. He went as far as to remark, in a travel journal for the lay public, on his theories of Black and White people having distinct ancient origins, saying, "tho' it be a little Heterodox, I am persuaded the black and white race have, *ab origine*, sprung from different-colored first parents." The prevailing ideas at the time pointed to all of mankind having a single origin, and Atkins used physical descriptions of the people he saw in Sierra Leone and his feelings about their otherness to state with confidence that there was no way White and Black could be related.[5]

TO SIERRA LEONE

Once the *Swallow* sailed down the river, Atkins noted evidence of the havoc the pirate Captain Howell Davis and his crew had wreaked in the area nearly four years prior. The seamen encountered a Black Christian trader called Seignior Joseph who had moved his entire operation further inland about nine miles where the larger pirate ships could not penetrate. He met them in European dress and showed them the small chapel he had built for his family. He and his wives caught and roasted a manatee for the *Swallow*'s sailors, and over the heavily spiced meal, Seignior Joseph told them that he had been to England and then Portugal and was baptized there. By 1721, many free West Africans had visited Europe on diplomatic missions, to work in churches or monasteries, or to enroll in the universities there. Often their parents or other kin sent them with the hopes that a multilingual education in Europe could give their people an advantage over the European slave traders whose numbers swelled each year, since the vast majority of the Europeans in Africa lacked a formal education. After the meal, Seignior Joseph sold them the wood from his initial compound closer to Whiteman's Bay so that they could patch the wind damage on the *Swallow*.[6]

Then they met with John "Captain Crackers" Leadstone (commonly called "Old Cracker" in the documents of the British agents and navy), who was the "most thriving" trader in the area because he had been most willing to support the pirates. Back in 1717, the pirates, commanded by Captain Howell Davis, had stayed with Captain Crackers. He had allowed them to use the compound as their base of operations for their attacks on Sierra Leone and the Royal Africa Company fort at Bunce Island. This was where the pirates captured the ship of slave-trading captain William Snelgrave. Davis had led the crew, many who served under Black Bart now, in a savage attack on Fort James. The English factor, Robert Plunkett, had barely escaped with his life, running into the brush as the pirates descended on the fort, raided it of all supplies and enslaved people within, and then set it ablaze. When the pirates finally left, Plunkett returned to the ruins of the fort and penned a sternly worded letter to the Royal Africa Company in which he placed the blame squarely on Captain Crackers's shoulders. He wrote about the "many rascals on shore that assist with boats & canoes to bring their goods on shore" at what he called the "Privateer Town."[7] He sent that letter to London with the first ship that approached him for trade and waited for a reply.

The report the Royal Africa Company sent to the queen later that year summed up the main concerns succinctly, claiming that Captain Crackers and the others "who live on Shore [are] worse than the pirates." Upon reading Plunkett's letter, the clerk who compiled the report agreed with the factor's assessments and recommended that all but two of the men who lived on the compound "ought to be tried for being accessories to the pirates."[8] According to the Piracy Act of 1698, for which the Royal Africa Company had lobbied, all those found guilty of being accessories to pirates would be executed with the same brutal and public spectacle as the pirates themselves.

After the pirate attack, the RAC officer Plunkett had been tasked by the company to rebuild Fort James. He had kept the wariest of eyes trained on the river for signs of Captain Crackers's pirate friends. When Ogle's ship arrived with letters and supplies, he squealed in relief and made the naval captain promise to return soon, for he knew the pirates would be back. Howell Davis had made him that menacing promise four years earlier. Ogle replied that he would sweep the entire coast from west to east before doubling back, confident that that would take care of it. Traders and other workers loyal to the deep pockets of Captain Crackers who were present at this meeting informed the old independent trader about what Ogle had said to the Royal Africa Company employee.

While Ogle reassured Plunkett, Atkins focused his attention on Captain Crackers. Atkins's description of the slave trade among Crackers and the other independent traders is stomach churning. He described frequent brutal beatings by Old Crackers with a thick strap made from manatee leather for the purpose of creating compliance among the African captives for sale. Atkins noted that in one of the pens where the enslaved were imprisoned, he could not help taking notice of one fellow among the rest, of a tall, strong make, and bold, stern aspect. As he imagined we were viewing them with a design to buy, he seemed to disdain his fellow-slaves for their readiness to be examined, and as it were scorned looking at us, refusing to rise or stretch out his limbs, as the master commanded. . . . [A]ll the company grew curious at his courage, and wanted to know of Cracker, how he came by him.[9]

Crackers told them that this man was called Captain Tomba, a leader of some villages by the river Nunez, who "opposed them and their trade." The closest part of the Nunez River to Whiteman's Bay is approximately five hundred kilometers to the north, which speaks to Captain Crackers's reach in the slave trade. Captain Tomba had led a group of rebels to raze a village of slave traders who were "friends" of Crackers and most likely who supplied him with captives to sell. African resistance to the trade was robust, as was slave traders' responses to it.[10] In retaliation, Crackers had sent reinforcements to kidnap Captain Tomba from his bed at night and told Atkins "from thence he was brought hither, and made my property."[11]

From the clues Captain Crackers gives John Atkins, Tomba was most likely from the region known as the Koinadugu Plateau. This plateau was home to fortified towns whose existence hinged on resistance to human trafficking. Captives from this region were valued by enslavers in the American low country for their extensive knowledge about rice cultivation; those who planted the rice had developed sophisticated irrigation techniques and knew how to get good growth from multiple varieties in various seasons. In Sierra Leone, rice cultivation was highly prized, and eating rice was a symbol of status. Atkins mentioned this when he was there, saying of the people in Sierra Leone that it was "he being the greatest among them, who can afford to eat Rice all the Year round."[12] This was also true in the Americas, where enslavers paid top coin for African experts in agriculture. Even under the harsh confines of enslavement, these specialists were able to transfer those skill sets to the American low country to turn rice into a cash crop, earning for their enslavers great wealth.[13]

As a result, the rice-cultivating regions of Sierra Leone became an attractive target for raiders. Slave raiding in the Koinadugu region was blatantly apparent in the landscape: the archaeology of the region of Captain Tomba's home shows how some of the towns were surrounded by thick mud walls, behind which guards kept constant watch. Other towns used living defenses, planting tall cotton trees around their town and filling the perimeter with thickets of *inthiri* thornbushes to control how people could enter and exit. People in other towns along the edge of the plateau used the topographical features to their advantage, founding towns on steep slopes that made raids difficult.[14]

Atkins was horrified by what he saw and by the story of how Captain Tomba became imprisoned, but nowhere else does Atkins make these types of observations, though the *Swallow* would stop at several of the British Royal Africa Company's trading fortresses where enslaved people were imprisoned and treated much the same way. The visceral depictions of the brutality of the trade were reserved for descriptions of the independent agents alone. In addition to this, Atkins discussed the brutal ways in which the local Africans treated the enslaved to ready them for sale. Though Atkins is often described as an antislavery advocate, he spares all royal British agents his judgment in the narrative, pointing fingers only at the violent actions of Africans and independent Europeans. This creates an impression in the journal that Atkins believed—or wanted the British public to believe—that the slave trade would be more humane if regulated by a company run by the British Crown. Any antislavery sentiment he might have harbored never stretched to abolitionism.[15]

Hunting Ghosts

While Atkins grappled onboard the *Swallow* with his feelings about Captain Crackers's inhumane display, the seamen on the *Weymouth* in the Gambia River experienced a different reception. With no recent pirate attacks or independent traders to speak of, the Royal Africa Company's gifts had been well received by the king of Barra.

Captain Mungo Herdman reported cheerfully that the king gave the Royal Africa Company permission to build a fort at Gillislee, "a town commanded by a woman, about 15 miles up the river, made a duchess by Captain Passenger." Captain Passenger was a local English-speaking caboceer who had worked with the Royal Africa Company before. Atkins explained that in trading towns, "the most deserving fellows" were given English titles of knight, colonel, and captain.[16] This originated with Portuguese tradition on the coast and was reinforced by the Dutch and Prussian slave traders who signed treaties with their local African allies to make them vassals of the Portuguese, Dutch, and Prussian kingdoms.[17]

The *Swallow* departed Sierra Leone and was rejoined by the *Weymouth* on May 1. They sailed south together, stopping at the towns around the Cestos River in what is now Liberia on May 10. Atkins observed "a whole town running away from a boat with white men" but failed to connect that to the practice of snatching Africans directly from the coast for the trade in which many European traders, company or independent, partook.[18] The kidnapping of Africans along the coast had occurred for more than a century and was a prolific enough practice that slave traders from all the European companies remarked on it.[19]

When they stopped at the first large settlement, the African king Pedro, "who commands there," expected gifts in return for allowing the European naval ships to collect fresh water and wood. Captain Ogle sent a lieutenant and a purser in their finest clothing with a handful of gifts for the king: a gun, two pieces of salt beef, cheese, a bottle of brandy, a dozen pipes, and two dozen congees, a type of textile made in England. After making them wait an hour, the king arrived and rejected their presents, saying that he had enough of these things, but what he really needed was more clothing. He had the English seamen strip so he could have their breeches. Then he dismissed the officers with a glass of palm wine and an "Attee, ho," a "salutation with thumbs and fingers mixed, and snapping off."[20]

In his journal, Atkins attempts to couch this action in the ignorance of King Pedro, but once the judgmental tone and descriptors are stripped from the narrative, it gives the impression that King

Pedro knew exactly what he was doing and what he wanted and sent the English naval officers back to the ship to get it. Based on Atkins's squeamish descriptions of what the sailors had said about the king's tardiness, knotted wig, patchwork coat, and dirty clothing, it sounded like King Pedro had wanted to put the scoffing English seamen in their place by keeping them waiting, not making a particular effort about his own appearance in receiving them, and forcing them to strip in front of him and return to their ship in the nude. It was likely a test both to gauge the British captain's intent as well as to assert himself: King Pedro wanted to reinforce that Ogle's seamen were not in a position to challenge his sovereignty. Though the king had been unable to get Ogle to come down himself, he learned that the English had accepted this treatment of their sailors. It was reassurance that Ogle cared very much about getting on his good side in order to gain access to water and wood and maintain the cordial relationship between Pedro's people and the Royal Africa Company.

King Pedro's son, Tom Freeman, later boarded the *Swallow* uninvited, and him they "dress'd with an edg'd hat, a wig, and a sword, and gave a patent upon a large sheet of parchment, creating him Duke of Sesthos." King Pedro sent a couple of goats to the ship in return and his younger son Josee for the same treatment, and the seamen onboard the *Swallow* obliged. In exchange, King Pedro allowed the *Swallow* and *Weymouth*'s seamen to trawl the Cestos River for fish and to visit his village, enjoying the amenities it offered.[21] King Pedro had a royal court but no standing army and nowhere near as many riches as John Conny and so might have used his alliance with the English to better position himself within West African politics. Often the English remarked that Africans with limited power and resources, like King Pedro, made better allies, though the reality was more complex, as they often remained loyal only as long as the English could provide what they wanted at a better bargain than anyone else.

By May 1721, Captain Chaloner Ogle and his squadron still hadn't heard about Bartholomew "Black Bart" Roberts's outrageous murder of the French governor in the waters surrounding Martinique. His intel was old—he had sailed from England to West

Africa with the understanding that the pirates were somewhere in the vicinity. No one had guessed that they would cross the Atlantic once more, heading straight for the Caribbean Sea, which was home to several naval shipyards of Great Britain as well as Spain and heaving with pirate-hunting naval ships from every European colonial power, at least when compared with the vast, unsupervised waters of the West African coast. In the past few months, three of the most notorious pirates of the era had been captured and either executed in Jamaica (Calico Jack Rackham and Charles Vane) or left to perish in a dank cell (Mary Read).‡ It hadn't even occurred to Ogle that a fleet of men could be convinced to set out on such a suicide mission, for he had to wield the threat of corporal punishment over his seamen to get them to perform their jobs on the best of days. So, for the past few months, his crew had stopped at Sierra Leone and every place with a British presence, only to be told that, yes, the pirates had been there, but it had been many months since. It just didn't add up. Where could the pirates be? In this case, what Ogle didn't know could absolutely hurt him.

The Return of the Pirate Fleet

Ogle had made his way southeast to the Gold Coast when Black Bart and his fleet, still high from their daring wins, execution of the governor, and escape in the Caribbean, approached the coast of Senegal in the first week of June. According to later testimony, Roberts's crew spotted two French naval ships, both cruisers, patrolling the French territory for Dutch smugglers. Performing a maneuver that they had perfected in Africa, most of the pirates re-

---

‡ The other name that often accompanies Read's is Anne Bonny. She, too, was captured with Mary Read and Calico Jack and imprisoned in Jamaica and, like Mary Read, claimed to be pregnant to be granted a stay of execution. Colonial Caribbean jails were notorious for poor sanitation, and Mary Read died of a fever before she could give birth. The fate of Anne Bonny, although the subject of speculation, remains unknown. At this time, many English and colonial British judges believed that motherhood softened so-called criminal women, and therefore many women who "plead the belly," as it was referred to, later were spared the death sentence upon the birth of their children. In England, many pregnant women found guilty of crimes ended up transported to the colonies. In the British Caribbean, local officials experienced more autonomy, and White women were significantly outnumbered by men and therefore in high demand, which often led to more lenient sentencing. See James Oldham, "On Pleading the Belly," *Criminal Justice History* 6 (1985): 1–64.

mained at sea while they sent out one ship as bait. Once the French pursued, the ship retreated, leading the two swift ships straight into the pirate fleet. By the time the black flags were raised, the French were outmanned, outgunned, and out of sight of land and anyone who could help them. No naval employees at the time were paid enough to attempt such an uneven fight, and so the French ships lowered their flags and raised a white cloth in surrender. The larger French ship, *Count of Toulouse*, was renamed *Ranger*, and the smaller storeship *Little Ranger*, and two of the boldest lieutenants in Bart's fleet—Thomas Sutton and James Skyrme—once more became captains of their own ships.[22] They pressed the French musicians onboard the naval ships into the pirate crew and forced them to create a more superior soundtrack of plunder in West Africa.

In a mood to celebrate and revisit old friends, the pirates voted to head down the coast to Sierra Leone. For Black Bart's crew, in particular, it was prime pirate country, and they were looking forward to plundering and catching up with old friends. Bart himself, however, was wary. Several weeks at sea meant that he may not have heard the latest news from West Africa. It was a rapidly changing political landscape, and that first time back on land after crossing the Atlantic always carried risks. He had hoped that the French ships would have some recently dated letters onboard that could hint at news but had no such luck. Although this victory over the French navy was an auspicious omen, he disliked not knowing what his fleet was sailing into. As the sober captain of a rowdy and reckless crew, Bart generally calculated many of those risks on his own. As his crew swelled in numbers, so did the burden of making the decisions that kept them alive.

The crew had unceremoniously discarded the body of the governor of Martinique some time ago, as corpses tied to yardarms tended to attract attention once the ships had sailed closer to land. The crew were spread comfortably across the fleet's newest additions, the *Ranger* and *Little Ranger*. While at sea, they flew the French tricolor to avoid suspicion, but as they pulled into the harbor at Sierra Leone and snaked their way through Tagrin Bay, they lowered the French tricolor and raised their new black pirate flag. They were within a few hours' sailing distance from a handful of Royal Africa Company factories down the river, but the pirate flag wasn't for them—it was for the locals who lived on the coast along the banks of the Sierra Leone River, who would take the news to their favorite English outlaw who made his living among them: the infamous John Leadstone, old Captain Crackers.

When Black Bart's crew found his compound, they rejoiced. Crackers spotted their flags and fired salutes from his cannons, and the pirates roared and fired a few celebratory shots back as they docked in Whiteman's Bay. The last time they had been there in 1718, they plundered the ship of the infamous London and Virginia slave trader William Snelgrave, who was now safely back in England lobbying for security in the trade and penning his manuscript for future publication while awaiting the pirate scourge to pass.

Black Bart had never before met this fabled Captain Crackers in person, though he had endured many tall tales about the cruel and boisterous human-trafficking outlaw during those long nights crossing the Atlantic. The pirates who had captured and recruited Bart back at Anomabo spoke frequently of the man and his ability to survive anything. When the two captains came face to face, however, their differences could not be more pronounced. The tall, sober gentleman in the waistcoat and wig cut a striking figure against the leathery rum-soaked Old Crackers, but that mattered little. In the short time that Black Bart had been a slave ship sailor and then a pirate, he had lost so many colleagues, acquaintances, and even what some might call friends to the brutality of the industry. Someone who could not only survive but also thrive on the fringes of the most violent trade was someone whose opinion he would not discount.

Captain Crackers was eager to trade with them and tell them everything he knew about Chaloner Ogle and his two warships. His gromettas, or English-speaking Africans whose marginalized ethnic statuses made the undesirable work for European-descended outlaws a necessity, slaughtered some cattle and hens kept on the compound, while the pirates fished and hunted turtles to bake directly in the half shell. In exchange for casks of spirits and wine, Crackers offered information, quarter, and what was, by all remaining accounts, a rollicking time.

This time around, the atmosphere was still festive but also strained in many ways. During the not quite three years that had passed, the political tension in both the Caribbean and in West Africa had reached an all-time high. The last time Black Bart's crew was here, the South Carolina pirate Blackbeard had been hunted down by order of Britain's governor Spotswood of Virginia, who had personally financed the hunt. Blackbeard's head had been severed and hanged from the bowsprit of Lieutenant Robert Maynard's navy ship. While Black Bart's pirates were evading naval capture in the Caribbean, the remainder of the most infamous and bulletproof of their Atlantic Ocean colleagues had been sentenced to death. Many of the men on Black Bart's ships had lost personal friends in Britain's war on piracy. Many of the colleagues they had sailed with before would never again share the Atlantic Ocean with them. Black Bart's crew had fled to Africa after killing Martinique's pirate-hunting governor, knowing very well that they were most likely next. Captain Crackers and Black Bart's crew drank to their fallen comrades and competitors alike, pouring out several measures of brandy onto the red earth for each name. They had known sailing across the Atlantic that this was their last hurrah, but now the full truth of it had sunk in.

Black Bart's stress threshold was high, as he had worked on-board slave ships and entered the business of piracy at its most dangerous period, but even he could feel the noose tightening. His pirates could evade capture and punishment in the Atlantic for only so long. That they had managed to sack more than two hundred ships during the short time he had led them was both a matter of pride and the biggest liability he had ever faced. No other pirate had been as successful as Black Bart. He counted on Captain Crackers for some intel that would give him the edge. Neither Black Bart nor his crew ever fully expected to get out of the pirate business alive, but they hoped that when it was time to go, it would be on their own terms.

While the crew prodded the French musicians and broke out the spirits for round two of heavy partying in Sierra Leone, Crackers told Bart that, indeed, the British navy had come knocking just a couple weeks ago. The old outlaw had watched Ogle's ship, the

Swallow, navigate past the hidden compound and down the river to Fort James on Bunce Island to check with the Royal Africa Company's factor there, Robert Plunkett.

After Ogle left, the locals of Sierra Leone who helped supply both Plunkett at Bunce Island and Captain Crackers down the bay eagerly shared the news that might earn them a favorable trading deal. Crackers passed all their gossip on to Black Bart and allowed the pirates to once again use his bay as a rest stop while they figured out their next moves. Knowing that people in pursuit rarely look behind them, Bart decided his fleet would head southeast along the coast right behind Ogle, but they would give Ogle some time to put some more distance between their ships. He allowed his men a two-month-long blowout courtesy of Captain Crackers but did not get too comfortable in Whiteman's Bay. After all the time spent running from the various naval powers in the Caribbean, he was eager to sack the wealth of the Gold Coast.

TERROR ON THE ONSLOW

While Ogle's squadron made its way slowly to the safety of the Royal Africa Company stronghold on the Gold Coast, Cape Coast Castle, Black Bart's pirates grew weary of sitting in place, harassing independent merchant ships bound for Bunce Island. It was time for bigger prizes. Black Bart had set his eye on the jewel in the Royal Africa Company's crown and for the very place where Ogle was heading: the Gold Coast. This was the inevitable test: either the pirates would perish and go down on their own terms, or they would win, upgrade their ships, and slip around the Dutch East India Company's Cape Colony at the Horn to plunder the wealth of the Indian Ocean world.

Tracking Ogle's route, the pirates found two great ships anchored at Point Cestos, where King Pedro and his sons, Tom Freeman and Josee lived. Like Ogle's crew had in Cape Three Points, the pirates were replenishing their fresh water and wood supply. One ship named the *Robinson* was, like that of Captain Snelgrave, a ten percenter, one of the private English slave-trading ships that paid the Royal Africa Company 10 percent of its profit in exchange for permission to trade. Roberts considered these ships to be sitting ducks. While his pirates had been able to take any and all ships, the owners of the ten percenters often had little protection against piracy, choosing instead to insure their ships and take the payout each time they were attacked. This gave them little incentive to fight back against pirates. Next to the ten percenter was a small and swift armed British naval vessel. Captain Canning of the *Robinson* had chosen to stop for water when he spotted a British naval frigate, the *Onslow*, doing the same in hopes of naval protection from the pirate danger in West Africa.

The *Onslow*, piloted by Captain Gee, was in the area because it was transporting soldiers headed from England to Cape Coast Castle to help defend Royal Africa Company fortifications against pirates, along with the internal threat posed by unhappy African trading partners and independent agents. All the European trading companies tried to keep standing armies that they could use to coerce local powers or more deeply engage in local conflicts in attempts to sway the trade to their favor. However, the European soldiers often found themselves underprepared for conflicts with West and West Central African armies, which by 1721 had become adroit with both African and European weapons and tactics.

Like all frigates at this time, the *Onslow* was built for speed and maneuverability and carried carriage-mounted guns. That made it both a more difficult prize, but also more valuable. The pirates already had two cannon-equipped French naval ships in their possession, but a state-of-the-art frigate from His Majesty's Navy would be the ideal prize with which to sail into Cape Coast Castle. The employees of the fortress would assume it was friendly and hold their fire until it was too late. Black Bart had every intention of using it to take a leaf out of the late Captain Howell Davis's book when it came to his sacking of the island of Príncipe.

What is known from this point until the pirates arrived at the Gold Coast with these two ships in tow is suspect, as sources become fewer and farther between. The source that historians primarily leaned on in the past for this swatch of time was Nathaniel Mist's fabricated Charles Johnson narrative, so unfortunately, the best source for what happened next comes from Elizabeth Trengrove, a determined Cornish woman onboard the *Onslow*. She survived sexual assault by one of Black Bart's pirates off the coast of what is now Liberia, gave evidence at Cape Coast Castle, and then, determined to watch her assailant's execution, made her way to London to give testimony to the High Court of Admiralty. The only reason we know with any certainty what happens next is due to her determination to seek justice, and these two pirate trials are the only times she appears in the historical record.[23]

Fortunately for the pirates, the crews of both the *Robinson* and *Onslow* were ashore, refilling their water casks. Though King Pedro and his sons were aware of these comings and goings, they did not get involved in European affairs unless it benefited them. When the pirates attacked the two ships, there were few onboard to resist. In no time, they were storming the decks and breaking open the crates and barrels in the hold, dividing the loot among themselves, until they heard Elizabeth Trengrove's scream. William Meade, one of the pirates onboard, had tried to force off her hoop skirt, and another named John Mitchell came to her aid and advised her to hide in the gunner's room until they could find the captain. While making her way there, some of the looting pirates had seen and threatened her. Black Bart investigated the noise and ordered her locked up on the *Royal Fortune* until he could figure out if she was worth a ransom and how to make the exchange. The pirate he assigned to guard her, David Simpson, became one of her assailants.

The pirates apprehended the remaining crew of both ships, including Trengrove's husband, when they returned from the water run and assembled them to sort them out. The soldiers they considered landlubbers and offered each a mere quarter's share of future loot if they wanted to join. The sailors didn't get this choice; the pirates pressed them into service. Roberts, a Sabbatarian himself, tried to convince the naval clergy to minister to his crew, but the reverend refused, and so Roberts took his prayer books, figuring someone else could read them out loud to the crew on Sundays. For two weeks, the pirates remained at Cestos, refitting the *Onslow* and ripping out anything that they considered unnecessary weight. *Onslow* was already fast, but she could be faster. Then they lashed forty guns to her blocks, turning her into a floating fortress. Proud of this swift and deadly ship, Black Bart gave Captain Gee his older *Royal Fortune* with which to get home and transferred that name to his newest prize. With this many cannons, the pirates felt confident that they could survive an attack on or by virtually anything in West Africa.

Chapter Five

———————◯———————

The Last Stand

WHILE THE PIRATES HAD BEEN CAROUSING with Captain Crackers, the *Swallow* and *Weymouth* sailed further away from them, southeast into the Gold Coast. They met up with an English ten percenter from Bristol, the *Robert*, which they stopped to ask about the pirates. Captain Harding had sailed the exact route that they had just a few days prior and hadn't heard anything about pirates. Rather, he told them about an insurrection onboard his ship that had cost him most of his crew. A few days after Ogle's ships had departed Captain Crackers's compound, Harding had snaked the slave ship *Robert* through the Sierra Leone River. The Royal Africa Company's factor on Bunce Island, Robert Plunkett, had no African captives to sell him, but Captain Crackers had a whole pen full of enslaved people on offer. Harding, uncertain whether he would find so many captives to buy anywhere else on the West African coast, cleaned out Captain Crackers's supply, which included none other than the guerrilla fighter Captain Tomba, who had burned a village of slave traders in Sierra Leone.

The next day, it was still dark when Harding woke to screams onboard. Tomba had convinced two enslaved men and an unnamed enslaved woman to attempt a takeover of the ship. The woman stole him a hammer that the crew had carelessly left in the open and kept watch until the sailors guarding the captives nodded off. Then she alerted the men, who used the hammer to kill three sailors sleeping on the forecastle. The third awoke and screamed before he died, which woke the captain and rest of the crew, who thwarted Captain Tomba's escape.

Atkins reported how Captain Harding boasted about quelling this insurrection. Because Captain Tomba, a physically large, strong man from rice country, would fetch the highest price on the auction block, Harding did not want to kill him. Instead, he ordered Captain Tomba beaten and scarred, then chained him up and made him watch as Harding tortured and killed one of his male accomplices and forced the other to eat the dead man's heart and liver. The woman Harding "hoisted up by the thumbs, whipp'd and slashed her with knives, before the other slaves till she died."[1] Atkins said nothing more about it, other than that it was a "melancholy story."[2] His lack of further analysis or insight in his published journal speaks to the ways in which Atkins, as an officer of the British navy, understood his place as someone who reinforced the empire's goals, no matter how gruesome or inhumane this enforcement became and no matter how he personally felt about it.

The *Swallow* and *Weymouth* left the *Robert* soon after and sailed further east. While Black Bart and the pirates followed Chaloner Ogle's route from west to east along the coast of Guinea, the naval captain fumed. He had begun the trip agitated back in February when he had departed Portsmouth with eight months of provisions for his crew. It was now the end of May, and all he had to show for his efforts was a ship empty of food and full of grumbling seamen. Other naval officers who had accomplished far less in their careers, like Lieutenant Robert Maynard, had been involved in the high-profile captures and executions of the most notorious pirates of the era. If Maynard could get Blackbeard, Ogle had to get Black Bart.

Besides this, Ogle felt the weight of responsibility for this piracy problem because he had not been able to stamp it out entirely in the Caribbean while serving during the War of the Spanish Succession a handful of years prior. Ogle knew that defeating the pirates wouldn't be easy. He had learned on this trip that they had formed a confederation under the charismatic Bartholomew "Black Bart" Roberts. Ogle knew that many of the pirates were recent recruits, and not all of them would be well-versed in seafaring or battle, but he didn't underestimate them. He would have to rely on his superior naval training to win against a sizeable crew with stolen cannons and a palpable vendetta. He and his seamen expected Black Bart's crew to put up the fight of their lives, because once the navy caught them, their lives would indeed depend on it.

What Ogle hadn't expected or prepared for was that a fleet of mismatched, stolen ships crowded with hundreds of drunk pirates flying every possible color under the harsh sun would have been able to elude him for the past four months on the coast of West Africa. The supplies that the navy had brought from Portsmouth had dwindled to a few weeks of food and hardly any water, though they had stretched their supply with supplements from along the coast at Cestos and other places. Each time they had stopped a ship or at a fortification, they asked about the pirates, and they asked about food and water. The surgeon John Atkins wrote of the great scarcity of food that stretched from Sierra Leone to Ouida. At some of the British forts where they stopped, like Anomabo or Dixcove, he found the factors to have "dwindled much" with "lank bodies" from scarcity of provisions. One of those factors, Atkins learned, later died from starvation ("he pined with a Vacuum of the Guts, and died"), though the director general at Cape Coast lived in comparable luxury, acquiring animal proteins from trading vessels and supplementing with a special garden of English fruits and vegetables tended by the enslaved for his private use.[3]

Aside from the director general's extravagance, every available scrap of food grown near the West African coast went into the trade. It must have felt uncomfortable for Ogle as a pirate hunter to beg for sacks of grain or bottles of brandy from governors whose ships had been sacked and whose trade was in ruins. Because of his standing with the navy, no one had the power to refuse him or outright accuse him of being a failure, but nobody had to, because the judgment was stamped on their ungrateful faces as they avoided eye contact while handing over their meager provisions.

By June, Ogle and his crew had entirely run out of their supplies from England and were once again out of water as well. The naval squadron of two approached Cape Three Points hesitantly. Fort Great Fredericksburg was in the process of changing hands from the Prussian Brandenburg African Company to the Dutch West India Company. Ogle knew that such exchanges often got messy as governors became deposed, and the local traders and people of the village surrounding the fort objected to the changes or took sides. Bystanders and third parties easily got pulled into conflicts, and he had enough on his plate. However, Cape Three Points was one of the best and nearest places to obtain fresh water, and his water levels were critical. The English and Dutch were of course consistent adversaries, but water was water.

In the early modern seafaring world, it was universally understood that to let seamen die of thirst was barbaric on all counts. It was one thing if a sailor died in defense of his ship and empire, but quite another thing for them to die of thirst with bloated tongues. At this time, dehydration, or "seawater poisoning" as it was called because the sailors often would resort to drinking saltwater to slake their thirst, was one of the most common causes of death of people on ships. Although the freshwater con became prevalent at this time as a way for pirates and other unscrupulous actors to gain access to ports in order to attack them, Ogle was confident that his seamen's request to refill their water barrels would not be turned down.

As his ships drew closer to the shore, he found no flag flying from Fort Great Fredericksburg at Cape Three Points. If his maps were correct, this fort had always flown the Red Eagle, the flag of the German-speaking Prussians of the Brandenburg Empire. He had been made aware that the Prussians had left and sold to the Dutch, but why then was there no tricolor flag of the West India Company? It was rare that operational European fortresses in West Africa didn't fly a flag to signal their affiliation to visitors. After all, an approaching ship might know a lot about a fort based on the flag: not just who owned it or worked within, but what its trading policy would be and whether the crew would be welcomed. Still, the sailors needed water, and this place was their surest bet. Ogle anchored both ships as close as he dared in the shallow bay and sent his sailors in rowboats with empty barrels.

As they took inventory and unstopped the barrels, a dark-skinned local agent approached them with a large gold-headed cane engraved with the name "John Conny." This agent quoted the sailors a price for the water: one ounce of gold, the going rate that Conny charged all ships.* The sailors did not recognize the authority of Conny, an African who was decidedly not Dutch, at this fortress. As far as they were concerned, only the Dutch governor of the fort had the authority to charge anything for the water. Rather than paying, the sailors roughed up this agent with "some opprobrious treatment" and sent him back to whomever this John Conny was.

At this point, it is important to think about the nature of historical sources. The only known account of this meeting was recorded by John Atkins, the surgeon employed by the English Royal Navy to take care of the men on the *Swallow* under Captain Chaloner Ogle's command. He kept a diary that he edited and ordered thematically, rather than chronologically, for publication in 1734, a dozen years after his tour of duty in Africa. He was not present at this meeting, but rather recorded what the seamen had told him. Something suspiciously missing from this account is the prior knowledge of John Conny and his watering policies by anyone in Atkins's crew.

As countless historians of this period have pointed out, sailors knew things. Those who didn't know things didn't last long in the rough waters of the Atlantic. In addition to knowing things, they knew each other. The entire seafaring industry relied on news and gossip by word of mouth, whether it concerned the weather, the availability of resources, or news about each other and key individuals of this time. The Atlantic Ocean and all its shores were a geographically wide world but also small in many ways. Each port city—whether that was Portsmouth in England, Amsterdam in the Netherlands, or Cape Three Points on the Gold Coast in West Africa—had just as much in common with the other port cities of the Atlantic world as they did with the nations or polities in which

---

* By all accounts, this was a modest and affordable amount to charge for a ship's worth of water, and most of that was for local laborers who helped point out the best watering holes and helped carry barrels to and from the shore. Conny charged the amount not because he needed it—or even because the laborers needed it—but because charging a fee gave him a reason to speak with a representative from every ship that stopped. It was one of the ways that Conny, who was more stationary at his castle than the pirates he traded with, collected news and gossip to remain relevant.

they were geographically located. With the amount of stopping Ogle's crew did while hunting down Black Bart's fleet, it is nearly impossible that someone onboard wouldn't have heard of John Conny's exploits.

John Conny was the hottest European gossip on the Gold Coast. He pops up in all their slave-trading documents with regularity. Among various spellings, the English referred to him as John Conny or Johann Kuny, the Dutch as Jan Conny or Johannes Conrad, the Prussians as Johann Cuny, and the French as Jean Cunny in their documents. By standards of the time, he had been around for an incredibly long time and was positioned for challenging the Europeans with the defeat of the Denkyira Empire. John Conny's people, the Ahanta, were Akan peoples who were consolidated into a united Asante kingdom, or even empire, under King Osei Kofi Tutu I in 1701. Tutu remained further inland in Kumasi, the seat of this new kingdom, as tenacious men like Conny paid tribute while challenging coastal power structures and vying for European allies. Conny looked for allies who were either flexible like the pirates or malleable like the Brandenburgers.

By 1710, Conny was responsible for the most dramatic deposition of the Prussian governor there: he plundered a ship that had stopped at the cape and his mercenary militia attacked the fortress with the ship's cannons supporting their rear. Rather than waste resources challenging him, the Brandenburg Company replaced Governor de Lange with Nicholas Dubois, an employee who was more to Conny's liking. Though Dubois often was too European for Conny's tastes, the two worked together for years as Conny's power and personal military grew. In their first disagreement, Dubois had tried to represent Conny in an agreement with the Dutch and English, but, embarrassed, he soon realized that Conny had no intentions of following through on agreements he himself hadn't made. After this, Dubois often wrote home about how it was better to do things Conny's way, and the Brandenburg Company agreed. They had dozens of Duboises that they could send from Prussia, but only one Conny to rely upon on the Gold Coast, and they dared not take his goodwill for granted. The caboceer's mercenary forces presented a threat to the African allies of the British and Dutch and interfered with their slave trade, and the Prussians didn't have the power to rein him in. Conny's Asante soldiers attacked British and Dutch forts, raided caravans, and prevented communication over land, while pirates made things difficult for the European empires at sea, stymieing much of the slave trade on all ends.

While the Brandenburg Company debated its role in the slave trade, it had recalled its European staff and left John Conny in charge. The Brandenburgers eventually sold their fortress to the Dutch according to European land and title conventions, without consulting John Conny. According to conventional customs in West Africa, however, European slave traders rented the spaces upon which they built their fortifications. They paid for the privilege of being there and negotiated other privileges (such as fishing) with each alliance they struck with the representatives of the African polities who owned the land. When the Dutch arrived to move into the Brandenburg Fort Great Fredericksburg and benefit from the alliance that the Prussians had built with John Conny, Conny did not recognize their right to be on Ahanta land and trained his cannons on the West India Company ships. Conny and his mercenaries had given the Dutch a brutal and bloody run for their money. Since 1717, Conny and his soldiers had been solely in charge of the fortress, running it like a free trade port for sailors, merchants, and pirates alike.

By the time the British Royal Navy arrived to replenish their freshwater supplies in June 1720, Conny had decided that the Prussians weren't coming back, nor were the Dutch, and he would become the new governor of the fortress. Pound for pound, he had done more damage to the British slave trade than Black Bart. All this is to say that even if the gossip network had failed Ogle's seamen, someone in Ogle's position almost certainly would have been briefed about Conny. It is impossible that agents of the British Royal Navy sent to West Africa on a mission to protect the trade would not know of the Ahantan ruler. Therefore, their decision to mistreat his agent at the watering station carried weight. And Atkins's failure to mention any of this long history in the journal was—as with many of his omissions—a choice.

The brutalized Ahantan agent climbed up Manfro Hill to Fort Great Fredericksburg and collapsed against the heavy Prussian-made mahogany desk in Conny's private chambers. After hearing what had happened, Conny took a group of armed soldiers with him to the watering station and seized all of Captain Ogle's water casks, along with ten of his seamen, whom he marched to the town as prisoners. Though he certainly had the power to mistreat them or avenge his agent, he did not. His treatment of these prisoners makes it clear that Conny was angling for an audience with Ogle. Later, when Ogle and Atkins came ashore to collect the men, they told Atkins, who copied the tale in his journal.

> The officer among them endeavoring to distinguish to John the difference of a king's ship from others, got his head broke: John (who understood English enough to swear) saying "by God me king here, not only for my water, but the trouble has been given me in collecting it. Drink on," says he to the sailors (knocking out the head of a half-anchor of brandy) "and eat what my house affords; I know your part is to follow orders."[4]

In other words, when the arrogant English officer tried to explain that he was with the British Royal Navy, Conny explained to him that British monarchy had no power in Cape Three Points. Everyone paid the same. Conny considered himself the king of the fortress and surrounding town in Cape Three Points and wanted to drive home his message that he would be granted the audience with the European men who were his equal. The mercy he showed the prisoners in offering them brandy (an important drink in negotiations between Europeans and Africans on the West African coast at the time) and food (something that was relatively valuable) demonstrated Conny's understanding of the seamen's positions as men with relatively little power and his willingness to make the English his allies if they could be reasonable. For Conny, it was a test.

Too bad Chaloner Ogle had never been any good at tests. When the sailors failed to return to the HMS *Swallow*, Ogle took Atkins and a handful of seamen to shore to treat with Conny directly. Atkins's description of the town of Pokesu and Fort Great Fredericksburg paints a lavish picture of a Prussian and African strong-

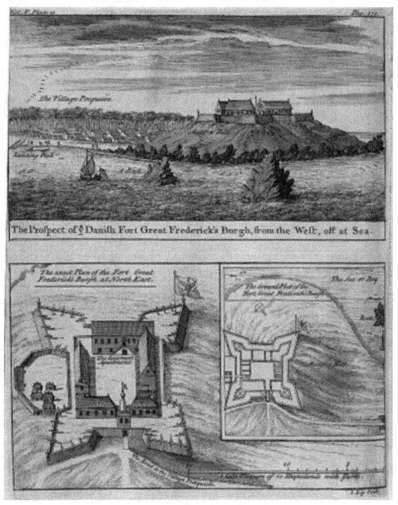

Images of Fort Great Fredricksburg (incorrectly labeled as Danish), also known as Conny's Castle, and the Ahantan town of Pokesu at Manfro Hill, Cape Three Points, by Johannes "Jan" Kip, 1732. Cf. *Koninklijke Bibliotheek, The Hague, inv. nr. 3032 B 10, opp. p. 577. Atlas of Mutual Heritage and the Koninklijke Bibliotheek, the Dutch National Library. The metadata of this file is in the public domain.*

hold. Pokesu was a wealthy town, bustling with soldiers and other fit people, flowing with palm wine, and full of nutritious foods: fish, nuts, citrus fruits, and "Canky" or kenkey, a type of steamed dumpling made from fermented cornmeal that is still a staple in Ghanaian cuisine. The five bastions of the fort could mount fifty canons. The garrison was fully operational, and the African soldiers wore European uniforms with brass buttons, and every soldier had a European musket in addition to his own African weaponry.

Most impressive though was Conny himself. Atkins wrote: "He is a strong-made man, about fifty, of a sullen look, and commands the respect of being bare-headed, from all the negroes about him that are worth caps."[5] In the trading ports of West Africa, status was often marked by European dress and accessories, such as those worn by Seignior Joseph in Sierra Leone or King Pedro of Cestos and his sons. A highly desired European item was lace hats for women and military-style caps and sometimes even powdered wigs for men. In some places along the coast, only the wealthy or those who had the rulers' favor were allowed to wear these. Atkins's comment refers to his realization that Conny didn't feel the need to dress in a European fashion to command the respect of the elites who did wear these items. Later descriptions of one of his wives decked out in nothing but gold chains covering her entire body show that her self-presentation was also highly politicized in this way. Conny was influential, connected, and wealthy enough to obtain for his wives all the latest European fashions, but he demonstrated that he was influential, connected, and wealthy enough to conspicuously refuse to parade in them.

Conny invited Ogle, Atkins, and the prisoners to feast with him in the courtyard of Fort Great Fredericksburg as they negotiated a price for the seamen's transgressions at the watering station. As the English officers needed water for their hunt and weren't in a position to refuse, they climbed the hill with Conny to his palace within the fort. Atkins the surgeon couldn't help but notice that the entrance was paved with skulls that looked decidedly human. He inquired about them and received confirmation that they were European in origin. Atkins didn't have to ask for more details: before getting to the negotiations, Conny had a few things he wanted to get off his chest. He had a captive audience of uneasy, inebriated Englishmen, some of whom were paralyzed in fear by his power play.

As the seamen feasted with Conny and the people of Pokesu, he told them the story of the skulls. As Atkins recalled it, after the Brandenburgers left West Africa, the Dutch claimed ownership of the fort. They sent several armed frigates to demand Conny's surrender, but being a "bold and subtle fellow," he demanded evidence of ownership. Even if they had provided it, which they had not, Conny presumed their guilt, telling Atkins he saw no reason for them to come so heavily armed if they had any rights to the space. The Brandenburgers had paid him rent for the ground beneath the fort, and he told Atkins, "I do not design to tenant it out to any other White men while I live."[6] Those words would later come back to haunt him.

Atkins reported that Conny told him when the Dutch came ashore to try to take the fort, Conny and his men were lying in wait, hiding behind the houses in Pokesu. They performed a successful guerrilla ambush and cut the Dutchmen into pieces and shortly after paved the entrance of Conny's palace with their boiled skulls. Conny's message was clear to Atkins: he was deadly serious about his claim to the lands of his people, and he had amassed a large enough force and sufficient arms that he could and would enforce this claim in the presence of Europeans. Ogle and his seamen could either honor this claim and become allies or challenge it and donate their skulls to his collection of paving stones.

As the meal wound down, Conny drove a hard bargain, and Captain Ogle agreed to pay six ounces of gold and an anchor of brandy for their transgressions at the watering station.[†] This was more than six times the initial cost, but the price was well worth the intel and gossip that he and his men picked up at the feast. It might have been an insult to His Majesty's Navy for Ogle to acknowledge Conny's power and sovereignty in this way, but Ogle had a mandate to find Black Bart. At Cape Three Points, he had learned where this elusive pirate and his fleet, which also had needed water in the

---

† An anchor is a measurement for wine and spirits equal to roughly ten U.S. gallons (37.85 liters).

past, were headed. To Ogle's mind, Black Bart was an immediate threat. Conny was stationary and could be dealt with later, hopefully by someone else. If Ogle ever saw West Africa again after this trip, it would be too soon.

For now, Conny and the English had come to an understanding. Atkins reported that once Ogle had agreed to the payment, Conny showed them "great civility" and permitted them to fish in his river while they refilled their water barrels. This is a significant gesture on the Gold Coast especially: in most written contracts between the European slave traders and their African business partners, fishing rights were a signifier of trust and kinship that denoted a relationship based on presumed good faith. Regular access to protein was not a given at this time, when every crumb of food was needed to sustain the lives of the enslaved during the Atlantic voyage. In the past, this point of negotiation had caused much contention and even some deaths. It is unknown if Ogle or Atkins, two men who were not directly in the human trafficking business, knew about this aspect of the trade, but Conny's offer demonstrates movement on his behalf toward an Akan-English alliance on his terms. Because Conny was so powerful, wealthy, and independent, it was a different kind of alliance than those the naval officers had struck with King Pedro of Cestos or the King of Barra and his Duchess at Gillislee.

From Conny's perspective, it made sense: they both hated the Dutch, they both had a large supply of cannons and soldiers, and both the Akan and the English could benefit from the removal of the Dutch in West Africa. England could gain the upper hand in the trade, and Conny could rule from Fort Great Fredericksburg without challenge. Conny could attack by land, and Ogle by sea.

The English captain with his imperial eyes did not see things that way. In his empire, people of Conny's skin tone were enslaved. He left Cape Three Points six ounces of gold lighter, with the understanding that such a powerful African could not be allowed to remain in place at Fort Great Fredericksburg.

While en route to Cape Coast, Captain Ogle called formation. One of the first names he called—Armstrong, Robert—did not respond.[7]

He called again, hearing no "Aye, captain!"

The crew shifted in silence on deck. Ogle set his jaw and moved down the roll call, and it happened three more times: his crew was missing a small handful of seamen. He ordered a search of the cargo deck and was unsurprised when his officers came up empty-handed. Life as the lowest-ranking people onboard a British naval vessel was hell, and it was unsurprising that Conny's Castle had seemed the safer option for them. Likely, Conny had helped the four to hide at his fort and escape the *Swallow* with intentions to utilize their knowledge or assistance in the future. Ogle was incensed by their insolence but had little time to process it or to act on it.

For now, he was fixed on finding the pirate scourge, and he finally had enough water in his hold that he would not need to stop again for a while. He had spent the past few months making his way down the West African coast from west to east, finding old evidence of plunder but nothing fresh. Other than the free trade city of Ouidah, there wasn't much that would have interested the pirates in this region, and he considered it all cleared because he still did not know that the pirates had made it to the Caribbean and back during the time he had spent searching for them in Africa. While Ogle retraced the pirates' trail from the previous year, the pirates were now inadvertently retracing his from a few months earlier. Instead of being in front of him, they were behind him, and the rear view was the last place Ogle thought to look.

The squadron arrived at the British stronghold of Cape Coast Castle June 16, 1721, and after meeting with the well-fed director general, Ogle agreed to escort some of the slave ships down the coast to Anomabo so they could safely complete their sordid business. They then moved on to the independent free-trade city of Ouidah in what is now Benin, the most easternmost point along that stretch of the coast that regularly drew European ships, but no one there had heard or seen anything. Anywhere further east than Ouidah in the Gulf of Guinea had rougher waters and less European presence, and so if Ogle were to think like a pirate, south would be the direction to go. He rationalized that heading toward Cape Lopez and the islands off its coast in modern-day

View (facing south) of the cannons protecting Cape Coast Castle from the ships of pirates and other European rivals in the slave trade. *Photo by author*

Gabon would be a sure bet because there was plunder there, and the ten-day trip meant that help would be slow to arrive. Cape Lopez, the Gabon River, and the isles of São Tomé and Príncipe all had robust international trade that would attract pirates. Furthermore, they were the last port of call along the West African coast before heading further south into West Central Africa, a region outside of Ogle's jurisdiction. If the pirates went there, they wouldn't stay— they would round the cape and flee into Madagascar and the Indian Ocean trade. They would be someone else's problem—Commodore Matthews's actually—and Ogle had seen enough of Commodore Matthews's smug face to last him a lifetime. There was no way that he was going to chase his prize into Matthews's waiting arms.

On July 28, 1721, both of Ogle's ships arrived at the island of Príncipe, off the coast of Cape Lopez, certain that they were hot on the pirates' trail. Governor de Sousa, who had been responsible for the dramatic death of Black Bart's mentor, the gentleman pirate Captain Howell Davis, was still the Comte de Príncipe, though the island certainly looked and felt different when Ogle arrived. Madalena de Lancastre, de Sousa's wife, had died during the time between the pirates' visit and Ogle's arrival. The city was still rebuilding after the fiery vengeance Black Bart had wreaked upon it. The Portuguese were now wary of all foreign ships captained by men with fancy coats.

Still, any enemy of the pirates was at least a temporary ally, if not a friend to the Comte de Sousa. The British seamen stocked up on Portuguese bread and careened their ships. Ships that were in heavy use, as the *Weymouth* and *Swallow* were, needed to be brought onto land for regular maintenance even if there was no damage from cannon fire. This ensured that their ships remained fast enough in the water. The seamen, excited to leave the cramped quarters of the ships, went ashore and stayed in tents. They soon drank the island dry of the palm wine the locals made specifically for visitors. Atkins believed that this excess, combined with the aqueous vapors that accumulated in the mist on the island at this time of year, brought on the epidemical malignant fever that ravaged the crew.

He was half right. Yellow fever, the disease that burned through the crew, is spread through mosquito bites, and the rainy season had created the stagnant water that attracted mosquitos and provided ideal breeding conditions. Under the conditions Ogle's crew faced in 1721, the expected death rate was up to 50 percent, and the disease often permanently disabled those who survived. There is no treatment other than the management of symptoms and fluid levels, so dehydration due to weeks of excessive drinking likely would have made the disease more deadly, as would any impurities in the drinking water.[8]

Ogle's crew suffered extreme fevers, vomiting, delirium, and the jaundiced tinge to their pale skin and eyes that gave the disease its name. Some seemed to recover, only to be stricken again, relapsing with internal bleeding that put them into comas before they died. Every day those that remained buried three to four seamen.

Atkins wrote that this illness "reduced us in a short stay of two months, to some deliberations whether we could proceed to sea safely without a return of men from England."[9] Their crew had been so decimated that they barely had enough healthy seamen to steer the ships. Atkins reflected that by the end of their voyage, the *Weymouth*, which had left England with 240 men onboard, had recorded 280 deaths: the disease had ravaged the crew faster than the sailors could be replaced.

Seeing what the disease had done to the crew, Atkins recommended that they take whatever help they could to get their ships away from Príncipe. In August, the sailors had rented two houses to use as makeshift hospitals to quarantine their sick, but it did nothing to stop the spread of the fever. By September it became clear that their numbers would continue to dwindle, stranding them on the island if Ogle did not take Atkins's advice. The sailors hired twenty locals to help them weigh anchor so that they could outrun the fever. Thus a skeleton crew of the seventy-two remaining seamen wearily sailed north for Cape Coast Castle on the Gold Coast in hopes that England had sent some reinforcements by way of sailors, soldiers, or supplies.

On October 25, they arrived at Cape Coast Castle. The director general rejoiced when Ogle's ships appeared on the horizon. He was anxious about the reports of Black Bart's heavily armed fleet. While Ogle had gone south and suffered the epidemic, the pirates had swept through the Gold Coast, west to east, decimating every ship and European presence. The pirates hadn't tried to storm the well-fortified Cape Coast Castle as they originally considered, but they had attacked every other coastal European stronghold and ship in the area, and Cape Coast Castle was filled with refugees and dread. The director general could not hide his dismay when he found that on the short journey from Príncipe to the Gold Coast, Ogle's already threadbare crew of seventy-two had been reduced to fifty-seven.

Fifty-seven was not enough to sail two warships, much less actively man them. Atkins had turned the *Weymouth* into a quarantine ship, isolating the remaining sick sailors while the survivors piloted the *Swallow*. Ogle took it to Sekondi to repair and scrape clean the hull so that she could move unencumbered once they found the pirates, while Atkins went with the *Weymouth*, now all but a ghost ship, around the Gold Coast, with all the doors and hatches open to air it out. Once free of disease, his objectives were to help the officers gather intel, supplies, and any Englishmen he could impress to replace the lost crew.

The *Weymouth* encountered fresh evidence of the pirates everywhere it sailed. Atkins didn't know yet that while he and Ogle were sailing north from Príncipe, Black Bart and his crew headed south from the Gold Coast. On intersecting courses, they unfortunately were far enough away to miss each other entirely—literal ships passing in the night. Ogle's earlier instincts about the pirates' movement south were correct; the timing had just been off.

At every fort and factory where Atkins stopped for intel, he heard more stories of missing ships, plundered goods, and men who had joined Roberts's fleet. Atkins forcibly enlisted the landlubbers that Roberts had rejected, hoping that the *Swallow* and *Weymouth*'s surviving naval officers could teach them the essentials in the short time they had left. There was no way to know how many ships and pirates the naval squadron would have to go up against to stamp out the threat for good. The only certain thing was that they were forever two steps behind the pirates and needed a new tactic fast.

Naturally, Atkins returned to Cape Three Points to see John Conny. He did not expect the caboceer to inform on the pirates, but perhaps Atkins, a rather observant man, could infer something, either about Roberts or, failing that, about the handful of sailors who had defected at Cape Three Points, or perhaps something regarding Conny's next moves. This time, the surgeon was more respectful in his approach. He had seen Conny's militia and guns. They had come to an understanding last time, and Atkins—onboard a decimated ship full of people who didn't want to be there and didn't know how to fight—wanted to ensure that the African trader–turned-king received the respect he demanded. Without Ogle there to bungle the meeting, he felt confident.

They fired their guns in salute, an acknowledgment of Conny's sovereignty at Fort Great Fredericksburg. Upon firing the cannons, Conny himself came to the shore to greet the English sailors and officers, and with a guard of twenty to thirty men, escorted them to his home in Pokesu. His home had been built using Prussian bricks and stone from Fort Great Fredericksburg, and Atkins spent quite some time describing it in his journal afterward. Conny led them through his home and into the courtyard, where the houses for his officers and servants were. Atkins emphasized the way Conny imitated the grandeur he had observed from the Prussians in the ceremony he put on for the sailors. This time, he fed them kenkey, salt butter, cheese, palm wine, and beer. Atkins also mentions the presence of one of his wives, who was pregnant at the time and clothed entirely in gold chains, including gold drops in her hair, which he estimated must have amounted to a total eight to ten pounds troy weight of gold on her body.‡

That wasn't the most shocking thing, however. After making quick mental calculations about how much that gold was worth, his eyes shifted to one of the trees in the courtyard that was adorned with what looked like human jawbones. When he asked Conny, the caboceer replied that about a month earlier, he had felt bad about the Dutchmen's skulls paving the road, so he had given them a proper burial with pipes, tobacco, and brandy. Their jawbones he had kept in case warnings were necessary. Atkins hadn't learned anything about Black Bart on this trip, but after reflecting on the spiritual and ethical concerns among the West Africans that Conny spoke about, he mused that their morality kept them from injuring one another, but it had "little or no influence in respect to us; whom they rob, cheat, or murder, as best answers their conveniences." Then he wrote the phrase that would damn Conny and his men. Atkins said that their beliefs were "like the Articles of Pyrates, which keep up a sort of honesty among themselves, tho they despoil everybody else." With the flick of a wrist and stroke of a pen, he had done to King Conny what the British Crown had done to the Maratha Navy's Admiral Kanhoji Angre in India: reduced a local powerful sovereign ruler to the status of a mere pirate to better suit the desires of empire.[10]

---

‡ The troy pound is an English unit of mass mostly used to weigh precious metals. A troy pound is roughly equivalent to 0.82 imperial pounds, making the amount of gold mentioned here anywhere from 6.5 to 8.3 pounds.

The desires of empire became apparent in how Atkins wrote about Conny, Pokesu, and Fort Great Fredericksburg in his report. It reads like an intelligence briefing. The surgeon thoroughly covered everything that one needed to know about the people within to launch a successful assault. He addresses the tactical mistakes of the Dutch, whose bones ended up as paving stones and decorative wind chimes. He thoroughly described the setup of the fortress and the town surrounding it, and the number of cannons and soldiers Conny had at his disposal. Most interesting is what he wrote about how these soldiers—Asante mercenaries mainly—had been trained in the battle tactics of both Prussian oblique formation with muskets and Asante pincer formation with swords. Finally, he discusses the sheer wealth on display, for instance, the descriptions of foods reserved for the wealthy West Africans, the gold that bedecked Conny's wife, and the ways in which the caboceer recruited allies. Though Conny divulged nothing about the pirate Captain Bartholomew Roberts, Atkins found much value in the meeting. These pages in his report are a warning to not underestimate this African threat to the efficacy of the British slave trade.

Atkins never wrote about how Ogle received this news, but we do know that soon after they departed from Fort Great Fredericksburg, both ships headed back to Cape Coast Castle to regroup. There, they found nothing but a stack of letters from factors and traders along the coast warning about the possibility of attack at Ouidah. Ogle already had some inkling of it, as he had been stopping at every conceivable point along the coast after scraping clean the *Swallow*, only to find wanton destruction and stranded Europeans whose wide-eyed testimony hinted at larger pirate aspirations. The captain didn't think Black Bart would be foolish enough to try to storm the well-fortified Cape Coast Castle, so the next logical target would have been the city of Ouidah, a three- to five-day journey by naval frigate. With their numbers still few and illness onboard, the sick stayed behind with Captain Mungo Herdman on the *Weymouth* anchored at Cape Coast Castle, while the able-bodied were transferred to the *Swallow* with Ogle and Atkins. They set sails and moved as quickly as they could to try to intercept the pirates.

As the navy recovered and regrouped on the Gold Coast, Roberts had continued eastward down the coast of Guinea that early autumn, taking a couple of smaller prizes while adjudicating the mayhem that descended over his crew as it grew larger and unwieldy with all the new recruits. As Ogle moved what remained of his crew north to the Gold Coast, Black Bart's fleet had left the Gold Coast to come south. When Ogle reached Cape Coast Castle, the pirates stopped at Cape Lopez, a place with many great hiding spots near the coast and in the river, to regroup and prepare for the taking of a large prize that could tide them over for a few months. Other than Cape Coast Castle, which had been built to withstand a sustained naval assault, there would be no prizes along the 1720s West African coast better than those anchored at the port city of Ouidah.

OUIDAH

Ouidah was an exceptional city during this period. It was arguably the most cosmopolitan West African port city of the early 1700s. It was arranged in four quarters: the original village of Hueda, and Portuguese, French, and English quarters, each marked by a fort not much more than a mile apart from the others. The forts doubled as warehouses and homes for the lower-ranking personnel of the European slave-trading companies, their families, and the African captives to be sold, all of whom were responsible to the king of Hueda, who resided in the larger inland city of Savi. Around each fort were families, many international and interracial, who provided services for the forts. Although the Europeans mostly came from Portugal, France, or the British Isles, the African population was more transient. Many came from other coastal areas, especially the Gold Coast, where they had acquired the languages and skills necessary to European trade, and there was always a steady stream of merchants from Savi as well. The Kingdom of Hueda separated the trade between these two cities; most of the merchandise and enslaved were kept in Ouidah, but to do business there, traders had to trek to Savi to deal with the king. The highest-ranking European slave-trading company officers, therefore, also had homes in Savi, whereas their underlings worked on the coast. This combined business resulted in around fifteen thousand enslaved captives moving through Ouidah each year at this time.[11]

Unlike Cape Coast Castle, the English Royal Africa Company stronghold, Ouidah was comparatively underfortified. This was because King Huffon maintained this city as a neutral port, and the 1703 treaty forbade all European hostilities in the city. Europeans who did not abide by this treaty could be denied access

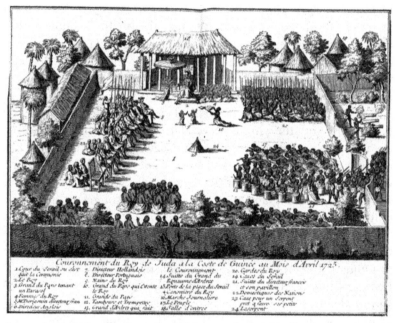

Coronation of King Huffon of Ouidah. On the left-hand side sits a row of directors of the various European slave-trading companies. They are labeled with numbers and a corresponding key: 5 is French, 6 English, 7 Dutch, and 8 Portuguese. The walls surrounding the ceremony are indicative of the architecture of both Ouidah and Savi, which limited the movement of Europeans and emphasized African design and control of the space. *Jean-Baptiste Labat, "Voyage du chevalier Des Marchais en Guinée, isles voisines, et la Cayenne, fait en 1725, 1726 et 1727," Paris 1730, t.II, p. 70. Public domain*

to goods and enslaved people obtained in the region. In a forced show of goodwill, the Portuguese, French, and English companies were allowed to maintain their presence with their forts, but these forts lacked the number of cannons or barracks for auxiliary troops boasted by each company's stronghold.

The pirates knew this, of course, because many of them were former slave ship sailors who had anchored at Ouidah in their previous lives. Although there is less information about the Black pirates onboard, it is likely that some of them either had been enslaved on a ship with other captives from Ouidah or had worked as canoe men or in positions that required knowledge of places like this. Many of Roberts's crew, Black and White, had witnessed or experienced the type of subhuman treatment at Ouidah that they no longer accepted as pirates. This made sacking Ouidah the equivalent of a grudge match for many in Roberts's fleet. Roberts, with his clearheaded vision, understood that Cape Coast Castle and Ouidah were the centers of the British slave trade at this time and that a solid hit at the business they were so desperate to protect would hurt the empire most. He also knew that because of the relationship between Ouidah and Savi, many of the slave ship captains would be holding gold from Cape Coast Castle onboard for the king. He figured that this gold from the company would be worth less to the captains than their ships and cargo, but there was only one way to find out.

Shortly after the New Year in January 1722, the pirate fleet left their camp at Cape Lopez and sailed north into the natural harbor at Ouidah. Roberts stood on the deck of his new, deadly *Royal Fortune*—the modified former English naval frigate *Onslow*—surrounded by his fleet, both the musicians and the pirates making as much noise as they could. Rather than flying false colors and sneaking into the harbor, they flew the Jolly Roger, confident that none of the three European forts would be a match for their fleet. The crews on the eleven anchored trading ships in Ouidah harbor immediately surrendered as the captains jumped into African canoes and European rowboats with their gold, hoping to make it to a fortress on land. Roberts's crew overran the ships and searched them, but as suspected, slave ships didn't carry much more than what was necessary for the transport of their human cargo. Although Roberts happily would take the best of the ships for his own use, he wasn't going to do it without all the real wealth that had disappeared into the fortresses on land.

He did something that only a man who had worked in the slave trade and knew its inner workings could have known to do: he ransomed the ships. At this time, ransoming and redeeming, or "panyarring," as it was called, was a common practice in the slave trade due to the frequency of miscommunication and the absence of trust between Africans and Europeans. If all terms of a trade agreement hadn't been met, a trader could temporarily hold ransom an object or person of importance until all the obligations of the agreed-upon deal were met. Both European and African people could be panyarred. Often the Africans who were panyarred were sold into the Atlantic slave trade if their family and friends could not free them before the ship weighed anchor.[12] Europeans who were panyarred often were sold into the service of local Africans and could be redeemed by anyone willing to pay the debt—usually another European company employee, though not always. According to this practice, Black Bart had pirated the ships that had not defended themselves, fair and square. They were his now, free to burn if he wanted to. So he sent some of his fastest runners to the forts to let the captains know that they could have their ships back for the bargain price of eight pounds of gold each, or they could watch their ships and careers go up in flames.

By 1720, both the gold and the ships of most of the English slavers were insured: the gold through the royal trading company and the ships through insurance companies like Lloyd's of London, still in business today.[13] The captains hiding in the forts would have made quick calculations. None of them owned the gold, but many of them owned the ships or were employed by the shipowners. If the ships were burned, they and their crews would be out of a livelihood for however long it took to collect insurance money and buy, refurbish, or build a new ship. If they lost the gold, they might lose the contract with the Royal Africa Company, but most likely they would not be blamed for the actions of the pirates that Chaloner Ogle and the navy already should have taken care of. Besides, there were other ways into the slave trade and other trades that needed ships.

Most of the captains surrendered their gold and coins but asked for receipts for insurance purposes. Roberts, who generally had a sense of humor about the surreal tone his life had taken, agreed and signed them as the "Gentlemen of Fortune," and even added the signature of a witness, Harry Gillespie, as well. One of these receipts, the one given to Captain Dittwatt, exists still in the records of the Royal Africa Company in the British National Archives in Kew, London.[14]

One captain, however, had not paid. Like several other captains, he had used all his gold to fill his ship with the enslaved Africans he was tasked with purchasing. Some of the other captains had been able to get loans from the company employees in the forts, but Captain Fletcher of the *Porcupine* had either been unable or unwilling to do so. The ubiquitously infamous 1724 narrative written by the fictional pirate Captain Charles Johnson described the scene. It states that Roberts sent two men, Harris and Walden, to release the enslaved to shore and then burn the ship to call the captain's bluff. Walden ordered the carpenter to unlock the shackles while Harris spread flammable tar across the ship's deck. The carpenter claimed that he had lost the key—perhaps he was calling the pirates' bluff, or perhaps he really had. In the eighteenth-century slave trade, the well-being of the enslaved chained below was certainly not a priority for many slave ship employees, who feared the living people they considered cargo and the inevitable revolts that happened onboard. The *Porcupine* went up in flames a moment later, and then the harbor was filled with the screams of the enslaved trapped below. Johnson insists the pirates burned the ship and all the enslaved trapped within.

However, the documents from later pirate trials suggest that wasn't the case. The trial paperwork did mention that some of the accused were covered in pitch and that a fire was set. One of the men, Edward Evans, who had been a sailor onboard the *Porcupine* when the pirates coerced him to join them, said that "the ship being on fire, he was glad to get onboard the pyrate to save himself, many of the negro slaves being burnt or drowned, unable to help themselves being fetter'd," while another sailor from that ship, Richard Wood, said that "the pyrates set him to work to unshackle the negroes on board the Porcupine." The Newfoundlander John Walden (aka Miss Nanny), whom the pirates had scooped up a year prior, admitted to setting the fire.

However, a couple other pieces of evidence cast some doubt about whether the enslaved were in fact burned. Robert Haws, one of the Porcupine's crew, found himself on trial for being one of Black Bart's pirates. He testified that from the burning ship, he was ordered into a rowboat. The quartermaster told him to "take out the Porcupine's Negroes, and carry them on board the French Ship."[15]

In addition to this, a peek into the Chancery Records suggests Haws was successful in saving the captives. Chancery courts in England decided matters of equity. The records indicate that Captain Fletcher of the Porcupine had 273 enslaved people onboard when Roberts attacked. Of those enslaved, 236 arrived and disembarked from the Porcupine in the Americas just five weeks later on February 24.[16] This discrepancy reflects the average rate of death during an Atlantic voyage onboard a slave ship. Of course, it's difficult to know what exactly accounted for those numbers or if the people who disembarked were the same who were onboard when Roberts's crew attacked. We may never know exactly what happened onboard the Porcupine, but we do know that the Johnson pirate narrative and all the tales it has spawned cannot be relied upon without additional confirming documentation. Some of the pirates certainly weren't above committing murder, but the trial records indicate that a mass burning of innocent Africans may have been a step too far for many of them.

Black Bart and his crew left Ouidah that day heavy with the gold that otherwise would have been used to trade for the lives of human beings. Roberts knew that none of this made his actions morally just, but he must have figured: who on the West Coast of Africa except the enslaved had any room at all to criticize his morals?

Captain Chaloner Ogle, of course, wouldn't have agreed because he was the military arm of empire. Like Black Bart, he had his own aspirations for using his position and his time spent pirate hunting in West Africa to cash out. To Ogle, Roberts and his crew were the perpetually growing thorns standing between him and any number of glories that could one day be his: knighthood, admiralty, a seat in Parliament, and a beautiful manor home with stately grounds to pass down to his descendants.

Two days after Ouidah's sacking on January 13, the *Swallow* sailed into its devastated harbor. The flotsam of burned plunder floated all around them. The angry British factors and residents of Ouidah wanted to know what the navy was going to do to protect them. Ogle's officers shook down anyone present, trying to figure out where Black Bart's pirates might have absconded. The answers Ogle's officers brought back puzzled him. The pirates had planted loud, obvious stories about heading west again, perhaps to Jacqueville, an island a few miles west of Cape Three Points. Ogle had just come from that region and knew it had to be a lie. With a pirate fleet that large hugging the coast, coming directly at them, the *Swallow* or *Weymouth* would have spotted them.

No, after the boldest and most costly sacking and ransoming at Ouidah, only a fool would make his fleet a target by remaining within view of the coast at all. As much as Ogle despised Black Bart, he knew that the pirate king who had taken the most ships and avoided capture for so long was made of more strategic stuff. The naval captain would have sniffed out a less disciplined and skillful leader by now. Ogle was certain the pirates would seek out someplace more concealed, like Captain Crackers's compound in Sierra Leone, where they would have land at their back and could monitor approaching ships at a choke point. What clinched Ogle's decision was a persistent French captain who had lost both his ship and the eight pounds of gold dust he paid in ransom to get it back. Ogle knew his ships and that the ship the French captain had described sounded like a top-of-the-line vessel. Indeed, such vessels were more rare in Africa. With a careening, she would be able to sail around the storms of the cape and into the Indian Ocean without a problem.

Later in April 1722, Chaloner Ogle confessed in a letter to J. Roberts Publishers that this missing French ship out of Ouidah was the clue that tipped him off to the pirates' most logical location. Once he heard what had happened from the French captain, he realized that the pirates wanted to trade in the *Ranger* for something better. He wrote, "I judged they must go to some place in the Bite [Bight of Benin] to clean and fit the French Ship, before they would think of cruising again; which occasioned me to stretch away into the Eve, and look into those places which I knew had Depth of Water sufficient for his majesty's ships."[17]

He headed to Príncipe on a gamble that the pirates would have stopped there en route to the Bight of Benin. It took ten days to reach it. During those ten days, Ogle fought to keep his doubts at bay. If he guessed wrong, this would be his last opportunity to catch them. Losing ten days plus the trail of the pirates would almost certainly give them sufficient time to leave his jurisdiction.

When they arrived, the rainy season had passed, but Ogle kept his men onboard in an abundance of caution. He didn't want them to come down with another bout of yellow fever, and after several of his crew mysteriously went missing after their visit to John Conny at Cape Three Points, he was concerned about further flight risks. At this stage, Ogle's crew consisted mostly of men who had been victims of the pirate fleet and had been forced onto Ogle's ships to replace his decimated crew. Not everyone wanted to be there, so Ogle made decisions with an eye toward preventing flight. However, for every man on the *Swallow* looking to get away from the navy, another looked forward to the opportunity to recover what the pirates took or to satisfy the baser desire for revenge. To those who had lost everything in a pirate attack, a few months of discomfort onboard a naval frigate may have been worth it.

Unfortunately, the Portuguese traders at Príncipe hadn't seen anything, so the squadron moved east to the Gabon River (now the Ogooué River), where the Old Cracker–types of this region tended to congregate just far enough from the coast to avoid being spotted. Ogle sent a few seamen in boats to navigate the difficult terrain, who soon found evidence that the pirates had been there but found no quarter so had moved on. As with Ouidah, they had missed Black Bart by only a couple of days. The difference was that this region was more isolated, so there were fewer places the pirates could be. Cape Lopez was the next logical port of call, and it was there that they finally found three of Black Bart's ships anchored in the natural harbor.

Had the *Weymouth* been around and had the *Swallow* been staffed with trained sailors and seamen, Ogle might have given the orders to attack point-blank. Three ships in a harbor were no match for two fully armed naval frigates, even if some of those onboard were unfamiliar with naval battle tactics. However, the *Weymouth* was still indisposed and Ogle had only the poorly staffed *Swallow* and no way of knowing how many other functioning pirate ships were out of view, how many arms these ships carried, and how prepared the pirates onboard were to fight. He did have extensive experience and training on his side, and now that he had invested the better part of a year of his life hunting them, he would leave nothing to chance. On February 10, 1722, Captain Chaloner Ogle sat down with his remaining officers around a nautical map of the region, and together they drafted a strategy to divide and conquer. There was nowhere left for Black Bart to run.

THE BATTLE OF CAPE LOPEZ

A merry life, and a short one.—Bartholomew Roberts, 1722

February 5, 1722

The fateful morning at Cape Lopez was warm and muggy like most winter mornings on the water in West Africa. Captain Bartholomew Roberts was awake though most of his crew still snored. There were so many souls onboard now, more than two hundred, that the ship itself sounded like it was snoring, though that also could have been the creaking of all the hasty adjustments the carpenters had nailed in place to transform the *Royal Fortune* into the ultimate weapon at sea.

Roberts was filled with frustration. He missed having refined and intelligent men like Captain Howell Davis around to plan with. At least Davis had been able to hold his liquor. How was he supposed to plan the next, most important part of their journey with a ship full of sailors who contained more brandy than a Christmas pudding?

His former lieutenant Walter Kennedy had been a big drinker, too. Ever since the Irish pirate had disappeared with half of Black Bart's crew in the Caribbean, leaving his loyal men with nary a drop of water or crumb of biscuit, the stress of leadership had been wearing away at Roberts and both paranoia and resentment had grown steadily. Roberts no longer accepted Irish men onboard his ship (later, one of his crew explained to the naval officers that being Irish "was against pyrates rules to accept of, because they had been formerly cheated by one Kennedy an Irish Man who run away with their Money") and he no longer ate with the crew, choosing instead to allow just a handful of trusted men in his mess.[18] His lieutenant, James Skyrme of the *Ranger*, adopted the same practice, keeping a tight inner circle while the newer recruits were left to their own devices and to the cruel leadership of the quartermasters.

This drastic change in leadership style was not without consequences. After Black Bart's crew had burned the *Porcupine* at Ouidah and Black Bart ransomed each ship for eight pounds of gold, a handful of the crew under James Skyrme discovered that one of the slave ships they ransomed used to be a French privateer and sailed well enough to go anywhere in the world. New ships like that were hard to come by in Africa, where slave traders preferred larger berths and cheaper voyages to faster sails. The pirates thought back to Black Bart's second *Royal Fortune*, which had been a French naval ship taken at Sierra Leone, and how they had taken full advantage of its power in their exploits. Black Bart was on his third *Royal Fortune* (the ship formerly known as *Onslow*, which had been carrying English soldiers to Cape Coast Castle and had stopped to water at the Sestos River when the pirates took her), so Skyrme's pirates thought it only fair that they upgrade their *Ranger* to a better ship, too.

Without conferring with Black Bart, who had already taken eight pounds ransom for this ship from its captain, Skyrme had ordered twenty men into the former privateer and sailed her out of Ouidah as their captain. The French captain clutched the useless ransom note and cursed them from shore. Black Bart was now guilty of both robbing a ship's worth of gold and the ship itself. Now that the pirates were nestled away at Cape Lopez, what was done was done. But Roberts would not forget that Skyrme had made an ass of him. Roberts had his own moral code and had given his word that if the ship captains paid in gold, they could keep their ships. Was it even worth sailing to the East Indies with men who lacked honor among thieves?

Not only that, but some of his ungrateful men, feeling the heat of the British navy at their backs, also had tried to escape at Cape Lopez. Christopher Granger had been trouble ever since Roberts conscripted him from Captain Rolls in the *Cornwall* at Calabar. First Granger put on a terrible Irish accent so that the pirates would leave him behind, but he was betrayed by one of his shipmates. Roberts assigned him to work with the carpenters, as there were never enough onboard. By Granger's own admission, he hated it, saying that he "was kept to work as a Negro among them, and ill used."§ When they arrived at Cape Lopez, he was one of the first pirates off the ship, using the excuse of washing clothes, but when he and his friends tried to run, they were caught by four of the "old-timer" pirates and forced back onboard, their land privileges permanently revoked.[19] This had all happened after several failed escape attempts at Sestos, Calabar, and Ouidah.

There had also been infighting among his men about workloads, their next steps, and personal feuds carried into Roberts's crew from other ships on which the men had served together. John Stevenson got into a fight and was slashed with a cutlass so badly that he ended up disabled, unable to walk properly onboard a ship.[20]

Roberts wanted to assess the four vessels (his third *Royal Fortune*, Skyrme's *Ranger*, the French privateer ship that would become Skyrme's second *Ranger*, and a smaller Dutch square-rigged flat-bottom pink that they had taken at Axim for its ability to navigate shallow water), split up the provisions, and decide on the best course of action. He didn't have time for frightened men behaving like children and threatening the integrity of his plans before he had even made them.

Daylight had well and truly broken by the time Roberts had kicked the cook awake to boil up some mess. The smell of food got

---

§ This was not an uncommon complaint and phrasing by the White people who the pirates pushed into jobs requiring heavy manual labor.

some of the less drunk fellows stirring. While the cook ladled into bowls generous portions of stewed African forest buffalo, which had been hunted by some of the pirates two days ago, one of the men keeping watch shouted, "A Portuguese!" The *Royal Fortune* came to life as hungover pirates reached for more brandy and rubbed the sleep from their eyes. James Skyrme, onboard the new *Ranger*, was anxious to see how the former French privateer sailed and called on his men to board her and prepare to go. Roberts shrugged and ate his breakfast while he watched more than a hundred board the *Ranger*, eager to break up the monotony of chores and drinking with some sea robbery. Maybe this was the diversion they needed to vent some steam before they buckled down and finished attending to the ships while they were anchored at Cape Lopez.

A GRISLY END

Meanwhile, on the *HMS Swallow*, Captain Chaloner Ogle's rancid mood finally lifted. Sure, the provisions of beef, pork, bread, and wine that the lord commissioners of the admiralty had promised to him back in August never made it to Cape Coast Castle—undoubtedly long gone in the bellies of these pirates whose ships they had spotted—and, sure, Ogle lacked a crew of competent seamen, but he had created a plan for capturing the pirates that even the impressed men onboard could carry out. Slowly the *Swallow* left its secluded hiding place and sailed into the open as if it were heading for Príncipe, just like any other Portuguese merchant or slave ship. The English surgeon John Atkins looked through the spyglass and reported that one of the pirate ships had weighed anchor and raised the sails. They had been spotted! Atkins reported that Skyrme's ship was "bending some of her Sails as she came out," a sure sign of rashness.[21] The pirates were in pursuit, expecting easy prey.

Ogle glanced up at the Portuguese flag he had ordered hoisted on the *Swallow*'s mast, and his stiff mouth twitched into an unfamiliar shape that might have passed for a smile. He shouted to his quartermasters to keep the course slow and steady. This allowed Ogle to lure the pirates far from their friends while appearing to give the pirates opportunity to catch them. Then he sat back, crossed his white stocking-clad legs, and watched the *Ranger* come to him.

When the *Ranger* got within gunshot of the *Swallow*, Skyrme commanded the pirates to fire several chase guns. Ogle noticed that they were flying the red English ensign, the king's Jack, a Dutch pendant, and a black flag. Ogle lowered the Portuguese flag and raised his own Union Jack to let them know that this was one of the king's naval ships. It was the equivalent of a trump card. Doing this would terrify some of the pirates onboard, and they were likely to give up, as many had done when Ogle fought in the War of the Spanish Succession. Even if they decided to try to attack, they would certainly lose, and when they lost the fight, they would come up on charges of firing on a king's ship and hang for it. As predicted, several of the *Ranger*'s thirty-two guns failed to fire as many of the men quartered to them refused to sign their own death warrants by raising arms against the British navy.

Once the two ships came within musket shot of one another, Ogle ordered the *Swallow*'s first mate to steer a hard right in order to expose her broad side, so that their side canons would be pointed directly at the *Ranger*. Ogle ordered the gunners to fire at will, confident that he could destroy their ship if they did not surrender. After a quick volley of shots targeted at both the body and sails of the ship, the *Ranger*'s mizzenmast broke in half and toppled into the sea. There was no point in fighting anymore, because the navy had taken away the pirates' ability to flee. Yet several in James Skyrme's crew chose to continue.

After an hour and a half, however, the pirates were done fighting. The men who had wanted to continue the fight had been killed, seriously wounded, or restrained by other crewmates calling for common sense and hoping to be spared. James Skyrme had been hit by a cannonball, and his leg needed to be sawed off during the conflict to save his life. Thomas "Bright Tom" Withstandyenot was wounded by powder that blew up in the steerage, which he said was "set a fire by a pistol by one Morrice, since dead."[22] After the fire was controlled, the two Williams, Petty and Main, got into a fight with David Littlejohn, the "long-stander" who had raised the pirate flag at the start of the conflict. Thanks to his actions, the navy now had everything it needed to charge everyone onboard with piracy and hang them.

Petty and Main would have shot Littlejohn had another pirate, Peter L'Fever, not intervened. Instead, they shrugged and fired into steerage to ignite the gunpowder and blow up the entire ship and all the pirates onboard rather than be taken alive. Littlejohn swore later that had there been enough powder left in the steerage, the shot would have done it. He had been with Black Bart long enough to witness his captain blowing up ships as part of grander heists, once at Príncipe to avenge the murder of their former Captain Howell Davis and again in Brazil when they stole the *Sacred Family* from the Portuguese treasure fleet.[23]

Without the ability to blow themselves up and no way to win against the navy's ship, the pirates raised a white flag, and those who had been armed threw down their cutlasses, poleaxes, and pistols. They allowed Ogle's fumbling landlubbers to board the *Ranger* and, under their supervision, threw their dead comrades into the sea before being transported to the *Swallow*'s hold as the navy's prisoners. A somber hush washed over the pirates as the sharks frenzied below, consuming the bodies of their dead crewmates before the weights sewn into the sailcloth and hammocks covering them had a chance to sink them down into Davy Jones's locker.¶

Ogle, who had seen the sharks feasting many times, was unfazed. Instead, he scrutinized the faces of every man taken from the pirate ship to the *Swallow*, disappointed that Captain Bartholomew Roberts wasn't among them. The surgeon John Atkins was glad that he hadn't been. He mused that without someone to organize the pirates, "their Drunkenness, Inadvertency, and Disorder, [made] them fall an easy Prize to us."[24]

Ogle interrogated those in the crew who agreed to speak to learn more about the pirates anchored under Black Bart in the river estuary at Cape Lopez. His captives all knew that they were facing gallows, and a few who claimed that they had been forced by the pirates to join the crew became willing informants in exchange for

---

¶ Atkins's journal describes in gruesome detail how the slave trade had exacerbated the shark problem on the coast and up the rivers of West Africa: "I have seen them frequently seize a corpse, as soon as it was committed to the Sea; tearing and devouring that, and the Hammock that shrouded it, without suffering it once to sink, tho' a great Weight of Ballast in it."

a chance at life. Ogle ordered the disabled *Ranger* to be sent to Príncipe, where the Portuguese governor whose fort and town had been burned by these same pirates three years ago willingly accommodated Ogle's mission. The captain would return to collect her when he was done with the rest of the pirates. He considered what he knew about the area and what the pirates-turned-informants onboard the *Ranger* told him until he was satisfied that returning to Cape Lopez wouldn't open his sole ship an ambush.

Captain Ogle took the *Swallow* and doubled back to Cape Lopez on February 9. Ogle later reported that he waited overnight until first light to make his attack on the three ships anchored at the estuary flying the Jack, ensign, and pendant. Pirate prisoners, locked in the hold unable to see, would soon experience the roar of cannon.

Ogle got within random shot, but the wind took him ahead, so he had to double back. He was a seasoned naval officer in the age of sail—he was trained to find a way to turn the ship so that its broadside with all the cannons faced his opponent rather than taking chances with firing any of the random guns. Once he doubled back and the *Swallow* got within pistol shot of the *Royal Fortune*, Ogle hoisted her proper colors so that Black Bart's pirates would recognize that the *Swallow* was a naval ship and then turned her broadside.

James Skyrme hadn't returned to the pirates, and now it became clear why. At that point, there could be no doubt in the minds of Black Bart and his crew that to fire upon this ship meant certain death for everyone onboard. In a panic, some of the pirates sought to flee. David Simpson, one of Black Bart's higher-ranking mates, approached Robert Armstrong, who, along with three other seamen, had abandoned Chaloner Ogle and the navy when they were anchored at Cape Three Points visiting John Conny at Fort Great Fredericksburg. Simpson asked the *Swallow*'s former seamen if they knew its weaknesses. Armstrong told Simpson and another of Black Bart's officers, Henry Glasby, that "the best of the *Swallow*'s sailing was on a Wind; and advised them to go away large," or swing wider than they normally would in order to force the *Swallow* to turn and give the pirates some options.[25] Black Bart heard them and agreed, ordering the ship to give Ogle a wide berth and open a chance for escape. Unfortunately, the winds at Cape Lopez were less predictable in the wintertime, and the time it took for the third pass gave Ogle the favorable wind to mitigate this problem Black Bart was causing for him, and he caught up to the *Royal Fortune*, blocking her escape into the estuary of the Gabon River.

At that point, several pirates threatened to surrender. It was one thing to exchange a mostly harmless volley with a merchant ship that could write off its losses. It was an entirely different thing to fire upon the king's ships. Everyone knew that was a one-way ticket to the gallows. But Black Bart was a charismatic man who could be threatening when the occasion required it, and no occasion had ever required it more than this one. With their escape route blocked, the pirates onboard the *Royal Fortune* had no choice but to turn with the *Swallow* until the ships were parallel to one another and ready for a cannon fight.

The firing began, and the *Swallow* disabled the *Royal Fortune*'s sails, and then shot down her mizzen topmast. The pirates scrambled to adjust the rigging and find some way to keep her steady and facing the *Swallow* in the gusty winds. For two hours the ships exchanged volleys, the *Swallow*'s naval officers Lieutenant Sun, Boatswain Baldrick, and First Mate Mac-Laughlin swearing that the pirates gave as good as they got. The firing didn't stop until the *Swallow* managed to shoot down the main topmast, disabling the *Royal Fortune* completely.

Finally, the pirates raised a white flag of futility and surrender.

Captain Ogle was surprised. The *Ranger* had lasted longer in battle than this, and it was in worse shape when the pirates had finally permitted the navy to board. He had expected—nay, perhaps even hoped for—more from the infamous adversary that had been eating away at his sense of self for the past year and a half.

While Ogle's men prepared to board the *Royal Fortune*, pirate James Phillips found some matches and ran to the powder room. He was seen with the matches "swearing very prophanely [*sic*], let's all go to H_ll together."[26] Several pirates who did not want to be blown up heard what he said and alerted Henry Glasby, a pirate they had come to know as a level-headed leader. Glasby rushed down to the powder room, where he found three men in a scuffle surrounded by piles of gunpowder. Hugh Menzies, who had been assigned to the powder room during the conflict, assisted Stephen Thomas in wrestling a lit match from James Phillips. Phillips, who was drunk and reeking of spirits, had preternatural strength in that moment and smashed Stephen Thomas against the ladder, injuring his hand. It took all three men to subdue him and snuff the match. Glasby recruited another man he trusted, Robert Lilburn, to keep watch in the powder room to ensure there would be no more attempts to explode the ship. With as much powder as the *Royal Fortune* carried, both pirate and naval ships would be engulfed in flames in a matter of minutes.

Ogle was the first to board the ship, eager to gloat to the infamous Captain Bartholomew Roberts that his pirate fleet had been decimated by just one naval ship. He most likely had an entire speech in his head, ready for this very moment. But when he called out to ask which among them was the captain, no one stepped forward.

The crew sheepishly shuffled as a chill passed over Ogle, considering what it meant.

Had Black Bart not been onboard his *Royal Fortune* this morning? Unthinkable. But what if he was on another ship hiding among the mangroves in the river, waiting to ambush the *Swallow*? Could there be another five ships? Had Ogle been too arrogant?

Perhaps not that last question—Ogle never thought he was too arrogant.

He asked about Black Bart again, this time more loudly, and Henry Glasby stepped forward and informed him that his captain had died from grapeshot. Once it became apparent that the pirates could not win this battle, his crew had hefted the body of their captain, with his golden Portuguese royal cross still around his neck, overboard to the sharks rather than allow the navy to handle his body or retrieve the gold.

Ogle felt robbed. It was just like Black Bart to deny him the satisfaction of capturing him or of dying at Ogle's hand on what should have been the naval captain's very best day. He set his jaw, not wanting his crew to see him lose control, and then shook his head.

It didn't matter. Black Bart had been killed in the Battle of Cape Lopez. Ergo, Chaloner Ogle had killed him. He had won. That is how he would write it in the letters home, and that is how history would remember it. Perhaps he would become *Admiral* Chaloner Ogle. That had a nice ring to it.

With Black Bart dead, Henry Glasby was the only one of the higher-ranking pirates onboard who had a reasonable chance of acquittal, so he made Ogle a deal. Although Glasby had helped Black Bart make decisions and taken care of the crew, he had been careful to toe the line from the start: he never went onboard prizes and he never took anything that wasn't his. He had even prevented the explosion of the *Swallow*. Surely that counted for something.

His pirates knew him to be clearheaded, reasonable, and kind. Black Bart had allowed some truly reprehensible people, like the careless drunkard James Phillips, onboard his ships, and Glasby was willing to leverage all the goodwill he had built to help Ogle and the Royal Africa Company nail them if it meant that he could save his friends and the decent men among the crew from the gallows and return home with them a free man.

Ogle had time to consider the offer Glasby had made him. He ordered the *Royal Fortune* to join the *Ranger* while he took the *Swallow* to investigate the remaining anchored ships and to take on fresh water at Cape Lopez. The ships the pirates had left behind were empty of people with signs of significant ransacking and refitting. Ogle's hunch had been correct: the pirates were most likely planning an escape to the East Indies. He had caught them in the nick of time.

One week later, on February 18, they finished and headed for Príncipe with the empty ships in tow to pick up the demasted *Ranger* and *Royal Fortune* and all their waiting captives. Finally, the seamen had everything in tow and set the course for Cape Coast Castle, the headquarters of Britain's slave-trading operations in Africa.

Ogle had done it. He had brought down the notorious Black Bart and made the African coastline safe for Britannia again.

Part Two

THE BIRTH OF
AN AMERICAN
INSTITUTION

Chapter Six

―――――○―――――

Who Were the
Gentlemen of Fortune?

IN A FICTION BOOK, the concluding blow at the Battle of Cape Lopez might feel like the end. We've had tragedy and triumph, death and destruction, twists and turns, and a chaotic climax. But as in life, every ending is a beginning, and the beginning that the Battle of Cape Lopez ushered in had some wide-ranging and tragic consequences for the trajectory of what would become the United States. The rest of this book takes us from the battle's conclusion, through insurrection plans and pirate trials, to the fall of the Ahantan John Conny, the rise of William Snelgrave's human trafficking career, and into the changing landscape of slavery, a truly American institution, and the consequences thereof that we still experience today.

When Black Bart's pirate crew tore through Ouidah and ransomed the slave ships anchored there, they created, upon request, receipts that slave ship captains could present to their trading companies to prove that they had been extorted by pirates. Black Bart and his officers facetiously signed these notes "Gentlemen of Fortune," referring to themselves as the gentlemen who lived and worked onboard the pirate ship *Royal Fortune*. Of course, they knew that fortune wouldn't always be on their side. Throughout this half of the book, I openly question—and invite you, the reader, to question, too—Who were the real gentlemen of fortune here? And who are they today? Who benefits from global extraction-based exploitative processes that change the face of the entire world?

And who among us ("us" meaning the national as well as the global population) are left behind?

In this part of the book, we explore how the Battle of Cape Lopez rearranged trade in West Africa. Britain had finally rid herself of the pirates who had caused millions of pounds of damage to British shipping and nearly bankrupted the empire's insurance and banking industries. With Black Bart and his pirates defunct, John Conny in Fort Great Fredericksburg lost a large amount of revenue. The Ashanti, his perennial allies to the north, began to explore other venues of trade once Conny no longer could offer them the best selection of the freshest wares the pirates had brought him. With Conny weakened, the English and Dutch saw their chance to eliminate him once and for all. To the east at Ouidah, political transformations drew more of the trade that had once flowed through Conny's territory, and English traders like William Snelgrave bypassed the western region of the Gold Coast, where Conny's Castle sat, to flock eastward instead. These European traders caused mass devastation and the removal of captives from Africa to the Americas in record numbers.

These changes, instigated by the loss of the pirates to this fragile economic ecosystem in West Africa, resulted in a clear British advantage in the trade. Gone were the days when it was anybody's game and nations like the Netherlands vied with Britain for supremacy of the trade. In turn, Britain's settler colonists in the Americas grew wealthy as British ships delivered larger numbers of enslaved Africans for the auction blocks of British colonies. This gave the British American colonies significant economic advantages over the Spanish and French in what would become the United States. As the British American colonies grew in both population and wealth, the British model of slavery—the chattel model—became the predominant one and with it came the virulent institutionalized racism that protected it.

The chattel system required everyone—enslaved and free—of every race and origin to be active participants in maintaining the objectification of Africans and their descendants. For centuries, peoples in the Americas were conditioned to think of—and therefore treat—Afro-descended peoples as things rather than humans. The ability to live with this level of cognitive dissonance has touched every human interaction since. The rest of this book explores how exactly this happened and how a pirate battle, which few people have heard of, contributed to such an all-encompassing American tragedy.

It starts in the aftermath of the Battle of Cape Lopez, with plans of a racially motivated insurrection that were brewed onboard the *Swallow* en route to Cape Coast Castle and the subsequent kangaroo court in which the pirates were tried.

Captain Chaloner Ogle and his crew and pirate prisoners were two days from Cape Lopez when the skies took on a pale green color and rains set in. The wind and rain grew so heavy that Ogle and his seamen could no longer distinguish between rain and the ferocious gales that sucked up water from the sea. The same wind that had aided the naval captain during the Battle of Cape Lopez had now turned against him. The hurricane hit Príncipe and the smaller neighboring isle of São Tomé so swiftly that his crew of landlubbers barely had time to cut loose the sails of the *Swallow* to prevent her from being swept up. The pirate prizes in tow—the *Ranger* and the *Royal Fortune*—with damaged sails and masts, didn't fare as well.

By the time it was over, Ogle scanned the horizon to find the *Swallow* completely alone on the seas, with none of the other ships in sight. Ogle kept the course and sailed his ship to the Royal Africa Company's stronghold of Cape Coast Castle, trusting that if his officers in charge of the prizes had survived the hurricane, they knew enough to chart a new course and meet him there.

INSURRECTION ONBOARD THE *SWALLOW*

On the way back to Cape Coast Castle, Atkins wrote in his journal that "the number of our prisoners gave a great deal of fatigue and uneasiness, during a six weeks passage, lest the danger of a Halter should prompt them to some desperate Attempt for their liberty."[1] In other words, the naval officers and seamen worried that the threat of the nooses awaiting them at Cape Coast Castle would spur the pirates to attempt something drastic to escape.

This is the point when both the documentary evidence goes strangely silent and the most intriguing event occurred: discussions of insurrection onboard the *Swallow*. It's important to understand the origins of the historical record of the Battle of Cape Lopez and the trip to Cape Coast Castle and how the crucial context of the Atlantic slave trade in West Africa offers a way to fill in some of these historical blanks.

Most of what we know about this battle and its aftermath comes from Captain Ogle's report, the surgeon John Atkins's journal, or records from the farcical trial (more on that in the next chapter) that Black Bart's pirates faced at Cape Coast Castle after their defeat by Ogle's crew. These court papers also were penned by John Atkins, who acted as the sole register and scribe throughout the entire six weeks that the pirates gave depositions and were sentenced. Though problematic and biased, these are the only surviving sources that were created by people who were physically present during the Battle of Cape Lopez and who interacted with the accused. A few more eyewitness testimonies were created after the fact: seventeen of the pirates with more complicated or incomplete evidence and motive—or better connections back home—were referred to the Marshalsea Prison in England to stand trial there. Everything else—newspaper articles, the Charles Johnson/Nathaniel Mist narrative, and so forth—was written later based on hearsay, rumors, and these few primary sources.

Conspicuously absent from these court papers created at Cape Coast Castle are the voices of the Black people who were captured by the navy at the Battle of Cape Lopez. My use of "Black" here refers to people of Africa and Afro-descended people of the diaspora. In the documents created by the British navy, everyone with visibly dark skin to Ogle and Atkins's eyes was labeled "negro"; no distinctions were made regarding whether they were enslaved or not or whether they were from Africa, Europe, or the Americas. It is unclear whether the pirates had purchased or kidnapped any of the Black people in their crew and kept them enslaved, whether joining the pirate crew (voluntarily or not) had liberated them, or whether any had been legally free to begin with. Most ship crews in the golden age of piracy contained a diverse group of Black people from all over the Atlantic world, some enslaved, some formerly enslaved, and some never enslaved. Most crews also had extensive experience with trading captive Africans, and as Black Bart's crew demonstrated when they captured the ship of slave trader Captain William Snelgrave, they were willing to treat at least some Black people as cargo to be bought and sold for profit. In short, enslavement was a fluid status in the pirate world, but slavery was the central reason Europeans and American colonists found themselves in West Africa and remained an ever-present threat for pirates with dark skin.

In comparison, Ogle and Atkins treated the Africans and Afro-descended people they caught onboard as a monolith. They never referred to them as pirates or charged them with piracy, but I refer to them as such in this book because, from what little evidence there is, they committed acts of piracy onboard pirate ships before being caught by the navy in a pirate battle, and every White person they were captured with who did the same was accused of this crime. Ogle had financial incentives for erasing the Black pirates, and his combined lack of education and lack of concern about the geopolitics of the slave trade made those incentives possible. In short, the distinctions that were so crucial to European survival in Africa in the 1600s had become less important to Europeans and their colonial descendants over time as the institution of slavery created a Black underclass. It was incredibly convenient—and therefore an often-unspoken goal of empire—to conflate Blackness with enslavement, and the British navy was arguably the strongest agent of empire in the 1720s.

This was why Ogle chose to separate the people onboard the pirate ships by skin color at Cape Coast and sell all of those with visibly dark skin into the Atlantic slave trade. He gave no regard to whether they had been enslaved before, whether they were treated as pirates or as enslaved cargo while with Black Bart's crew, or what roles they had played in the battle of Cape Lopez. If he asked about any of their origins (African, Caribbean, American, etc.), he did not record that anywhere. Rather, he allowed readers to make the presumption that all the Africans and Afro-descended people onboard were "slaves." A slave, when used as an immutable noun, is someone whose entire identity is dictated by their unfree labor.[2] In the British Atlantic world, the term was increasingly being used to refer to someone with no personhood at all.

On the other hand, the adjective *enslaved* describes a state of being, which, prior to the 1720s, mostly African and Afro-descended people could and did slip into and out of throughout the course of their lives. Many British people and their descendants in the Americas found it troubling that what they considered cargo could wield weapons and commit crimes against the empire. The very notion of Black pirates challenged the order of empire, and Atkins and Ogle, two men charged with preserving it, chose the path of least resistance and took action to convert Black pirates into gold by selling them as chattel into slavery. A closer reading of the documents related to the Battle of Cape Lopez and the subsequent trials challenges the assumptions underpinning Atkins and Ogle's erasure.

In Ogle's short summary letter of the Battle of Cape Lopez, Black people are mentioned only in reference to their numbers: twenty-three Black survivors on the *Ranger* with Captain Skyrme and twenty-five with Black Bart on the *Royal Fortune*. He makes no mention of how many had perished in battle. In the testimony the 165 Euro-descended pirates gave during their trials, most mentions of the Black pirates' and enslaved people's actions had been scrubbed. The only times Atkins allowed such references to remain in the record was when they could be used as proof of a White pirate's guilt or innocence. The Black people onboard the *Ranger* and *Royal Fortune* were prohibited from giving testimony, standing trial, or entering the historical record as actors in their own rights. Ogle intended to profit from their existence without allowing their voices to emerge, but because their stories were so entwined with those of the White pirates, some of their missing history can be reconstructed.

For example, the trial of pirate surgeon Peter Scudamore offers many details about an insurrection that White and Black pirates planned together onboard the *Swallow* while Captain Ogle ferried them to Cape Coast Castle for trial. Scudamore had survived both the battle and hurricane. He had been held in the *Swallow*'s dank hold for weeks while being fed starvation rations, then he had been locked into the holding cells reserved for enslaved captives at Cape Coast Castle. From the ventilation shafts in the dungeon, he could see the gallows that Royal Africa Company (RAC) employees had erected on the beach. By the time Scudamore was tried on April 5, the first group of pirates—among them many leaders like Christopher Moody, Valentine Ashplant, and Thomas Sutton—already had been found guilty and hanged. Their bodies were wrapped in chains for the birds to pick at. As days passed, the pirates' testimony grew more desperate, because those who assisted the navy by producing enough testimony with which to find their peers guilty could count on either a not guilty verdict themselves or a commuted sentence. During Peter Scudamore's trial, many witnesses willingly turned on the surly surgeon from their crew.

Peter Scudamore initially had been onboard the slave ship *Cornwall* under Captain Rolls. Slave ship surgeons had miserable jobs. They treated tropical diseases, which had high morbidity rates, and patched up sailors who became injured by any number of traumatic events: acts of resistance by enslaved people, conflicts with Africans on shore, pirate attacks, injuries from severe weather, or corporal punishment meted out by the captain or first mate. Worse still, surgeons were expected to physically humiliate and examine enslaved people during the purchasing process and to keep them well—or at least to confer the appearance of wellness—so that they could fetch a higher price when they were sold in the Americas. Often when enslaved people took ill on the journey due to maltreatment or willful refusal to eat or drink, surgeons prescribed and supervised brutal force-feeding. They invented means of torture, which they called "discipline," that didn't leave permanent visible damage, which would offend enslavers on the other side of the Atlantic and allow them to haggle down the price. They often addressed symptoms of dehydration or disease with potentially damaging treatments, and it was not unheard of for some to test their hypotheses for new scientific breakthroughs on the unwilling bodies of the enslaved captives.[3]

Other surgeons worked with or observed the enslaved populations onboard to learn African medical practices, which they then forced upon the entire captive population. This was how the West African practice of live smallpox inoculations became widespread throughout the Atlantic world.[4] The slave ship surgeons' medical knowledge and willingness to attempt experimental treatments made them highly desirable on pirate ships, so slave ship surgeons could count on being forced into a crew if their ships were captured. Because it was a highly undesirable position, the men who found themselves ship surgeons bound for Africa tended to be those who could not get work as doctors elsewhere. It was a last-resort job, which created significant resentment among the surgeons.

Scudamore certainly carried a lot of resentment, too, which he had taken out on the pirates. Even after sufficient evidence had been collected to find him guilty, other pirates stepped forward to share their experiences with the surgeon to ensure that he would find no mercy in the makeshift courtroom. William Child, another surgeon taken by the pirates from a different ship, reported that while they were imprisoned onboard the *Swallow* after the battle, Scudamore, who had been seeking out people well-versed in navigation for a plot with the Black pirates, "asked him whether or not he had a mind to go to Cabo Corso [Cape Coast Castle], and be hang'd and sun-dry'd?" Unlike Scudamore, Child hadn't been seen participating in any illegal acts while with the pirates, so he intended to take his chances in court. Scudamore thought Child to be a naive fool and told him to rethink whether the navy could be trusted to render a fair verdict. He "proposed of rising with the Negroes, telling, they could demolish the white men, and afterwards go down to Angola and raise another company [of pirates]."[5] As far as insurrection plans went, this one wasn't terrible. Although West Africa was decimated from pirate attacks and naval presence, locales south of Cape Lopez in West Central Africa offered more opportunities for pirates to rebuild a multiracial crew away from the watchful eyes of the British.

William Child declined to participate in the insurrection and that night told the *Swallow*'s commanding naval officer what Scudamore was planning. He told the officer that Scudamore "had been talking to the Negroes in the Angolan language all night" and that Scudamore had told him that "if they the *Swallow*'s people were not demolish'd that night, they should be the next."[6] One of Ogle's officers said that he overheard Scudamore ask pirate James Harris "whether it was not better to endeavor the raising a new company [of pirates] than to go to Cabo Corso, and be hang'd like a dog," but when an officer approached, Scudamore changed the topic to horse racing. The naval officer reported that most of his colleagues onboard the *Swallow* slept with their loaded guns beside them that night.[7] In his journal, Atkins confirmed this, writing, "the Pyrates in this Passage were very troublesome to us, from a Project or two they had formed for their Deliverance, and hoped by the Weakness of our Ship's Company [i.e., the short-staffed inexperienced crew], would have succeeded."[8]

Scudamore defended himself, accusing Child of purposely misconstruing a conversation the two of them had about insurrection in order to point the finger at Scudamore in exchange for an innocent verdict at Cape Coast (Child was indeed acquitted). Scudamore insisted that they both were discussing what might happen if the Black prisoners attempted an insurrection and turned the ship around. This, of course, was on the mind of every White person onboard the *Swallow*, pirate and seaman alike. All of them had spent months, years, or even decades in West Africa, working in or adjacent to the slave trade. All of them had heard the stories of insurrections onboard slave ships. Many of them, like those pirates who were taken from the slave ship *Elizabeth*, had survived one. They had all seen vivid atrocities committed in the name of the trade, which they filed in the back of their minds and drenched with brandy or rum to avoid thinking about them. And all of them knew that if they were the ones facing a lifetime of chattel enslavement, they would attempt the same.

Scudamore had reassured Child that if indeed the Black pirates rose up on the *Swallow*, he was confident that the Africans would not harm their White crewmates. He confessed that he was speaking with them, but only because they were teaching him how to count in an Angolan language to pass the time while imprisoned on the *Swallow*. As for his conversation with James Harris, Scudamore said that Harris saw him talking with the Black captives and approached him to ask him if they had mentioned anything about an insurrection.*

This story of potential insurrection and how both the White pirates and naval officers reacted to it and later spoke about it while on the witness stand at Cape Coast provides more information about the Black people who were captured onboard the *Ranger* and *Royal Fortune* than any other source from the Battle of Cape Lopez. In his report, which Atkins compiled while en route, Chaloner Ogle makes every attempt to minimize the presence of the Black pirates and to insinuate that they were nonentities, like cargo. A casual reader might assume that they were the enslaved captives gathered at Ouidah, because that's what Ogle implied. He had every reason to do so, both for profit and praise. Selling the Black pirates was lucrative. Shifting blame entirely to the White pirates and subsequently vanquishing them was a more impressive achievement than a victory over Black Africans who were not considered human by the Crown. In other words, overthrowing Black pirates wasn't going to get Ogle the promotion he was after.

Ogle's loyal surgeon John Atkins went one step further in his journal, referring to all of the Black people onboard as "slaves," for if they weren't enslaved when the *Swallow* captured them, they would become enslaved when Ogle sold them into the trade for his own profit. Even before the trials began, the victors wrote the history as it suited them, simply because they could. Even if Ogle accidentally sold an influential free African from the pirate crew into the trade, the fallout wouldn't be his; he had orders to leave for Jamaica as soon as the pirates were all hanged. Ogle didn't have to investigate the Black population onboard the pirate ships, because it was the job of the Royal Africa Company employees to know about African geopolitics and kinship networks, not his.

THE PRISONERS ARRIVE AT CAPE COAST CASTLE

The insurrection never came to pass, though this did not prevent the pirates from being punished for it as if it had. After the hurricane

---

* The court didn't feel like it could convict James Harris on the testimony available and so referred him to Marshalsea prison in London to await another trial with the admiralty.

and several grueling weeks at sea, getting paperwork in order and living in continual fear (the naval seamen of insurrection and the pirates of enslavement or the gallows), West Africa's Gold Coast finally appeared on the horizon. The *Weymouth* had moved down the coast to collect supplies, leaving the view of Cape Coast Castle unblemished. It was an impressive and oppressive fortification located centrally and painted completely white, which glowed in the sun like a beacon. During the past year and a half, the pirate prisoners had passed the bright and impenetrable fortress many times as they marauded along the Gold Coast, giving it a wide berth to stay out of cannon-shot. As the seat of the Royal Africa Company's human trafficking network in West Africa, it was the central hub of information and trade, with large stores of trade goods, gold dust, and a large population of enslaved Africans, all secured within four reinforced stories sitting atop a dank dungeon space that could accommodate thousands. Built much like a European castle, it had courtyards and bastions and spacious, airy suites where the administrative heads of the RAC enjoyed relative comfort while the enslaved suffered, hidden away below, out of sight.[9]

One of the dungeons of Cape Coast Castle, headquarters of the British Royal Africa Company. Normally reserved for enslaved captives, this is where Black Bart's crew was imprisoned while awaiting their trials and executions. *Photo by user Kwameghana at Wikimedia Commons*

Within the castle was a smith's shop, cooperage, storehouses, a chapel, and houses for the officers and servants of the company. Atkins described the space where they held the trials: "The General's Lodging communicates with the Chappel: a capacious Hall, which serves to preach and dine in, pray or drink, serve God or debate on Trade." From the window, they could watch the company's servants, and with a spyglass, see all the ships that passed by or made their way to the Dutch West India Company Headquarters at El Mina.[10] Just outside the castle was a bustling African city with a large trade market that had attracted the locals who allied with the RAC and Africans from further inland who traveled to the coast to conduct business. Gold dust was the main unit of currency, and most people carried small scales to weigh it out in transactions.[11]

On March 15, 1722, the *Swallow* dropped anchor, and the pirates were transported via canoe to the coast and then force-marched amid jeers in the bustling city uphill to Cape Coast Castle.[12] For the next two weeks Ogle waited for "witnesses" to arrive while the pirates remained locked away in dungeons usually reserved for enslaved captives. The place reeked of human waste and unwashed people, as well as the festering wounds sustained during the Battle of Cape Lopez or incurred while onboard the naval ship *Swallow*. There were a total of 169 White pirates in one of the dungeon spaces; the 48 Black pirates were housed separately alongside African captives being held for forced transport across the Atlantic. Only the White pirates would be tried for their crimes. They were split into two groups: the group that followed James Skyrme on the *Ranger* to pursue Ogle's ship and the crew that remained behind on the *Royal Fortune* with Black Bart. Each group was charged together with the testimony of three of Ogle's naval officers who had fought in the battle, and everyone charged pleaded not guilty to the crimes of piracy.

Four of the accused had died of battle injuries while waiting in the slave dungeons of the castle for their turn to take the makeshift stand. Several of the amputees, however, including James Skyrme, commander of the *Ranger*, John Walden (aka Miss Nanny) from the

Swallow, and Israel Hynde,[†] on the *Royal Fortune*, survived. They were a credit to the foresight of Black Bart and the high number of ship surgeons he had forced to join the crew.

As the assembled people at Cape Coast Castle waited for the witnesses to arrive so that the trials could begin, they made preparations, building a long gallows so that the pirates could be hanged in groups. The Royal Africa Company had determined that Black Bart's crew had plundered more than four hundred ships in total. The crew shrugged, as no one had bothered to keep count. Each time that Ogle had returned to Cape Coast Castle during his year-and-a-half-long game of cat and mouse with Black Bart, the running total of pirate attacks had increased, sometimes exponentially. RAC officials had written letters about this pirate crisis to the king, shareholders, and agents all over the empire. Now that they had the pirate menace in their grasp, they were prepared to interpret the 1700 statute of the 1698 Piracy Act as generously as possible and to taunt the pirates about it during feeding time.

The statute had been created in response to the surge in piracy and the inability of the English courts to accommodate the sheer volume of accused pirates. It allowed any acts of piracy—including pirate-adjacent acts, like assisting and advising people to commit piracy—to be examined and tried anywhere in the British Empire, rather than forcing accused pirates to be transported back to

---

† Hynde's presence on the *Royal Fortune* has divided many pirate scholars about whether he could have been the infamous pirate Israel Hands, who had sailed with the late Stede Bonnet and Blackbeard. The Nathaniel Mist narrative, published in 1724, claims that Israel Hands died a beggar in London but provides no evidence, nor is there an obituary for him in any of the available English-language British or colonial American newspapers. No overlap exists during Hands's time with Blackbeard and Hynde's time with Black Bart, so Hands and Hynde could be the same person. May 1719 is the last time Israel Hands appears in the documentary record—he informed on Blackbeard in exchange for his life in South Carolina. In the trial at Cape Coast Castle three years later, Hynde was said to be boatswain of the *Ranger*, giving commands onboard for Skyrme while the *Swallow* shot away her mast. Hynde was said to be an enthusiastic pirate, swearing, brandishing a cutlass comfortably, and forcing useful people to join the crew. Hynde admitted that he initially worked on the slave ship *Mercy Galley* at Calabar when she was taken by pirates, whereupon he joined them, voluntarily signing the pirate articles, and fought with a cutlass during the battle. Another man in Black Bart's crew, Isaac Russell, who did not go on the *Ranger* with Hynde but remained on the *Royal Fortune*, was given a referral to Marshalsea rather than sentenced to death for his crimes, because he was among the men who captured Blackbeard, so it's certainly not outside of the realm of possibility. Often pirates bragged that they had a connection to legendary figures like Blackbeard, but the ones who actually did knew to keep their mouths shut if naval officers asked.

England for trial. It permitted commissioners to assemble a court of admiralty whenever and wherever they deemed necessary, with full power and authority to issue warrants, summonses, and "do all things necessary for the hearing and final determination in any case of piracy." Of course, very little infrastructure existed for any type of fair jurisprudence of this nature to occur.[‡]

The RAC had already received all necessary permissions to hold its own trial, and even though a lawyer was present, no one at Cape Coast Castle had full legal understanding of the Piracy Act or its detailed instructions for holding these impromptu admiralty trials. The one British lawyer present in West Africa, James Phipps, glanced at the worn naval officers and the barely literate seamen and merchants employed by the navy and RAC and charged himself with reading and explaining the act. He convinced Ogle to remove himself from the proceedings and place his underling, Captain Mungo Herdman of the *Weymouth*, in charge to at least give the illusion of impartiality. However, this certainly didn't prevent bias, since both the RAC and the *Swallow*'s seamen would benefit financially from each guilty verdict, because the piracy laws allowed seamen and their captains to keep a percentage of the pirate loot. This fact had motivated Captain Herdman to return to the castle for the hearings to preside over them and for his sailors to give witness testimony regarding all the plundered ships they had come into contact with despite the *Weymouth* never having been present at the Battle of Cape Lopez. The trials that would decide who would live and die would begin immediately.

---

‡ The statute states that any act of piracy could be "examined, inquired of, tried, heard and determined, and adjudged in any place at sea, or upon the land, in any of his Majesty's islands, plantations, colonies, dominions, forts, or factories." *An Act for the more effectual Suppression of Piracy, 11 Will 3 c 7.*

Chapter Seven

———————————○———————————

The Pirate Trials

MUCH OF THE PROCEEDINGS of the pirate trials from the Battle of Cape Lopez went contrary to the laws and freedoms British citizens enjoyed in 1722. A small handful of the *Weymouth*'s officers served as jurors, while three of the officers who saw combat onboard the *Swallow* (Lt. Isaac Sun, boatswain Ralph Baldrick, and mate Daniel Mac-Laughlin) provided all testimony for the mass prosecution of every defendant, despite, of course, their obvious inability to personally observe the incriminating actions of more than two hundred pirates in the heat of battle.

Questions were leading. Subjective evidence of feelings or attitudes held weighed equally—or even outweighed—objective evidence of acts committed. When the commissioners explained their verdicts in the court documents, they took into account the accused pirates' criminal histories, ages, and character. The "character" of the accused or their witnesses was a determining factor of guilt or innocence and, naturally, the understanding of "good character" in eighteenth-century Britain relied heavily on classist, cultural, and racist assumptions. The court conjectured as to their economic backgrounds and prospects and appealed to the importance of "British values," as they understood them, in making their sentences.

For example, many of the accused who were married or had children were judged more leniently than those who had no families. However, marriage was neither as accessible or even desirable for men who made a living on the sea.* The gender ratio, which was near fifty-fifty in Britain, was nowhere near as favorable in the colonies or at sea. Men without land, money, or favorable steady employment had very few prospects. The pirates were also tried in groups that made them seem guilty by association; the accusers lumped the accused together for trial each day based on seniority in Black Bart's fleet or on the defendants' perceived slights against the empire. Those who ended up on the stand together with confirmed murderers never had a chance. Furthermore, the court denied prisoners' rights to cross-examine witnesses of the court and to select their own witnesses. The court encouraged a heavy amount of hearsay, which it accepted at face value if it resulted in a guilty verdict, while shifting the burden of proof to the accused: the pirates were all guilty until proven otherwise.

According to the impromptu admiralty court that assembled in March and April 1722 at Cape Coast, there were few ways to prove innocence. Prisoners could provide a letter from their captain dated from the time of capture testifying that they did not go with the pirates voluntarily. This was difficult; often there wasn't enough time or paper onboard for captains to create dozens of such affidavits (that is, if the captains even survived the pirate attack). Failing that, the accused could produce a notice of their involuntary capture by pirates from a newspaper. This was even more difficult, necessitating a captured sailor to beg someone who was released by the pirates to expend money and time sailing to a place where newspapers were published and paying a fee to place the notice. Then the accused must rely upon that paper being available in some nearby repository for the court to consult in time for the trial.† The court also accepted testimony from witnesses who had been previously deemed reliable; for example, reports about the accused loudly and frequently complaining about being impressed by the pirates and refusing to take a turn going onboard captured prize ships or to accept a share of plunder from them. Finally, the

---

* And, of course, a life at sea was appealing to many who intentionally dodged the expectations of heterosexual marriage and/or children.

† Several accused pirates swore that they attempted to place a notice but didn't have money of their own to pay for it, because they refused to take their turn plundering ships. Others said that they gave money to sailors or captains to place notices, but the notices were never placed. They were found guilty and hanged.

court accepted evidence of escape attempts, provided again that a
reliable witness saw it. Some of the more seasoned pirates knew
about the court's requirements for evidence and were therefore
able to produce them, while many of the newer pirates who had
joined more recently weren't aware or didn't have the opportunity to
create, find, or provide this evidence. If the evidence provided was
deemed weak, the Royal Africa Company (RAC) employees and
naval officers who made up the court delivered a guilty verdict and
sent the accused to the gallows within a day or two of conviction.[1]

As one might imagine, some of Black Bart's men were sentenced to death because they didn't have the money to place a
notice in the paper, while others were acquitted for having had
the foresight and opportunity or funds available to do so. Those
sentenced to death were hanged in groups every few days, which
shrunk the pool of potential witnesses and increased the number
of guilty verdicts as days passed in later trials. The court did not
find that problematic, since someone found guilty of piracy could
no longer be a credible witness in their eyes. Impromptu overseas
admiralty trials like this became the norm as European and colonial
governments worked together to eradicate the people no longer useful to the empire. The entrepreneurial maritime behavior that was
rewarded during the sixteenth and seventeenth centuries became
the reasons seafarers swung from gallows in the eighteenth century.
Now, looting was reserved solely for people wealthy enough to have
no need for it and the agents of empire they appointed through
Crown-sponsored organizations like the Royal Africa Company or
His Majesty's Navy.

Henry Glasby, one of the pirates who had prevented the *Swallow* from being blown up and who had witnessed some of the
pirates' insurrection plot while en route to Cape Coast Castle, was
among the first to be tried. Glasby was master of the *Royal Fortune*
and comported himself according to British middle-class norms
of civility among the mostly working-class sailors who had been
recruited on Black Bart's flagship. He was also incredibly calculating, sowing a story of regret and reluctance to the former slave ship
captains who had been obliged to join his crew. During the trials,
the former merchant captains among the pirates were acquitted, as
were the people those captains vouched for, and during Glasby's

trial, a string of former captains testified on his behalf. As one of the pirates who had been with the crew the longest and knew the men, he also cooperated with the navy by helping them sort out criminal from repentant captive. Lieutenant Isaac Sun of the navy swore that "the prisoner has since shewn the Involuntariness of his Actions while with the Pyrates, by declaring the vilest Characters among them." In essence, Glasby positioned himself as the right hand of the naval investigators, making their jobs easy for them by saving his friends and damning those with whom he had conflicts. As Lieutenant Sun "heard a very good character of the prisoner," it was presumed that the man with the gilded tongue could be trusted to help convict the most guilty, saving everyone some time during the trial process.[2]

Glasby understood that for him to be able to save any of the innocent men that had sailed beneath him, the other leaders among Black Bart's crew would have to die. He did not attempt to intervene in the trials of his equals, James Skyrme, Thomas Sutton, David Simpson, Christopher Moody, or Valentine Ashplant. These men were among the first to be sentenced. Mungo Herdman told them:

> Ye and each of you are adjudged and sentenced to be carried back to the place from whence ye came, from thence to the place of Execution without the Gates of the Castle, and there within the Flood-marks to be hanged by the Neck, 'till ye are Dead, Dead, Dead; And the Lord have Mercy upon your Souls. After this ye and each of you shall be taken down, and your Body hung in Chains.[3]

Many of the other pirates were found guilty under evidence that today might be considered absurd. For example, some of the evidence that sentenced George Smith was the testimony of Jacob Groot, who complained that he came onboard their Dutch prize and spoiled "some very good sausages, he and the others ludicrously stringing them about their Necks for a time and then throwing them away."[4] Likewise, two witnesses said that William Phillips "challenged a cheese from among the pyrates, that they had seized; and was so warm in his persisting about his having of it, as a share he claimed among them, that he quarell'd with the Quarter-master and was beat by another of the pyrates."[5] John Ouchterlauney went down because of his love of wigs (he stole two from Captain Trahern when his ship was plundered), as did William Williams. Unfortunately for them, the British took markers of class distinction very seriously, and the theft of captains' wigs at sea fell under piracy statutes.[6] Joseph Mansfield, a habitual heavy drinker, staggered onto the deck of the *Royal Fortune* after the pirates had surrendered to the *Swallow*, spirits heavy on his breath. As the somber defeated pirates huddled under their broken mast watching Captain Ogle's men preparing to board the *Royal Fortune*, Mansfield came "vapouring with a cutlass, to know who would go on board the prize?" It was "sometime before they could persuade him to the truth of their condition."[7]

John Stevenson was one of the soldiers being transported on the *Onslow* to Cape Coast, where the pirates took him, telling him that it would be a shame for a big, strong man like him to be starved to death like the other soldiers of the Royal Africa Company. He claims the pirates took his clothes and beat him, so he complained to Black Bart and asked for some new clothes and a gun. He had been injured by another pirate and was unable to fight during the Battle of Cape Lopez, but because he had accepted plundered clothing and a gun, he was sentenced to death.[8]

The insurrection plans made onboard the *Swallow* also played a sizeable role in the proceedings. Like many of the insurrections that enslavers and slave ship personnel feared, the one to which Peter Scudamore may or may not have been privy never occurred. William Child's tip-off gave the naval officers the opportunity to thwart the rebellion and ensure that the pirates all made it to Cape Coast Castle to stand trial. It took a month and three days to get there, and when they arrived, there was no sign of the prize ships that had been blown away in the hurricane. However, awaiting Ogle and his men at the castle was a giant shipment of wine and dry provisions, which he had begged for nearly a year before.

Ogle feasted and sold the Black pirates to the first slave ship that stopped at Cape Coast Castle, pocketing the tidy sum, which was forgotten until the trial of the pirate surgeon, Peter Scudamore.

While collecting sufficient evidence to doom the surgeon, the court produced some details about the Black pirates that Ogle and Atkins's written testimony omitted. When Ogle captured the *Ranger*, 23 of the 132 onboard were Black. Nearly a dozen pirates confessed that when they saw the *Swallow*, only volunteers piled into the *Ranger* to pursue her; Black Bart and Skyrme didn't force anyone to go. This can be interpreted in two ways: either twenty-three Black pirates volunteered to follow Skyrme onto the *Ranger* to plunder this Portuguese ship, or the White pirates forced twenty-three enslaved people, whom the pirates considered chattel, onto the ship to help move the cargo. Both interpretations of this testimony were equally viable in this world. Both at the very least make the Black people onboard active participants.

There is overwhelming evidence of free Black pirates with full agency and power onboard many other pirate ships at this time. It was common knowledge that Blackbeard's most notorious and trusted officer, Black Cesar, was a Black West African and that sixty out of his crew of one hundred had been Black as well.‡ When they were caught at Ocracoke inlet, Virginia's governor tried them under the acts of piracy, same as any White pirate, indicating that they were there of their free will and possessed the capacity to make this decision and be punished for it. They were tried, found guilty, and then executed. After their deaths, North Carolina's governor called them "negro slaves" whose collected testimony could not be used as evidence. Here too was tension between recognizing the threat that Black pirates posed to colonial order versus the threat created by recognizing the personhood of Black pirates by sending them to trial. Chaloner Ogle wasn't the type of person to grapple with this if he didn't have to.

Similarly, the *Boston News-Letter* reported that the crew of French pirate Captain Oliver "La Bouche," or "the Mouth," Levasseur, one of the pirate captains who had worked with Captain Howell Davis in Sierra Leone before he recruited Black Bart, was Afro-descended.[9] Many of the other pirate ships during this time

---

‡ Many of those crew came from his ship, *Queen Anne's Revenge*, which had been a former slave ship captured by Blackbeard and his crew in 1717 near the Caribbean island of Saint Vincent.

sailed with crews that were roughly a quarter Black.[10] The Spanish and Portuguese maritime culture intentionally trained, armed, and deployed Black privateers—who later became pirates—against their empires' competition at sea.[11]

Despite this, pirates of all races treated enslaved Africans like cargo at times and bought, kept, and sold African captives. Enslavement and Blackness were flexible, context-dependent concepts in the early 1700s Atlantic world, with competing empires creating their own racial categories, rules, laws, and social norms regarding enslavement and, later, race. Pirate ships—with their diverse crews from many walks of life, countries, cultures, socioeconomic classes, genders, and religious and political affiliations—were spaces where race and slavery were negotiated continually based on the changing makeup of the crew, the location of the ship, and the circumstances. There were slave traders, abolitionists, and people who didn't think too hard about slavery onboard nearly every ship. This made the maritime world a space of both Black liberation and possibility, as well as Black anxiety and oppression.[12]

The fear that the *Swallow*'s officers expressed about the Black survivors of the Battle of Cape Lopez is telling, as they made up less than a third of the total prisoners. That same fear didn't make it onto the page with regard to the White captives.§ In regard to this fear, witnesses mention a couple of things that stand out: the Black pirates knew enough about sailing to sail the ship themselves, something that people who had been captured and marched directly from the interior of Africa and who had been kept as living cargo among pirates would most likely not know. It stands to reason that they knew about sailing because they had come from seafaring people, they had worked onboard other vessels, like those of the BAC, or they had learned how to sail as part of the pirate crew.

The testimony also implies that the Africans and other Afro-descended people onboard shared a common African language, whether that language was from Angola or from elsewhere.¶ This

---

§ The total number of survivors onboard the pirate ships was 217, of which 48, or 22 percent, were African and Afro descended.

¶ Often Europeans in West Africa used specific and general terms interchangeably. However, it's also possible that Scudamore spoke with the Black people onboard in a language from Angola. European and Euro-descended people who worked in the slave trade were

meant that they could communicate easily and coordinate efforts, something all slave ship captains and sailors feared and worked hard to mitigate by selecting at the forts and trading posts enslaved captives from different regions when possible. If the Black people onboard spoke a common tongue from West Central Africa (the area referred to then as Kongo-Angola, as opposed to West Africa where Cape Lopez and the Gold Coast are located), it stands to reason that this group included Africans from the coastal regions. Although the officers in the navy didn't know much about Africa, they did know about coastal Africans and were terrified of them.

Many of the White pirates even expressed fear of coastal Africans in certain regions, especially Sierra Leone. Individual White people in coastal Africa who weren't affiliated with a company generally did well only if, like Captain Crackers, they had networks and could find a way to make a place for themselves within the existing African systems. Many lone Europeans who found themselves stranded on the coast were taken in by locals who put them to work and allowed them to accrue debt, which another European had to pay before the person was allowed to leave Africa. For example, George Wilson, a pirate on the *Swallow*, was caught in bad weather

---

under constant threat onboard slave ships. The ones who survived the longest in this trade were the ones who had the most knowledge about Africa and its peoples, culture, geography, and, of course, languages. In addition to that, those who could humble themselves to work with free Africans on their terms tended to stick around longer in the documentary evidence than those who rigidly kept hold of colonial attitudes and behaviors. Local knowledge and, ironically, the willingness to treat African traders as equals was what kept the Prussian slave traders of the Brandenburg Africa Company safer at Cape Three Points than their Dutch and English competitors nearby. Another reason a language originating in Angola was plausible in this instance was that the pirates had taken several Portuguese and Dutch slave ships, and it was common enough practice that those ships would begin a voyage in West Central Africa. If they could not fill their cargoes there, they sailed to Príncipe and then back to the Gold Coast to check in with the Dutch and Portuguese forts there before sailing to the Americas with a full hold. Ships that went to Angola preferred to sail directly from Angola to Brazil, as it was the shortest and most profitable Atlantic crossing; however, many captains who had ensured ample provisions preferred the fullest hold possible rather than a short voyage. A peek into the Slave Voyages Database confirms that many of the Dutch slave ships that were in operation from 1720 to 1722 stopped first in the ports of Loango (in Angola), or Congo North, before stopping at the West African places Black Bart's pirates had plundered: Calabar and Axim. That ships were rerouted to begin voyages in the more stable west-central regions also correlates to the disruption of the slave trade caused by pirates in West Africa. See also Filipa Ribeiro da Silva and Stacey Sommerdyk, "Reexamining the Geography and Merchants of the West Central African Slave Trade: Looking behind the Numbers," *African Economic History* 38 (2010): 77–105, www.jstor.org/stable/41756132.

and left at Cape Mesurado, where he was forcibly indentured by the locals until he was redeemed by sailors from the *Elizabeth*, the same Humphry Morice slave ship that saw an insurrection onboard and that William Snelgrave visited. John Sharp paid three pounds and five shillings in goods to free George Wilson from his servitude in Cestos.

Wilson ended up back on the *Royal Fortune* with the pirates and participated in the Battle of Cape Lopez against the *Swallow*. When he was captured by Ogle, he informed the captain of another, different pirate insurrection plan. When he was found guilty, he "referr'd to the king's pleasure" (i.e., he begged for imprisonment for as long as the king determined rather than execution, because he had turned informant and possibly saved naval lives).

Then there was Thomas Ouchterlauney, who claimed that he did not attempt to escape the pirates because he was terrified of the West African cannibals (who did not exist, though White fears of cannibalism in Africa were incredibly common and founded on colonialist tropes readily accepted by those who stood to profit from empire).[13] Of course, it wasn't only the Black people in coastal Africa that the White pirates were afraid of. Thomas Diggles, a pirate in Black Bart's crew, admitted that, unlike many of the others who were considered a flight risk, he had been allowed to go ashore at Sierra Leone. The naval officers asked him why he didn't try to escape there, and he replied, "the whites there threatened to hang" him. Atkins and Ogle, who had met Captain Crackers and watched him torture the freedom fighter Captain Tomba, believed Diggles, and he was acquitted.[14]

Both coastal West Africans and West Central Africans were martial societies out of necessity. By 1722, the peaceful, non-slaving peoples who had lived along the coast had been overrun, sold into the trade, or amalgamated into larger polities that did partake in slavery and warfare out of necessity due to the culture that emerged in response to the demands of the Atlantic slave trade.[15] Africans who belonged to any of the coastal polities were incredibly familiar with coordinated warfare using both African and European weapons and methods.[16] Most had more martial experience than many of the White pirates.[17] As with modern racism, the racism forming at the time had cognitive dissonance baked right in: to upper-class imperial British minds, Africans were both nonentities to be enslaved, the majority not worthy of putting on trial or writing about, yet also fearsome soldiers who took European captives and could slip from shackles easily and overwhelm the armed officers.[18]

Six weeks later, the trials were over. Of the 217 people caught at Cape Lopez, 48 were sold into slavery, 4 died before they could stand trial, 74 were acquitted, 52 were hanged at Cape Coast. Two, who were found guilty but whose executions were commuted by asking for the king's pleasure, were sent along with seventeen defendants for whom the court could not find sufficient evidence for conviction to the Marshalsea debtor's prison in England for yet another trial. Another twenty were sentenced to death but had their sentences commuted to serving the Royal Africa Company instead.[19]

Of the seventeen sent to Marshalsea for retrial, one died in Africa before leaving for England and nine died onboard the ship en route. The seven who made it to Marshalsea pleaded for mercy and were granted pardons but had to petition the lords of the regency to waive the fees payable for their release because they were "naked and destitute" from their long imprisonment.[20] The twenty men sentenced to servitude with the RAC in West Africa died of malnutrition, disease, heatstroke, and overwork before serving out their seven-year indentures.[21] That meant that the death rate for those thirty-seven who were neither hanged nor acquitted but granted some type of "mercy" during the Cape Coast trials was more than 81 percent after seven years—far from merciful.

THE TRIALS IN MEDIA

All of this information about the Battle of Cape Lopez and the trials was spread liberally throughout the Atlantic world, as it was among the first major events to occur after the proliferation of printing presses in the Americas, which happened in the 1710s. Prior to that, there were only a handful of presses in the Americas and only one in what would become the United States: that of Cambridge, which the Puritans brought with them in 1638. For nearly a century, it printed mostly Puritan literature. Outside of that, the vast majority of the printed material circulating in North America, South America, and the Caribbean before the 1710s was from Europe. The news was old and expensive. The explosion of local American printing presses meant that newsletters, pamphlets, tracts, and the like could be copied on cheaper paper and that the Americas could produce their own news rather than waiting months for news to be printed and then shipped across the Atlantic Ocean in ships that didn't always make it. For the first time, the colonies that would become the United States had their own newspapers.** With the ability to print came the transmission of distinct American values: the news that was printed and shared with colonists was shared in ways that reinforced colonial, rather than purely European, needs and demands.[22]

The trial records were an especially sought-after printed commodity. The trials of Black Bart's pirates, the report written by Captain Ogle, as well as the journal written by his surgeon John Atkins were advertised for sale widely in both colonial and European newspapers. The reading public could not get enough about pirates. These pieces of literature were advertised and printed alongside the speeches and sermons of Cotton Mather, America's most famous Puritan preacher, who reinforced the need to quell piracy and was often called to record the last words of pirates sentenced for execution in New England. He called pirates a "generation of sea-monsters" who "perished wonderfully" and "haunt the sea."[23] His sermons consistently sold out and were published alongside the pirates' last words and accounts of their executions. During this time, the Nathaniel Mist narrative *A General History of Pirates* (1724) became wildly popular and the English trader, journalist, pamphleteer, and novelist Daniel Defoe, an ardent friend of Mist, published bestselling works such as *Robinson Crusoe* (1719), which featured pirates and blended fact with fiction.

** The first newspaper in what would become the United States was the *Boston News-Letter*, which began in 1704 and was the only newspaper in the British North American colonies until 1719, when the *Boston Gazette* and the *American Weekly Mercury* launched. All three papers published new information and reprinted old information about Black Bart and the Battle of Cape Lopez.

The English-reading public also read about similar trials of people accused of impeding British trade in the Indian Ocean world, where the accused were taken to Bombay (current-day Mumbai) to stand trial for piracy in the Asian capital of the East India Company. Commodore Matthews, Captain Ogle's long-term rival who had departed Portsmouth the same time as Ogle to hunt down Admiral Khanoji Angre and the Maratha Navy, was ultimately unsuccessful. Had he been able to capture Angre, however, the trials at Bombay would have been similar to those of Black Bart's pirates at Cape Coast.[24]

"Pirate" became the moniker du jour for anyone who impeded trade and therefore impeded empire, and printers grew wealthy reprinting and exaggerating reports of piracy to an eager public. Clement Downing, midshipman onboard several of the ships in Commodore Matthews's East India Squadron, later published his account of Admiral Angre (whom he called "the Great Mogul, Angria") and in the foreword admonished against this practice: "the World has been of late very much imposed on by fictitious Pieces, under the Titles of Voyages, Travels, Memoirs, &c. with sham Names prefix'd as the Authors." These forgeries were collected from various sources and altered, exaggerated, abridged, and "jumbled together," with "many improbable incidence added, to amuse the Imagination of the Reader." As very little truthful information had been published about Admiral Angre and the East India Squadron's antipiracy efforts, Downing felt it necessary to create a concise and factual account of only what he directly saw and heard.[25]

These points speak to a concerted public awareness of the administrative shift the British Atlantic empire experienced as it transitioned from one of many competing powers to the superpower during the long eighteenth century. This rapid expansion of the empire depended on unimpeded trade, especially that of enslaved Africans to British colonies with plantation economies. Enslaved Africans built the wealth of Great Britain and of each of her colonies. Black Bart's pirates were one domino in a longer chain that had to topple in order for Britannia to rule the waves.

WHAT HAPPENED TO OGLE?

If Black Bart and his crew were toppled dominoes, Chaloner Ogle was the agent of empire who would ensure the dominoes stayed down through self-elevation and relentless extermination of every similar threat. Once he had squeezed every shilling and gram of gold dust from the sale of the Black pirates on Black Bart's crew and the prize ships, he and Atkins left the RAC officials to dispose of the dead bodies, assign duties to those sentenced to labor, and arrange transport of the accused who would be tried in Marshalsea prison outside of London.

In a letter to the admiralty, Ogle claimed that the quantity of gold he recovered from all the prizes was three thousand pounds and asked the lords of the admiralty to ensure that the value of the prizes themselves (i.e., the ships) and anything left on them be shared with the crew of the *Swallow*.[26] In actuality, the value of the gold dust that Black Bart had robbed at Ouidah was worth far more than three thousand pounds, though a full account is nowhere to be found. Ogle reserved more than three thousand pounds for himself alone, explaining to the admiralty that the money was needed to support his elevation in status, which he would soon receive for his heroic actions.[27] He gave the crewmen two pounds apiece and left Cape Coast for Jamaica, neglecting to tell the men of the *Swallow* that they were entitled to anything more, although the king himself had set the sum at one hundred pounds for every officer who successfully fought the pirates at Cape Coast.

Once the *Swallow* made it back to England, a harrying account from the naval carpenter Thomas Anthony and his wife, Mary, who appealed to the admiralty court, provided some insight into the condition in which Ogle had left his seamen. James Morris, one of the crew on the *Swallow*, had once served under Thomas Anthony in the navy. When the *Swallow* returned to port in May 1723, it was reported that "most of the men were dead." Anthony went to look for his former colleague and "found him in a very low, weak & deplorable condition." He obtained leave to carry him ashore and "by this Morris's most earnest & pressing solicitations, was prevail'd upon to lett him be att his house." The Anthonys cared for Morris and took him to the hospital at their expense when he seemed to be getting worse. Mary Anthony sought out Lieutenant Isaac Sun of the *Swallow* for the debt due to them when Morris died.[28]

Those few among Ogle's crew on the *Swallow* who survived had to sue for the prize money they were due; their pleas made it in the *American Weekly Mercury* in 1725, four years after the Battle of Cape Lopez. The crown proposed a 100-pound reward for the commander, with less for officers and crew, for a total of 1,920 pounds. Officers on the ship did not know they were entitled to this reward until *A General History of Pirates* was published, and they read about themselves and their actions at Cape Lopez in it.[29]

In April 1725, Lord Townshend wrote to the admiralty on their behalf, and in February 1727, a petition of the "persons, wives, widows, children, and relations of persons lately serving under the command of Sir Chaloner Ogle" made it to the privy council. By then, at least two more men onboard the *Swallow* who knew they were due this sum had died and tasked their descendants to go after the money in their wills.[30] The remaining seven seamen and assembled surviving family members of the rest presented to the council their "most deplorable circumstances with Sir Chaloner's most severe oppression in unjustly detaining their proper dividends of such shares of the effects as were taken from the Pyrates" in the amount of around two thousand pounds that Ogle had "dishonorably held back." Even the officers received only small proportions of the share—slightly more than two pounds per person. They asked the privy council to "compel Sir Chaloner to pay to every one of the [party] their respective share of the said prizes over and above what has already been distributed to them."[31] They eventually got their money, but Ogle was never reprimanded for robbing his crew and leaving them to die. Rather, he was promoted for his actions regarding the threat to British trade posed by the pirates.

Perhaps too his promotion was earned through what he had done to help weaken King John Conny of Fort Great Fredericksburg at Cape Three Points, who had become quite the menace in the eyes of the RAC. The last time John Atkins and Chaloner Ogle were at Anomabo (in October 1721, three months before the Battle of Cape Lopez), Atkins wrote about a conflict between the Ashanti and the people living at Cape Apollonia, which they blamed on John Conny of Cape Three Points, their neighbor and competitor. Atkins wrote that "we found them preparing to revenge this Injury, buying up all our trading Arms at good Price, and giving a Fowl for every Flint we could spare." Atkins said that they were intent on getting the upper hand over Ahanta, "which, by accounts since, I hear they have accomplished against Conny."[32]

These were common ways that slave traders and other British agents in West Africa wrote about arms trading and other political interference in which they took part overseas in attempts to manipulate trade in their favor. Unlike the plainspoken Dutch, they rarely stated outright that they were furnishing one group of Africans with guns in attempts to wipe out another group that had become difficult trade partners, but the evidence exists in the time lines and results.[33]

Atkins casually mentions the encounter and the aftermath as if it were happenstance, but it was far from chance. Atkins was a naval surgeon on a ship tasked with hunting down Black Bart. He initially met John Conny after the Ahanta king ransomed his seamen (who had refused to pay for the water they were taking) and invited him up to his heavily fortified palace atop Manfro Hill in the town of Pokesu at Cape Three Points, treating them to a luxurious meal with both fresh butter and cheese, in the company of his wives decked out entirely in gold from head to toe. This was a show of wealth and martial might, intended to either persuade the British to ally with him or to convince them to back off and leave him to rule at Cape Three Points. Then King John Conny had made a clear threat by telling the unforgettable story of the failed Dutch ambush, the Dutchmen's skulls and jawbones serving as grisly props. To add insult to injury, Conny made Ogle pay the cost of the water several times over before the British naval captain was allowed to leave. Despite this fierce display, four of Ogle's crew were persuaded to stay behind, choosing the menacing but unknown Conny over the sure tyranny of Ogle, and then later to join Black Bart's crew when the pirates stopped at Three Points for water and intel.

The description of this entire evening had struck horror in the hearts of the RAC employees, whose slave-trading fort at Dixcove had already been ransacked by Conny's military. It was no coincidence that Ogle and Atkins found locals who happened to be preparing for war with Conny nor that Ogle and Atkins traded the arms provided by the RAC to forge alliances with Africans who were amenable to British trade. And it was certainly no coincidence that Atkins inquired about what happened later and then reported it in his journal for public consumption. This is not the only place in the journal where Atkins carefully crafts his role as enforcer of the empire against local Black threats to its economic well-being.

Atkins did it again a year later when he and Ogle left Cape Coast Castle in West Africa for Jamaica after the pirate trials per their orders. In his journal he casually mentioned a situation with the enslaved population and self-emancipated maroons, which was becoming a topic of intense interest in the British Atlantic world by 1723. Five years later, the British navy would be deployed there to fight in the First Maroon War (1728–1740)—a conflict between the mountain communities of self-emancipated Africans and Afro-descended people in Jamaica—and tasked with protecting the profits of Jamaica's planters and keeping the enslaved Africans on plantations and out of the mountains.[34] Ogle himself would become naval commander in Jamaica in 1732, right in the middle of the conflict. He would fight with and threaten Governor Trelawny in a squabble over impressment and stand trial for assault of said governor in Jamaica, though once again the empire would forgive him.[35]

As was the case with their interactions with John Conny, Ogle and Atkins visited Jamaica first to get a sense of the situation before acting on it. Ogle and Atkins stayed in Jamaica from August 1722 until January 1723. Atkins reported that the Black majority population in Jamaica "renders the whole Colony unsafe" and allowed "hundreds of them" to run to the mountains from which the formerly enslaved "commit little Robberies upon the defenseless and nearest Plantations."[36] He described planters who paid search parties for every maroon killed, provided they brought back ears as proof. If living maroons were brought in, however, the planters tortured them and burned them alive. This cruel reaction didn't deter the maroons, who were being "encouraged and supplied with Powder and Arms" from Spanish traders in Cuba.[††] Atkins writes, "The natural Remedy against this Evil, is an increase of Hands." The evil he referred to was the self-emancipating armed Africans, not the planters who mutilated, tortured, and burned them alive. Atkins was convinced that the best way to stamp out the threat posed by the maroons to British planters was to increase British military presence in Jamaica.[37] The Crown heard him and deployed Ogle a few years later once the conflicts has escalated to a full-scale war. This time, thanks to his actions in West Africa, Ogle commanded twenty-four ships of the line.

Ogle eventually become an admiral and was knighted for his antipiracy efforts. Sir Chaloner Ogle made it to Parliament in 1746 and became commander-in-chief of the navy in 1749. His estate remains in the English countryside. The entirety of his career consisted of combating threats to British trade and plantation slavery, and the way he conducted himself provides insights into his personality and way of operating. This in turn speaks volumes of the king who decorated and promoted him through the ranks. Ogle was a tenacious and forceful man yet brutish, short-sighted, and crude. Blind to his own privilege and with a giant chip on his shoulder, Ogle personified the British bulldog of empire.

The story of piracy in West Africa is the story of Britain's attempt to expand the empire, and nothing illustrates this more than the trials and punishments of Black Bart's pirates and of the Ahantan king John Conny. Speed was key if the British wanted to stay ahead of the other European powers, and forced labor was

---

[††] It was standing policy of the Spanish Empire to undermine the British in this particular way anytime the two powers were at war. The Spanish Atlantic world held different conceptions of race and slavery than did the English world. There was a significant population of free Black people and people of African ancestry in the Spanish Empire, and the Crown did not hesitate to furnish these populations with arms pointed directly at the English. In the Caribbean and most border areas, such as Spanish Florida and Louisiana, the Spanish colonial governors created policies that incentivized escape among the enslaved populations in British colonies: they promised freedom and citizenship equivalent to that of any Spanish colonist to any enslaved person in the British territories who self-emancipated, crossed the border, and converted to Catholicism. Then the formerly enslaved Africans and Afro-descended people often were given arms to point at their former enslavers and were expected to live at and defend the borders of the Spanish Empire in key areas, like Fort Mose near Saint Augustine, Florida. See Jane G. Landers, *Black Society in Spanish Florida* (Urbana: University of Illinois Press, 1999).

the only way to keep up with the breakneck pace of expansion. All impediments to trade had to be eliminated, as did anything that rendered the results of this trade unprofitable. Honoring the rights and the humanity of the enslaved was not profitable and slowed down the machine of empire. Furthermore, antipiracy measures did not come cheap. Financing Captain Ogle's crew and ships was an expensive investment that would be recouped on the backs of enslaved Africans. As the price of enslaved captives shot up—first because of the scarcity caused by piracy and then because of the costs of antipiracy measures, the rise in slave ship insurance, and other factors—enslavers calibrated the most cost-efficient ways to enact slavery. Planters demanded more affordable slave labor, and the British Crown, navy, and Royal Africa Company worked in concert to make this their top priority. As the British understood it, not only *could* a noose designed for Black Bart fit easily around the neck of John Conny, but it *had* to.

Chapter Eight

The Defeat
of John Conny

THE AHANTAN KING JOHN CONNY noticed the absence of Black Bart's pirates at his castle well before they were caught and hanged. The early 1720s were an increasingly unstable time for the western region of the Gold Coast, and Conny needed as many allies as he could get. The pirates hadn't exactly been allies, but they had been a continual source of valuable loot and free-flowing information at a time when Conny couldn't afford to be cut off from European gossip and news. Despite entertaining the English Captain Ogle and his surgeon, Atkins, twice now, Conny wasn't any closer to an alliance with the English or their Royal Africa Company.

If it were only a matter of conflict with the Dutch West India Company, Conny could handle it. He had been fighting them since the Prussians pulled out of Cape Three Points in 1717 and left Fort Great Fredericksburg in Conny's capable hands and then sold it to the Dutch without informing him. Unfortunately, that was the year that his dear ally, the first Ashanti king, Osei Tutu, died. Through the Brandenburg Africa Company, Conny had been supplying the Ashanti with munitions; in return, they had favored him heavily for their coastal trade.[1] Osei Tutu and the Ashanti had become Conny's lifeblood. Though he was wealthy beyond belief in every way that counted (gold, loyal subjects, soldiers, wives, networks, and property), his ability to retain that wealth was dependent on his role as middleman between the ships that anchored at Cape

175

Three Points and the new Ashanti Empire to the north, whose wars
of expansion provided Conny with enough enslaved captives to
supply the Europeans. Most of those Europeans didn't belong to a
company—Conny's clientele were pirates, free agents, and English
ten percenters who came for water but left with gold dust, ivory,
and enslaved captives in the cargo.[2]

ARMS TRADING

This steady flow of captives and goods from the Ashanti was now
being threatened. The death of Tutu gave the Ashanti dependencies such as Wasa, Twifo, and Aowin an opening to rebel and seek
their autonomy once more. The new king, or *Asantehene*, Opoku
Ware I opted to quell the uprisings one by one, which conserved
Ashanti resources and ensured a chain of morale-boosting victories
but prolonged the overall power struggle. This was bad for Conny—
the longer Opoku Ware was tied up in conflicts, the less military
support he could send Conny's way. While Opoku Ware was engaged with one of these uprisings, the Aowin attacked and sacked
the capital of Kumasi in 1718. High-ranking Ashanti residents

Modern view from Conny's Castle, or Fort Great Fredericksburg, of Cape
Three Points looking over Gold Coast canoes and the town of Pokesu (Princes
Town). *Photo by author*

were rounded up, and the Aowin marched the Ashanti of Kumasi to Cape Apollonia, the westernmost point of the Gold Coast, to sell them as enslaved captives. The Wasa, another group using this conflict in its own bid for independence, forged an alliance with the Aowin and followed them to the coast to run drills for a joint attack on Ashanti.[3]

This large-scale displacement of people from the north going south and west dramatically shifted the balance along the coast. The instability in the north, Conny's domination of the coast to the south, and the Aowin and Wasa military settlements in the far west boxed in the peoples who lived in the triangle between the three, causing many people to flee past Dutch Axim and settle near the mouth of the Ankobra River. The peoples already there, the Azane, feared that the Ashanti wars would arrive at their door and that their people would end up captives on ships to the Americas. The leaders of the Azane had discussed building their own fort at the mouth of the Ankobra River to keep out Ashanti if they attacked back in 1718. By 1720 the idea was floated again, and they approached the Dutch for help, asking them to build and control it jointly.* The Azane had hoped that as the Ashanti wars repopulated the coast with refugees, the Ankobra River region, which snaked all the way from the coast up into Ashanti territory, might have made a

---

* This wasn't such an unusual prospect. Many of the Prussian and Dutch forts were built in places where locals desired to get the upper hand and could make use of a bastion to hide and to ride out the worst parts of the warfare. Conny wasn't even the first Gold Coast African to have his own fort: Edward Barter, a man educated in England with an English father and Fante mother, became an important trader at the English fort at Cape Coast in the 1690s, before the pirates were hanged there. By 1700 he built a miniature fort-shaped house defended by cannons and flying the English flag. Before Barter, in 1693, the Danes reported a similar story to that of Conny: Asameni of Akwamu, someone who, like Conny, had served as middleman to European factors, seized the Danish Christiansbourg Castle close to Anomabo for himself and held it for a year. He used his expansive knowledge of Danish weaknesses (mainly greed) and the fort's layout to overrun it with soldiers who then refused to leave. They had been allowed into the heavily fortified castle in modern Accra, Ghana's capital, because Asameni had told the Danes that he had found a stock of so many affordable guns that it took eighty men to carry them all in. Such tactics were tried-and-true methods of asserting African trading rights and sovereignty and disregarding the European insistence on monopolies. See J. K. Osei-Tutu and H. W. Von Hesse, "Illusions of Grandeur and Protection: Perceptions and (Mis)Representations of the Defensive Efficacy of European-Built Fortifications on the Gold Coast, Seventeenth–Early Nineteenth Centuries," in *Power and Landscape in Atlantic West Africa: Archaeological Perspectives*, ed. J. Cameron Monroe and Akinwumi Ogunidiran (Cambridge: Cambridge University Press: 2012), 149–50.

potentially lucrative prospect for the West India Company (WIC), ensuring a win-win situation: profit for the Dutch and physical safety for the Azane.

Before the WIC could get permission from the Netherlands to build at Ankobra, war broke out between the rebel Ashanti dependencies of Wasa, Adom, and Twifa on one side and Conny's Ahanta, who were still allied with Ashanti, on the other. The WIC abandoned talks with the Azane to focus on fortifying its existing forts in the region lest Conny emerge victorious from this conflict and try to burn them down again. The Azane, furious at this Dutch betrayal, became Conny's most important lifeline, sourcing his military with the food and supplies needed to fight off Ashanti's enemies. This was crucial, as food along the coast was scarce because the slave trading companies bought every scrap to keep captives alive in the fort dungeons and in the bowels of ships. The Wasa, Adom, and Twifa didn't have a direct and reliable line to enough calories to sustain their militaries. WIC employees complained among themselves that Conny's distinctive canoes loaded with goods arrived daily at the mouth of the Ankobra River and that it was the Azane who filled them with grain and kept Conny and the Ashanti in fighting condition.

Between August and November 1721, Conny was winning the war. This period sees frantic correspondence among the Ten Gentlemen shareholders of the WIC in the Netherlands and the Dutch Elmina council on the Gold Coast, as well as among the slave traders at each of the Dutch forts.[†] They feared that they were going to be squeezed out of the trade entirely if they did not intervene more heavily. The Dutch observed that the English had more resources to expend with the pirates gone, and they were terrified that the English would use the chaos that had broken out in the western region to try to take possession of Conny's Castle at Cape Three Points once again. Willem Butler, an employee of the WIC, wrote to the Ten Gentlemen of the WIC that they needed to act quickly if they wanted to possess the former Prussian fort. If Conny

† The Ten Gentlemen (*Heeren Tien/Heeren X*) was the name given to the advisory board of the Dutch West India Company. The Ten Gentlemen were representatives from the various chambers of the company in the Dutch Republic, as well as a delegate from the States General, the legislature.

were separated from it, his power would soon wane. The Dutch already had sent two brand-new, cutting-edge mortar cannons to West Africa but prepared for more substantial actions. Since they had already paid the Prussians for the fort, they were determined to take possession one way or another, but for it to fall into English hands was just as bad as allowing Conny to remain there.[4]

Meanwhile, the conflict between Conny and the rebel Ashanti dependencies raged on. After a brutal loss at the hands of Conny's troops, the Wasa requested protection of the WIC, should the Ashanti demand they be handed over. Much of the population located in the fighting area fled to the west to escape captivity and enslavement.[5] The Dutch saw this as an opportunity to cultivate goodwill and dependency among the refugees who also wanted to see Conny—the African who was partially to blame for their displacement—gone.

The English had the same thought process. When Ogle and Atkins had stopped at Cape Apollonia, they found all their former African acquaintances were gone, forced to flee the area. What they did see were Conny's unmistakable canoes, which had become a regular presence at the mouth of the Akobra River in Cape Apollonia. Atkins wrote that the Ashanti (whom he called "Santies") who lived to the north enjoyed good trade with both John Conny and at the RAC fortress at Anomabo, the easternmost British point of influence in the eastern region of the Gold Coast. Atkins understood that the Apollonians had been interfering in the trade in an attempt to gain a favored position as intermediary between the Ashanti and the coast, though most likely it was the Aowin and Twifo, who had come to Apollonia to run drills together and had displaced the Apollonians. The Ashanti finally deployed a full military force in an attempt to unseat them. The Aowin and Twifo blamed John Conny for this Ashanti onslaught, saying that he, the most favored coastal trading partner of Ashanti, instigated this fresh conflict between them and the Ashanti.

The people at Cape Apollonia cleaned out Ogle and Atkins of every gun and flint they had onboard the *Swallow* and *Weymouth*, bringing things in return that were most prized in this area: cages upon cages of fresh fowl. The live birds were kept by every ship that could manage to keep them alive to guarantee unspoiled sources of valuable and rare protein during the long voyages and time spent anchored while filling their berths. The Wasa and Twifo were so desperate for sufficient arms to gain the upper hand on Conny that they paid Atkins a whole bird "for every Flint we could spare (there being no such thing in the country)." By the 1720s, good flints could last for the entire life of a musket or shorter gun, though the ones Ogle and Atkins had brought to Africa from England likely weren't the highest quality or necessarily the best fit for the Dutch, Prussian, French, and older English guns already in circulation there. The fact that the English navy was able to command such a dear price for small amounts of a raw material that required little processing, weighed almost nothing, didn't spoil on the voyage, and was plentiful in Europe speaks to how many older guns the various African powers already had access to from previous trades with Europeans.[6]

This was because the large numbers and sheer density of various European powers along the Gold Coast facilitated the military culture there. Each slaving company built strong fortifications, imported large numbers of weapons and some European troops, and relied on local African auxiliary troops or mercenary troops to supplement them.‡ Small numbers of arms made it to Africans via the Portuguese, but the arms trade to West Africa began in earnest with the English in 1646, who sold larger numbers of guns to a state opposed to Great Komenda and Fetu, two polities who worked with their Dutch competitors.[7] The English also made a habit of presenting guns as gifts to allies of the RAC. By the 1650s they were used by militaries further inland, who came to the coast directly to buy them. In November 1673, a RAC ship bound for the Gold Coast routinely carried more than one thousand muskets, and by 1686, the warehouse at Cape Coast had more than five thousand muskets in storage for trade to Africans.[8] The director general could use these at his discretion to trade and dole out among the English trading forts, posts, and factories as needed. By the time the Komenda

‡ Auxiliary troops were comprised of local soldiers hired out to the Europeans—who often rented the space upon which the European fortresses were built by African rulers—whereas mercenaries were free-agent career soldiers in Africa who hired out themselves as private militaries to the highest bidder.

Wars began in the 1690s, the soldiers of John Cabes—the caboceer after whom John Conny had styled himself—all had both guns and African-forged weapons.

Africans working with the Dutch demanded equal treatment, which meant more guns. In an account published shortly after his death in 1704, the WIC slave trader Willem Bosman remarked to the readership, "Perhaps you wonder how the Negroes come to be furnished with fire-arms, but you will have no reason when you know we sell them at incredible quantities, thereby obliging them with a knife to cut our own throats."[9] By the 1690s, it was common enough for Dutch ships to carry a thousand pounds or more in gunpowder, and those numbers kept rising. One captured Dutch interloper ship, the *White Moor*, in 1725 carried more than fifty-five thousand pounds of gunpowder in her hold![10] In retrospect, this is perhaps unsurprising, as Black Bart's pirates often seemed to have enough gunpowder onboard to blow up entire ships in their attacks.

With Conny's enemies thus armed by the English, Conny doubled down on his efforts to sell the Prussian-built Fort Great Fredericksburg, which had become Conny's Castle. In August 1722, however, the Azane, the suppliers of grain to Conny's military, declared war on Cape Apollonia. The Dutch WIC was convinced that it was Conny's idea. There's no real evidence for that, though the Azane must have made a small fortune supplying Conny's military, which put them in the financial position to be able to win this conflict.

THE PUNCH BOWL

It was around this time that another Englishman visited Conny's Castle at Cape Three Points. James Houstoun, another surgeon, was hired by the Royal Africa Company to come from England and give an honest assessment of the state of the English holdings in West Africa. Houstoun sailed the exact same route that Chaloner Ogle and Black Bart had taken, first to Sierra Leone and then eastward along the coast, giving Dutch forts wide berth and stopping at the English ones. When the ship he was on ran low on water, they dropped anchor at Cape Three Points, and agents of Conny canoed to him and were invited onboard. As with Atkins, these ambassadors had Conny's gold-headed engraved cane with them as a symbol of his sovereignty, and they quoted the prices for collecting water. They also mentioned that their Ahantan king was a great lover of the English but a "mortal enemy" of the Dutch. Houstoun's curiosity led him ashore to visit King Conny while his ship watered, who

> receiv'd me very kindly, with the usual Ceremonies of their Country Musick, Drums and Horns, and ask'd me what Wines I pleas'd to drink. He had several sorts of European Wines, but I chose rather to drink what I knew was more agreeable to him, Brandy, which he to compliment me, caused to be made into Punch. When he turn'd a little warm'd with Liquor, he shew'd me a Dutchman's skull, and ask'd me if I wou'd pledge him in a Bumper of Punch, to the Damnation of the Dutch, from that skull? I humour'd the Jest, but begg'd he would excuse me, the Draught being too large for me. If we had been empower'd to trade with him on Account of the Company, I cou'd have purchased from him a considerable number of Slaves, with what Quantity I pleased of Rice, the only Product of this Country, for the Soil seems agreeable for nothing else; and it's from hence that most parts of the Gold Coast is furnish'd with that Grain.[11]

This grisly punch-bowl scene with the Dutchmen's skulls of course echoes what Atkins experienced when he visited Conny the year before. Conny never stopped trying to court an earnest alliance with the RAC, and he did so in a similar way to his role model, John Cabes of Komenda, by enhancing his own perceived ferocity and styling himself as a consistent ally of the RAC who had no mercy for England's greatest competitor in the slave trade.

The skull punchbowl also played to another of Conny's strengths: styling himself as an African ruler who was not deferent to European rulers but their equal. Just as Europeans communicated their values of justice and the supremacy of capital with their fierce and gruesome displays (such as hanging pirates in chains so that they could watch birds consume the remains), West Africans used their own grisly displays to communicate theirs to great effect. Aesthetic displays of the remains of wartime foes had a long history in West Africa, and many considered this a mark of martial strength. The head, specifically, was considered the most vital part of a person, therefore the skulls of wartime foes often adorned martial paraphernalia, like sword handles, lances, battle dress, and musical instruments. Several important African soldiers were either buried with these wartime trophies or beneath carefully stacked pyramids of them.[12]

Nevertheless, Houstoun made his nervous getaway and later jotted down that he believed the "laborious Dutch" were the only real European competitors the RAC had to worry about. He wrote that "every True Briton" should "unanimously join" to ensure that the slave trade be centered in England and carried out by the Royal Africa Company, "who hitherto have been greater Losers than Gainers by it."[13] He spent several pages illustrating what a "glorious and advantageous trade" the English had and how the entire nation must take any measures necessary to remove any and all obstructions to it.[14] He also discussed how most of the English forts were decimated and depleted, though Ouidah had every luxury imaginable.[15] The way Houstoun constructed his rave made it likely readers would have inferred that Conny's insistence on sovereignty was one such obstruction to trade and responsible for the decimation of England's forts.[§]

Conny was wealthy, ruthless, smart, tactical, and old. From 1717 onward, his actions had monopolized all the Ashanti trade in the western region of the Gold Coast, leaving very little for the European traders. Outside of Ouidah, which was technically too far east to be considered part of the Gold Coast, no one traded as

---

§ Houstoun also blamed the employees that the RAC had placed in charge at the forts. They were not the kind of men who could resist Conny nor would they try. Houstoun mentioned that the forts "more resemble haunted Houses than garrison'd Forts, having one Ghost above Stairs, and perhaps 2 or 3 at most below, spinning out a life that is a real Burden to them, in a miserable condition, under Tyranny of a Despotick Power." The despot he named was Mr. Baldwin, the factor who robbed and cheated the company and regularly sold African girls younger than ten years old as "women" and pocketed the difference. See James Houstoun, *Some New and Accurate Observations Geographical, Natural and Historical. Containing a True and Impartial Account of the Situation, Product, and Natural History of the Coast of Guinea, So Far As Relates to the Improvement of That Trade, for the Advantage of Great Britain in General, and the Royal African Company in Particular. By James Houstoun, M. D. Humbly Address'd to the Honourable the Court of Assistants of the Royal African Company of Great Britain* (London: J. Peele, 1725), 25–33.

much as Conny. Conny's actions deeply hampered WIC trade. By Atkins's estimate, Conny had "reduced the Traders Profits to 20 per cent."[16] While England had resolved its pirate problem in the slave trade at the Battle of Cape Lopez, the Dutch were stuck with no real ability to maintain their grasp on the Gold Coast as long as Conny was in charge.

The next month, in September, Conny welcomed a delegation of Portuguese-descended traders from Brazil who brought him gifts and requested permission to settle in his state of Ahanta.[17] Europeans on the Gold Coast believed that whatever company occupied Fort Great Fredericksburg would naturally inherit the incredibly lucrative trade with the Ashanti. The RAC panicked, fearing they might lose their opportunity to inhabit the fort. They entrusted one of their African middlemen, Thomas Awishee, to negotiate for the castle, guessing that Conny would respond more favorably to an African than to a European in this matter.

Meanwhile, James Houstoun visited Fort Metal Cross at Dixcove, the nearest RAC fortification to John Conny, about fifteen miles as the crow flies. In 1717 Conny had sacked it to rescue a blood relative, a woman named Adjoba, from enslavement at the hands of his rival, Appre. In 1722, Houstoun found that little had changed since then. Fort Metal Cross contained "nothing in it but one poor Gentleman, a writer, who was chief factor, Writer, and everything; and two or three Creatures call'd Soldiers, just ready to expire for want of the common Necessaries of Life." The factor and two or three soldiers who were holding down the fort at Dixcove were slowly starving to death. They told Houstoun that due to the "Disturbances of the Natives amongst themselves, their Trade had been entirely interrupted for some time,"[18] and when they sailed down the road to the next British fort at Sekondi (slightly more than fifteen miles away), they found the RAC employee "reduced to Starving in a starved Country."[19] Like the Dutch WIC, the English RAC also needed a direct line to the Ashanti—and fast.

England's serious attempt to buy Conny's Castle caused traders of the Dutch WIC to panic. In desperation, they chose to finally recognize Conny's rights to the castle and barter with him for it. They said nothing about their 1717 agreement with Prussia, in which they bought the fort. It was, as historian Kwame Daaku wrote, "an open admission by the Dutch of their helplessness in achieving their aims without Conny's consent."[20]

According to the WIC, they agreed with Conny that the Ahantan ruler would renounce control over the former Prussian forts but would retain the power to nominate the governor of Great Fredericksburg. The Dutch would pay Conny damages, a monthly rent of two ounces of gold, and a yearly gift of forty-eight English pounds for his services. They also credited him with 192 pounds' worth of trade goods for his trading business, on the condition that he stop trading with the interlopers and stop collecting the water toll from ships that needed to replenish their stores.[21] The Dutch drafted an agreement and threw in a New Year's gift of gold as *scheepsgelden*, or ship money/ship fees.¶

This was a clear attempt to control who Conny interacted with, as all of his business prospects and interactions with European allies had been through European ships—like those of Chaloner Ogle, Black Bart, or James Houstoun—that stopped at Cape Three Points for water. He wouldn't be able to entertain other Europeans and make better deals behind the backs of the WIC easily if this practice were to end. This, of course, was no deal for Conny: his free-market policies won him the favor of the inland Ashanti Empire, and his established relationship with King Opoku Ware was more lucrative and important to him than any relationship with the revolving door of European traders who came and went.

¶ From the context, it is unclear what exactly this "ship money" or "ship fees" refers to. An educated guess suggests a duty or tax for each ship that comes into port. Most likely, the Ahantan canoe men were to continue ferrying goods, captives, and crew between ship and shore, and this levy would fund this fleet. Back when Conny worked with the Prussians, a large part of his financial empire was built on monopolizing a fleet of canoes and canoe men who were always available for ships to use when they wanted to trade at Fort Great Fredricksburg. This was necessary at Cape Three Points because large ships could anchor safely, but the coral reef and jagged rocks just beneath the surface of the waves closer to shore necessitated African canoes, rather than European boats, with local ferrymen who had memorized the safest routes and were attuned to the daily changes of the sea. This gives credence to the idea that the Dutch were hoping either to retain some kind of trade relationship with Conny or to preserve some semblance of a relationship with him. The unrequested New Year's gift lends further credence to that notion.

Conny signed the document. Some historians speculate that perhaps he did so without full knowledge of what it contained, though the evidence also could lead to the interpretation that he signed the contract with full awareness but chose to disregard this last clause because it was essentially unenforceable, and unenforceable clauses just didn't count in his eyes. Either way, a year after signing, Conny built a strong, eight-feet-tall, three-feet-thick wall around Pokesu as the Dutch-Ahanta relationship deteriorated. He used stones from the fort, which weakened it while strengthening the capital of Ahanta, showing again where his priorities lay.[22] Later in 1723, Conny dispatched a cadre of his masons, bricklayers, and carpenters to Kumasi, the Ashanti capital, to help Opoku Ware rebuild his royal palace after it was sacked by the Azane's raid.[23] At the height of Conny's power, some sources put his military at twenty thousand. Things looked good for Conny, even if he couldn't quite get the English to do his bidding.

FAMINE STRIKES

In the summer of 1724, an inevitable famine struck the western region of the Gold Coast. The sustained warfare in the region had prevented farmers from remaining on their lands and tending to their crops, and the various marching armies in the area had required large amounts of staples to sustain the multiple war fronts. As many as thirty thousand Ahanta people suffered during this famine when Conny was unable to obtain sufficient grain to feed them. Underlying tensions from within Ahanta, which had been simmering before, came to a rolling boil when Conny's former supporters, now in danger of starving, threatened to withhold martial assistance. Conny's relationship with the Dutch had broken down so badly that they would not have helped him if he had asked, which he did not.

In October Conny attempted once again to sell his castle to the Portuguese and to the English in last-ditch attempts to secure enough food to weather the famine. Once again, the Europeans sent agents to broker deals, despite the Dutch's signed contract with both the Brandenburgers and Conny for its use. Once again, the WIC's employees wrote to the Ten Gentlemen in a panic that the fort was going to fall into English hands.[24] These European attempts to buy the fort from under the Dutch yet again meant that the European slave traders had chosen not to recognize the Dutch deal as a legally binding agreement. Rather, they chose to honor Conny's sovereignty and deal with him directly in the hopes of finally securing that all-too-valuable direct trading line to the Ashanti.

The real estate talks were yet again interrupted by war: Wasa, Twifo, and Adom attacked Conny, this time with full and open support of the Dutch. Conny barricaded himself in his castle and used his allies, the Azane at Cape Appolonia, to import the grain he needed to feed his troops and the refugees from the famine. This ongoing siege slowly eroded local support for Conny. Conny sent a canoe man up the Ankobra River to ask Opoku Ware in Kumasi for help against their common foes, but the *Asantehene* was spread too thin quelling uprisings and could not offer any real aid.

In response, the Dutch provided Ashanti's old rival, the Aowin, with gunpowder when they approached the WIC seeking an alliance against Conny, Ashanti's most faithful ally. Emu of Aowin put himself forward as Conny's replacement if they managed to oust him jointly.[25] The Dutch agreed to bombard Conny's Castle with the heavy mortars the WIC had sent from the Dutch Republic for this purpose three years prior, and another faction used grenades. Allies of the Dutch at Elmina came organized in *asafo*—military units—which fought alongside the Dutch.** The Ahanta were surrounded with no rescue coming from the Ashanti to the north. It was unsustainable and, eventually, Conny's Castle—the impenetrable

---

** The people of Elmina were divided into three large and four small wards that each had their own *asafo*, which formed the foundation of the defense system of the town. These companies had political as well as martial roles, and they often fought alongside auxiliary troops, European soldiers, and mercenaries. One of the more powerful *asafo* of Elmina were the Denkyira, who were involved in many conflicts with European slave traders on the Gold Coast at this time. The *asafo*'s role in the conflict against Conny would create the foundation for the rapid evolution of a greater political role for the ward leaders in the town. This system is still in place in Elmina, though it has evolved significantly since 1724. Much of what we know from this period comes from the *asafo* flags which were created at the time, and are still being produced to this day. See Harvey Feinberg, *Africans and Europeans in West Africa: Elminans and Dutchmen on the Gold Coast during the Eighteenth Century* (Philadelphia: The American Philosophical Society, 1989),104–8.

African fortress that had decimated Dutch trade and suppressed English trading in the western region—fell. The unthinkable had happened: John Conny, the most powerful trader, king, and military leader on the Gold Coast, was a wanted man and was on the run.

CONNY'S ESCAPE

After Conny's Castle fell to the Dutch and the Aowin, the WIC reported that Conny had been forced to flee north, but before leaving, he massacred the remaining Brandenburgers inside. No other sources corroborate this, though any Prussians left behind in Africa for that many years would not have been a priority for the Prussian elector prince in Europe, who considered the matter over in 1717, when he sold the fort.[26] The WIC finally claimed possession of Conny's Castle and renamed it Fort Hollandia. The Dutch dug up several places around the fort searching for a firkin of gold dust said to be left behind by John Conny when he ran away to no avail.[27]

All the locals who agreed to remain at Pokesu had to contend with striking deals with the Dutch. The WIC ultimately reaped the bitterness it sowed that day. For decades, uncooperative, resentful locals at Cape Three Points continued to trade the way in which Conny had encouraged them to, despite what the Dutch wanted. Fort Hollandia remained an ancillary trading port for the Dutch, never bringing in as much profit as the surrounding ports. That didn't stop the Dutch from waxing poetically about this victory, however. Pastor Lucas Crimpelman wrote to the Ten Gentlemen exalting, "We have here at the coast also reason to thank God Almighty that the weapons of this Noble Company have so remarkably separated the coast from that violent godless Negro John Conny, and banished him like a second Adoni Zedek (Joshua 10: 1–28)."[28]

For many years, historians speculated that Conny died in this attack, but there's a bit more to the story. Rather than running north to seek refuge with his Ashanti ally Opoku Ware (too obvious a move for the strategic caboceer), Conny escaped to an island on the Ankobra River and became a fugitive on Fante land. His allies the Azane, who had grown wealthy supplying his military during prior years, vouched for him. With the Ankobra River at Cape Appolonia acting like a moat around his island, he slowly regrouped and began networking to find more allies.

The Dutch wanted to prevent Conny from getting too comfortable and fomenting further anti-WIC sentiments in the region, so they provided arms and gunpowder to Conny's remaining rivals, which sparked some unexpected repercussions for the Dutch but did successfully rearrange the political forces in the region. Opoku Ware, unable to help Conny militarily, sent an envoy to the WIC to help negotiate a settlement and pressure the Dutch to come to a peace agreement with Conny. Ware threatened to withhold all Ashanti trade from the Dutch unless they signed it, and they agreed to stop hunting Conny in exchange for a share of the trade that had formerly been his.[29]

This fragile truce didn't last long. From his refuge in the Azane's land, Conny built up a solid power base and managed to turn some of the WIC's allies away from the Dutch. Still, it wasn't enough. In February 1726, locals from Axim who were aligned with the Dutch attacked his stronghold on the Ankobra River, and Conny was forced to flee once more. This time, he did flee to Opoku Ware's palace in Kumasi. The Ashanti ruler lacked either the desire or resources (or both) to help Conny regain his power on the coast, and Conny was forced to remain inland. This is where the documentary trail runs dry. None of the Europeans in Africa ever heard from or of Conny again. There is speculation that he lived out the remainder of his days in Kumasi.

CONNY'S LEGACY

In the western region, Conny's absence was felt. At first, taking such drastic action against Conny had a deleterious effect on Dutch trade and damaged the WIC's reputation locally. It made some of the Africans inland, especially the Ashanti, reluctant to turn to the Dutch for alliances. The few treaties the WIC was able to craft with Africans inland were aimed at securing military assistance in actions against uncooperative coastal powers or in keeping trade routes open among the various trading forts, posts, and factories of the company. As a Dutch maritime historian put it: the European slave trading companies deeply underestimated the power that John Conny commanded.[30] Because of their desire to deal with African agents who would trade with only them, the Dutch missed the opportunity to access the interior markets. Without that, there would be no supremacy in the trade. It was a fact the Brandenburgers had instinctively known, but eluded the Dutch.

The Dutch assumed that they would be able to use Conny's Castle, renamed Fort Hollandia, to enjoy unrivaled power and access to inland trade the way Conny had. They foolhardily assumed that Conny's power derived from the European fort, not from his strategic allegiances and various business investments, which kept most of the peoples in the western region of the Gold Coast reliant upon him in some way. The power vacuum left by the Ahanta ruler's absence attracted other important locals who wanted to replicate Conny's successes and enjoy the unrivaled wealth that he had enjoyed. They, however, did not have his upbringing or breadth of experience nor did they have the connections he had inherited by birth. The region remained unstable, with frequent conflict between Aowin, Wasa, Ashanti, and their various allies. This instability continued until the 1760s, with the formation of the Kingdom of Apollonia, which meant that from 1724 to 1760, the expanding trade in captives of these wars moved away from the Cape Three Points and Ankobra River regions and gradually focused to the east, between Cape Coast Castle, Elmina, and Ouidah (the modern regions of southeast Ghana and Benin).

Although the story of John Conny ends here, his legacy lives on in the African diaspora through the Caribbean festival of Junkanoo (or "John Canoe"), a street parade with costumes and choreographed dance, which takes place in the Bahamas and other places in the English-speaking Caribbean on the days between Christmas and New Year's Day. It is said that enslaved Ahanta people likely brought the festival to the Caribbean in the first decades of the 1700s, when enslavers like Edward Long first remarked on it. That was roughly the time that John Conny was amassing his fleet of canoes that he used for river trade as well as for ferrying European ships at Cape Three Points. Long wrote:

> In the towns, during Christmas holidays, they have several tall ro-
> bust fellows dressed up in grotesque habits, and a pair of ox-horns
> on their head, sprouting from the top of a horrible sort of vizor,
> or mask, which about the mouth is rendered very terrific with
> large boar-tusks. The masquerader, carrying a wooden sword in
> his hand, is followed with a numerous croud of drunken women,
> who refresh him frequently with a cup of aniseed-water, whilst he
> dances at every door, bellowing out John Connu! with great vehe-
> mence. . . . This dance is probably an honorable memorial of John
> Conny, a celebrated cabocero at Tres Puntas [Three Points] in
> Axim, on the Guiney Coast; who flourished about the year 1720.
> He bore great authority among the Negroes of that district.[31]

Historically, this week between Christmas and New Year was the time of year that enslaved people in the Caribbean could not be expected to work and also the time that the Ahanta threw fancy

Junkanoo festival celebrants, Kingston, Jamaica, Christmas 1975 (digitized from Kodachrome original). *Photo by WikiPedant at Wikimedia Commons*

dress festivals on the Gold Coast. Like the carnival traditions that occur later in the winter, such festivals were often used to subvert the social order, providing a controlled time and place for people at its very bottom to vent some of their frustrations with support from their wider community and protection from the wrath of the enslavers and others with power over them. Over time, as Caribbean nations took their independence, the festival was used as "an agent for social change and as a vehicle to prod the Government into effective action."[32] In post-emancipation Jamaica, Black Jamaicans who were excluded from the formal political process used the festival as a vehicle of expressing their concerns to the Kingston Common Council.[33]

As a result of John Conny's eventual downfall in 1726, the remaining unaffiliated European slave-trading merchants who cut into the profits of the official European slave-trading companies found themselves without their main trading partner in Africa. Without Black Bart's pirates to draw the attention of the naval ships, these free trading ships also increasingly found themselves the target of harassment, and their numbers declined. The Dutch West India Company was able to reenter the trade as England's largest competition.

With Black Bart and John Conny—the two largest threats to the nationalized European slave-trading systems—eliminated, the Dutch and English rivalry reinvigorated, each nation once again vying for the most favorable trading relationships and forts on West Africa's coast. To remain competitive after having fallen so far behind their initial goals, the Dutch and English sought to systematize and grow their trade, and the other slave-trading nations followed suit as demand in the Americas vastly outstripped supply. With the instability in the Gold Coast's western region, Europeans turned to markets further east. William Snelgrave, the English ten-percenter slave trader sailing under Humphry Morice who in 1719 had been captured by the pirate Captain Howell Davis in Sierra Leone, began writing once more about his ventures on the coast of West Africa. Like Houstoun and Smith, he was convinced that a new, glorious era in human trafficking had emerged for the British Empire.

Chapter Nine

―――――――――――――――○―――――――――――――――

The Return of
William Snelgrave

IN 1727, HUMPHRY MORICE sent arguably the most seasoned English legacy veteran of the Atlantic slave trade, William Snelgrave, back to West Africa. Snelgrave took the three-hundred-ton slave ship *Katherine*, which had space for more than six hundred enslaved captives in its hold. Politically, much had changed in the decade since Snelgrave had been attacked by Captain Howell Davis's pirates in Sierra Leone.

Although the route to West Africa from London was always the same, his stops were different. The *Katherine* sped past Sierra Leone and Cape Three Points and the fort formerly known as Great Fredericksburg (now called Fort Hollandia) without stopping for water. Snelgrave ignored the seat of Britain's trade in West Africa, Cape Coast Castle, and then also Anomabo, formerly the premier location for ten percenters to fill their holds. Instead, he sailed straight for Keta, in the Volta River region in the easternmost shores of the Gold Coast, making a brief stop to take on imprisoned captives before weighing anchor at Ouidah.* The city he found had changed drastically since he had last been there.

――――――――――――

* In US history, the port of Ouidah is perhaps most famous for being the port from which Redoshi, also known as Sally Smith, one of the last known American living survivors of the Atlantic slave trade, was taken. Redoshi was a captive from Benin who was kidnapped and smuggled to Mobile, Alabama, in 1860, more than fifty years after the slave trade to the United States had become illegal. She was twelve years old when her village was attacked by Dahomey and sold to the captain of the slave ship *Clotilda*, the last known ship to bring

When Black Bart sacked the town of Ouidah five years prior in 1722, the city had been the capital of the coastal Kingdom of Ouidah, and most of the enslaved captives sold there came from trade with the neighboring inland kingdom of Allada. The city of Ouidah served as the port and commercial center of the Kingdom of Ouidah, and four of the European slave-trading companies were allowed a presence there: Portugal, England, France, and the Dutch Republic. King Huffon lived further inland at the administrative center of Savi, where representatives from each of the European slaving companies jostled for his favor and gifted him expensive luxuries to be allowed access to his best trading partners and enslaved captives.

It was there that the Europeans built their forts, and the king's palace wrapped around the European forts so that he could surveil the movements of their employees. About twenty European personnel staffed each fort, plus one hundred or more African *gromettas* who took care of trade and kept alive the enslaved captives imprisoned there before they were marched down to Ouidah. Also serving the various forts were enslaved soldiers hailing from the Gold Coast because they were considered superior fighters.[1] To the north of the palatial compound and forts was the rest of the city, also walled off from the outside. Coastal Ouidah also was divided into various European sections, with a surrounding African town. It contained warehouses that could house thousands of captives and tons of trade goods. Many of the coastal residents were immigrants who had come seeking opportunities and jobs, such as canoe porters from the Gold Coast, as well as transient merchants, messengers, administrators, fishers, farmers, and religious clergy.

The layouts of Ouidah and Savi together provide many clues about the power dynamics in the city where Europeans were com-

---

enslaved Africans to North America. Redoshi lived through emancipation, Reconstruction, Jim Crow, and the Great Depression and was mentioned by Zora Neale Hurston in *Barracoon: The Story of the Last "Black Cargo."* She was one of the founders of AfricaTown, a historic community formed by Africans who were on the *Clotilda*, three miles north of Mobile. In 2019, Redoshi became famous nationwide when Newcastle University issued a press release highlighting her life (www.ncl.ac.uk/press/articles/archive/2019/04/slave/). See Sylviane A. Diouf, *Dreams of Africa in Alabama: The Slave Ship* Clotilda *and the Story of the Last Africans Brought to America* (Oxford: Oxford University Press, 2007).

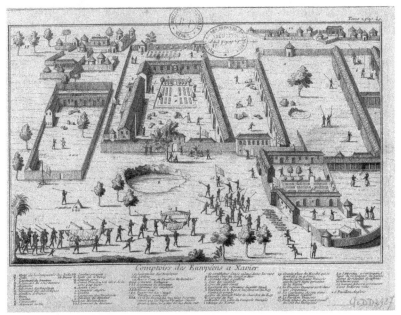

Trading posts of the Europeans at Savi, compiled by Jean-Baptiste Labat in 1730. European traffickers were kept separated in their assigned quarters, and their movement was restricted according to the will of the king. Some labels of note: (A) trading post of the French; (1) Trading post of the English; (aa) Trading post of the Dutch; (aaa) Trading post of the Portuguese; (eee) Lodgings of the enslaved captives (each European company had its own lodging place for captives); and (17) the entrance that Europeans used to access the space. *Comptoirs des européens à Xavier. View of Savi (Benin) published in Paris by Jean-Baptiste Labat based on material by Renaud des Marchais. Bibliothèque nationale de France, département Cartes et plans, GE DD-2987 (8233). Public domain*

pelled by treaty to get along.† European slave traders navigated the labyrinthine corridors of Savi to arrange trade and payments with the king, while employees at Ouidah managed the loading and movement of captives and goods. More than ten thousand enslaved

---

† In fact, in 1714, King Huffon had an English slave trader forcibly deported after a spat between the French and English traders in Ouidah. The intense competition among the Portuguese, French, Dutch, and English there made it possible for him to assert his authority in this way, and after the western region of the Gold Coast became unstable, his power only grew.

captives left Ouidah each year by the 1690s. King Huffon believed that allowing stone forts on the coast would make the Europeans "masters of his port," so he refused them until Black Bart's devastating 1722 attack.[2] This attack made clear some of the disadvantages of concentrating the trade in enslaved captives in one port, rather than spreading it throughout multiple ports like the English and Dutch were able to do on the Gold Coast.

Two years after Black Bart's attack in March 1724, the Kingdom of Allada, which used the city of Ouidah as its main port and market for the captives it sold, experienced a crisis similar to that of the Ashanti—several dependencies wanted either to become independent or to usurp the throne. Allada was sacked by a joint force including the new young upstart, King Agaja of Dahomey. Bullfinch Lambe, a slave trader with the Royal Africa Company (RAC) taken captive during this conflict described it to William Smith in a letter, telling him, "there was scarce any stirring for Bodies without Heads; and had it rain'd blood, it could not have lain thicker on the ground."[3] Dahomey's forces took eight thousand prisoners of war and a large quantity of guns and cannons.

If it weren't for the Alladan captives of war, this conflict would have stalled the slave trade at Ouidah. The new King Hussar of Allada didn't have the trade connections of his brother, so once the war captives from Allada had all been sold into the Atlantic slave trade six months later, his power waned. This allowed the Dahomeans to return, with King Agaja at the helm, and take Allada from Hussar. The deposed Hussar appealed to the neighboring Oyo Kingdom for help, who sent a horseback cavalry, but Agaja's forces prevailed, and in 1726, he became the new ruler of Allada. Normally, this type of violent instability kept Europeans away, but King Agaja was a different sort of ruler who piqued the interest of Humphry Morice, William Snelgrave, and the European powers desperate for strong allies.

DAHOMEAN CONQUEST

King Agaja annexed Allada and claimed the royal compound as his new seat of power. He took advantage of the bitter historical divisions among the southern leaders who had competed with one another for decades and therefore didn't aid one another when Agaja's forces attacked, conquering them one by one. As the late Yoruba historian Isaac Adeagbo Akinjogbin wrote, "The presence of the European in Aja country not only weakened internal administration but made inter-kingdom co-operation well-nigh impossible."[4]

On March 9, 1727, Agaja took and destroyed Savi, the seat of Ouidah's kingdom. The European factories burned to the ground. Encouraged by this easy defeat, King Agaja's troops marched to the coast and attacked the forts at the city of Ouidah. Although the Portuguese fort was destroyed and its cannon carried north into the interior, Agaja ordered the White slave traders of the compound to remain unharmed.[5]

The Dahomean conquest of Allada and Ouidah are considered watershed events in West African history. King Agaja developed an expansionist policy to rival that of King Opoku Ware of Ashanti. Like the Ashanti, the Dahomey took the European slave trade into account throughout their expansion process: the Ashanti had taken advantage through their fort controlled by their loyal ally John Conny at Cape Three Points, and the Dahomey used Ouidah to access European arms and offload war captives and others they deemed undesirable. When Agaja took Savi and Ouidah, five thousand were killed and more than ten thousand were captured, most of whom were fed into the slave trade. Forty European traffickers were among the captured, though they were released two weeks later.[6]

William Snelgrave's 1727 visit to Ouidah coincided with the first year of King Agaja's reign there. The last time Snelgrave had been sent to Ouidah was a decade before in 1717, right after he was released from his ordeal with the pirates in Sierra Leone. Back then, Snelgrave wrote of the previous king, Huffon, in the least flattering terms, calling him "a monster of nature."[7] Huffon had created a series of cumbersome rules and regulations around the trade that made life difficult for the Europeans at Savi and Ouidah. Snelgrave had survived being taken by pirates, having most of his cargo stolen by them, losing members of his crew to them, and then encountering the similarly pirated *Elizabeth* in time to witness and punish a deadly revolt instigated by the enslaved, only to discover that, thanks to the pirates, most of the forts on the coast where he usually stopped were emptied of enslaved people to bring onboard. After all of this, he found King Huffon's policies incredibly inconvenient. Like many European slave traders, Snelgrave resented powerful Africans who were able to thwart his goals and outright deny him his objectives.

This time, Snelgrave's visit felt decidedly different. He had been given the ship *Katherine*, a behemoth of a ship that easily could carry six hundred or more captives onboard. Snelgrave was under instructions from Morice to leave Africa for the British-controlled island of Antigua only when its hold was full.[8]

When Snelgrave arrived at Ouidah and witnessed the effects of the Dahomean conquest, with vast fields strewn with human remains, he commented on the devastation he saw in Ouidah, Savi, and Allada, which he called "a very great ruin'd Town."[9]

Seeing that there was nothing for him at Ouidah, he sailed forty miles onward, hoping that the port town of Jakin (now called Godomey) might have the large number of captives that he was after. At Jakin, however, a messenger from Allada found him and invited him to meet with the new king. When Snelgrave wavered, the messenger threatened that to refuse King Agaja might mean the end of his career, so Snelgrave packed his bags with the best Persian linens he carried onboard, as well as the ship's drum and some pocket pistols as gifts for the king. He also brought along a notebook so that he could create a diary that would help other slave traders working for Humphry Morice secure the best deals at Ouidah under its new rulership. He then hired a hammock carried by servants and traveled more than forty miles in this manner, which he called the "usual way of travelling in this Country for Gentlemen either white or black."[10]

Upon Snelgrave's arrival at Allada, he was struck by the large number of flies that seemed to be everywhere. When he was accompanied to King Agaja's gate, he understood the source: two large piles of human heads, which, the interpreter told him, were from sacrifices for Agaja's gratitude for his victory during the conquest of Ouidah. Naturally, this left an impression on the English slave trader. Still, when he was granted his audience with King Agaja, he was ready to bargain and get on the new king's good side. In his typical fashion, Snelgrave regaled readers with colorful details. Of his first meeting with Agaja, Snelgrave said that the King was

> full bodied; as near as I could judge about forty five years old. His face was pitted with the Small pox; nevertheless there was something in his countenance very taking and withal majestic. Upon the whole I found him the most extraordinary Man of his Colour, that I had ever conversed with.[11]

Each day, Snelgrave wrote down the conversations he had with Agaja, creating the only source that extensively quotes the king's words. That makes it a very uncommon, if untrustworthy source, since so few words of coastal West Africans from the 1720s were recorded and preserved. Snelgrave mentioned that the king stated, "as I was the first English Captain he had seen, he would treat me as a young Wife or Bride, who must be denied nothing at first."[12] Decidedly flattered, Snelgrave lowered his guard, which had the effect King Agaja had hoped. This part of the diary—in which Snelgrave and Agaja negotiate customs, prices of captives, and trading gifts—is the most well-developed section, revealing that Agaja was incredibly savvy and not as vulnerable to Snelgrave's attempts at flattery as Snelgrave was to his. Snelgrave tried to negotiate lower customs and better prices for captives, but the two men went around in rhetorical circles. As the historian Neil Polhemus says, "Agaja responded as we would expect from a powerful warlord that had just slaughtered some ten thousand innocent [Ouidahns] to gain unrestricted access to the European coastal trade."[13] Snelgrave also tried to secure deals for all the Humphry Morice ships, but Agaja rebuffed him. Snelgrave noted that the king told Snelgrave he should "be satisfied with my own good fortune."[14] Snelgrave attempted to complain about Ouidah's previous King Huffon, hoping that Agaja would want to differentiate himself from his predecessor, but Agaja refused to take the bait. In the end, Snelgrave failed to meaningfully lower the custom requirements or the price of enslaved captives or to achieve a bargain for other Humphry Morice ships. Still, Agaja did promise to protect the European traders that Morice sent his way and agreed to fill the hold of the *Katherine* with hundreds of captives—a significantly large number for a single stop on the West African coast.[15]

Throughout his narrative, Snelgrave often gave the impression that the Dahomeans were a warrior culture that enjoyed the slave trade and conquest as a way of life. He greatly admired King Agaja and the stability in trade that his consolidation of power could bring to the British. He waxed enthusiastically about the militaristic culture of the Dahomey, and how their entire society was set up around the slave trade, because it was something the Dahomean and English cultures had in common. However, William Smith, the surveyor tasked by the RAC with assessing their forts in West Africa, described it differently. After his visit to Ouidah in the same year as Snelgrave, he wrote, "The discerning natives account it their greatest unhappiness that they were ever visited by Europeans. They say that we Christians introduced the traffick of slaves and that before our coming they lived in Peace."[16]

As before, Snelgrave's political and economic interests as an active slave trader and antiabolitionist account for the inconsistencies between his observations and those of other Englishmen present at the time. Snelgrave blamed Ouida's previous King Huffon for his own conquest, claiming that Huffon had refused to grant Agaja and the Dahomeans access to coastal trade. However, Snelgrave also mentioned two Dahomean agents of Agaja, named Zunglar and Buttenoe, who were stationed at Ouidah under King Huffon and trading on Agaja's behalf.[17] In these inconsistencies are key insights into the ways the bloody conclusion of the Battle of Cape Lopez reshaped aspects of the trading culture in West Africa, which pushed Britain to the forefront of the trade and enabled them to spread their preferred form of chattel slavery throughout the Americas.

Historians are in agreement that Snelgrave's accounts were exaggerated and contradictory in order to both paint the old Kingdom of Ouidah as a failure and to promote the favorability of the slave trade at Ouidah under the Dahomey. Long-term African self-governance and sovereignty was no good for the Europeans, who feared another John Conny. Under Huffon, there had been more peace. Now, Agaja was a usurping newcomer on the throne with many fires to put out in the hinterlands, and Snelgrave hoped this might give Europeans, especially the English, a bit more room to maneuver.

For example, later that year, a horseback cavalry of the Oyo, Dahomey's rivals, attacked a caravan that was carrying several of King Agaja's wives, whom the cavalry beheaded. Agaja left the coast, heading north to hunt down the Oyo regiment and secure his new expansive kingdom. In his absence, the English—both employees of the Royal Africa Company and those of Humphry Morice—were able to grow their spheres of influence in the region. King Agaja often left Savi and Ouidah to protect the swelling borderlands of his empire; keeping the Europeans in line upon his return presented a difficult problem.[18]

EUROPEAN BODY HORROR AND THE SLAVE TRADE

Finished with negotiations, Snelgrave packed his things on April 12, 1727, at noon, when the captains of Dahomey returned to Ouidah from the country of Tuffoe in the north with their troops. The soldiers were decked out in shields and military gear more elaborate than what Snelgrave had seen on the Gold Coast among the professional soldiers ("the best Soldiers of all the Blacks," he wrote[19]). The Dahomey army consisted of three thousand regular troops armed with muskets and swords, attended by "ten thousand, at least, who carried Baggage, Provisions, dead Peoples Heads."

Snelgrave described this grisly procession and the ritualized nature of the soldiers' behavior at the king's gate (which he described as four times as large as Tower Hill, the execution site next to the Tower of London), which involved a procession, a drill, prostration, gunshots, and the sacrifice of a number of enslaved captives, which he believed was the reason King Agaja had kept him there for an extra day—to witness the spectacle and report home of the king's might. Snelgrave duly reported that four hundred war captives were sacrificed that day, and then repeated an exaggerated claim that four thousand had been sacrificed when Dahomey conquered Ouidah.[20] He wrote that war captive sacrifice "had ever been the custom of their nation."[21] In later parts of the text, however, he seems to agree that it was King Agaja who introduced this practice earlier in the 1720s.[22] Indeed, King Huffon was not known for engaging in this practice. Snelgrave remarked "this sight was well worth seeing even by us Europeans."[23] Of King Agaja, he said that aside from allowing his people to "slaughter the poor slaves as they did," he saw "nothing else that could be reckon'd barbarous in him."[24]

By invoking Tower Hill, the site of execution of prisoners of status back in England, Snelgrave reminded the reader that both he and Agaja came from cultures in which public spectacles of death were common tools of state control. He also drew a comparison in the readers' minds between Dahomean ritual sacrifice and British execution. This differentiated King Agaja, who engaged in human sacrifice that was "well worth seeing," from other African rulers who engaged in human sacrifice, whom Snelgrave described as "barbarous" and "brutish." The distinction between the two for Snelgrave seemed to lay solely in whether the act served or hindered the European trade in enslaved Africans.

Human sacrifice existed in the earliest history of almost all peoples in the world, including the English. Not only that, but Snelgrave himself was an agent of death, making gruesome examples of captives who resisted their enslavement onboard Humphry Morice ships and ordering captives who became weak or died thrown overboard to the shark frenzies.[25] The description of the militarized ritual of killing of war captives was placed in Snelgrave's narrative to serve a direct purpose that was adjacent to but separate from the other instances of human sacrifice that he described in other parts of his published narrative. These depictions had little to do with the way Africans were but spoke more to the ways Europeans were.

Most contemporary European sources about this phenomenon are unclear about what the eyewitnesses had witnessed. Many Europeans did not understand the societies or the function that ritualized killings of any type played within them. The lack of understanding in turn created myths about the slave trade during the early half of the eighteenth century, when numbers of enslaved captives being sold into the trade increased exponentially in many regions of West Africa, courtesy of the Battle of Cape Lopez and defeat of John Conny.

Several European sources also lumped in the practice of human sacrifice with cannibalism, about which Europeans—such as the pirates in Black Bart's crew—expressed terror, despite no recorded instances of the cannibalization of Europeans in precolonial West Africa.[26] Most likely these fears originated from the Caribbean, where the practices of anthropophagy among the Indigenous populations took on a mythology among Europeans and their descendants. This mythology was deeply intertwined with exploitation and colonialism among conquering settler populations beginning with the Spanish contact: Spain's queen had allowed Indigenous peoples of the Americas to be enslaved only if they were found to be engaging in cannibalism. The economic advantages of the enslavement of Native populations caused the Spanish to greatly exaggerate and fabricate reports of the practice, and so Europeans of other nations followed suit to justify Native enslavement.[27]

Similar justifications for enslavement occurred in West Africa, regarding both cannibalism and human sacrifice, both of which Snelgrave certainly sensationalized in his narrative. In the preface, he claims that it was practiced not only by Dahomey, but other places where he had seen this "most incredible and shocking" practice.[28] In several places in his account of sailing the West African coast, he made note of it. How and where in the narrative he did so reveals more about the European projections and interests in the eighteenth-century slave trade than anything else.

Take, for example, the story relayed to the naval surgeon John Atkins by Captain Harding, an English ten percenter who piloted the slave ship *Robert*, which first appears in chapter 5. Captain Harding stopped at Sierra Leone and purchased enslaved captives from Old Captain Crackers, including Captain Tomba, the freedom fighter from northern Sierra Leone's rice country who had been leading raids against the slavers attacking his homeland. Tomba led a shipboard insurrection that Harding thwarted by exercising vicious corporal punishment, including forcing the rebels to consume the raw and bloody internal organs of one of the victims while the other African captives were forced to watch. This wasn't an act of African barbarism or cannibalism, but a European one, and it wasn't an isolated incident, but one of many.

Take also the account of the surveyor William Smith of the RAC, who left England the same year as Snelgrave, in August 1726 on a RAC ship, to take inventory of the changes in their settlements on the coast of West Africa. Like Snelgrave, he too noted the most shocking things he saw and heard during his travel along the West African coastline from Sierra Leone to the Gold Coast and further east. (In fact, a couple of phrases in his paragraph-long title promise and advertise the salacious details: *Whatever Else Is Memorable among the Inhabitants* and *Great Variety of Entertaining Incidents, Worthy of Observation*). In 1979, scholars found Smith to be a plagiarist, cherry-picking many of the shocking events from similar narratives to pad his own.[29] This makes his source one of the more valuable ones for analyzing the European slave traders' obsessions with body horror, cannibalism, and human sacrifice, as the incidents he chose to steal from others are what he deemed most memorable.

When Smith arrived at Cape Three Points (at which point John Conny had been gone for more than two years), he mentioned that he stopped at Conny's Castle, now named Fort Hollandia, and a canoe came to his ship to let him know that if he wanted wood or water they would supply him "at a very dear rate."[30] Smith recorded some gossip that he had heard about John Conny, there still being much talk about the war between Conny's people, the Ahanta, and the Dutch in the area. According to Smith, the war:

> lasted some Years, and cost the Dutch a great deal of Blood and Money. On the other Hand, Conny, flush'd with many Victories over the Dutch, became a mortal Enemy to them, having pav'd a little Path from the Outside Gate to the Inner Apartments of his Castle, with Dutchmens Sculls, slain in his Engagements with them: He had a large Dutchman's Scull tipp'd with Silver, which he us'd as a Punch Bowl. However, in the Year 1724, he was beaten out of his Castle, and fled up in the [Fante] Country from the incensed Dutch.[31]

These ghastly details—the skull paving stones in an area where Conny would tread on them daily and the use of a skull as a punch bowl—are some of the most repeated and emphasized details in English depictions of King John Conny. They echo the words of the surgeons John Atkins, who first noted a similar story in 1722, and James Houstoun, who visited Cape Three Points in 1724 and declined to sip punch from the silver-plated Dutchman's skull.‡ The reasons for these repeated details across many narratives are partly because they are so shocking and made for great reading back in Europe and the Americas. Another reason was that savvy West Africans were masters at exploiting European fears of body horror and grisly depictions of extreme violence that played on or brought to mind the deep-seated terror in Europeans of cannibalism.

Along with the trope of the cannibal came connotations of ferocity and the inability to bargain or reason with Africans on European terms. This tapped into bigger colonial fears that existed in the minds of Europeans everywhere: that the peoples of Africa, Asia, and the Americas would hold onto their sovereignty. Europeans wrote the same way about John Conny of Africa as they did about Admiral Khanoji Angre of the Maratha Navy in India, the Barbary rulers of North Africa, and the many Indigenous American and Australian rulers with whom they struggled for territorial control and access to resources.[32]

Extreme violence was not uncommon on the Gold Coast (and indeed became more common as the slave trade ramped up), and prior to Conny's taking of the castle as his own, there was no evidence that he was a particularly bloodthirsty or violent ruler. In fact, the Brandenburg factors who worked with him during the first years of the 1700s expressed admiration of his keen business sense, wisdom, and networking capabilities, even though he often conflicted with them. Even Nicholas Dubois, who frequently found himself undermined and outmaneuvered by Conny, wrote flatteringly about him in his letters to Prussia. Conny had lived a long time among Europeans—Portuguese, Dutch, English, and Prussian—and

---

‡ It also echoes an event that happened in Saint Anne, Jamaica, in the early 1700s. Some "Coromantin Negroes"—the English term for the Akan people of the Gold Coast, of which John Conny's Ahanta also belonged—attacked a "Mr. B.," a "gentleman distinguished for his humanity toward his slaves"—as the enslaver and historian Edward Long put it—while he was sleeping. The rebels cut off his head, sawed his skull in half, and "made use of it as a punch-bowl." Edward Long credits this same group of Africans with the creation of the Junkanoo or "John Canoe" festival in honor of John Conny. See Edward Long, *The History of Jamaica or, General Survey of the Antient and Modern State of the Island: With Reflections on Its Situation, Settlements, Inhabitants, Climate, Products, Commerce, Laws, and Government*, vol. 2 (London: T. Lowndes, 1774), 424–25, 446–47.

understood their desires well. He styled himself like John Cabes, the powerful Komendan intermediary who played favorites but ultimately valued himself and his people ahead of his European business partners. For decades, Conny traded and warred with various European groups, furnishing his allies with all they demanded of him. Would it not make sense that he also understood their fears just as well as he understood their desires and that he manipulated the Europeans to serve his purposes? Conny was, after all, older and more experienced than the European traders on his coast, with a lifetime of European interactions under his gold belt.

During the earlier, seventeenth-century slave trade, there is comparatively little mention of cannibalism in sources. When it occurred, it was most commonly thought of as fetish—a substance that contains innate magical power or essence that can be transferred. In the documents of the European slave traders in both the Kingdom of Ouidah and on the Gold Coast, there are numerous mentions of the fetish and of Europeans partaking in the fetish before being allowed to trade. For example, when the Prussian soldier Otto Friedrich von der Groeben attempted to establish trade relationships in Ahanta with John Conny's people during the late 1600s, one of Conny's predecessors demanded that von der Groeben "take fetish with him." This fetish was an object or a piece of an object that had significance to the wearer. For example, someone who held the leopard sacred and wanted to become imbued with the characteristics of the leopard might carry its claw or tooth as their fetish. When promises were being made, the person would shave off a tiny part of their fetish and mix it with ingredients believed to have special powers, which would be swallowed by both parties. The ingredients varied from culture to culture and even person to person; on the Gold Coast among people dealing with European slave traders, gunpowder was very popular. The fetish ritual assured that the persons making a deal pledged their honesty to the highest power. Once von der Groeben understood this, most traders with the Prussian Brandenburg African Company insisted that the ritual swallowing of the fetish became part of the contractual routine between the Ahanta and Prussians. The Prussians equated African fetish with Europeans valuing signatures on written contracts, and believed in doing both when making deals in Africa.[33] On rare occasions, that fetish could come from the body of a person whom the fetish wearer greatly admired, and this was the extent of European slave traders' depictions of human-eating practices on the seventeenth-century Gold Coast.

The practice of the fetish was part of a collection of animistic beliefs prevalent in coastal West Africa. The Kingdom of Dahomey was located entirely in what is now the modern nation of Benin, the spiritual birthplace of West African vodun. Vodun is the umbrella term for the collection of ancestral beliefs and practices from West Africa that traveled with enslaved populations across the Atlantic and birthed a variety of syncretic religions in various places in the Americas, particularly in Haiti, the Dominican Republic, Cuba, Brazil, and the United States; in Louisiana, it is referred to as the more commonly recognized practice of voodoo.

An idea that evolved alongside these ancestral practices was that actions by the living could secure the favor of supernatural beings.[34] For example, a belief emerged that a person could be killed in order to deliver a message from someone in the living realm to someone in the non-living realm. Another belief connecting ritualized killings to ancestral practices was that a person sacrificed in this way could join someone recently deceased in the afterlife. For example, in Allada, some widows sacrificed themselves when their powerful husbands died.[35] Among the Ashanti on the Gold Coast, this practice also occurred at the funerals of powerful people. This made "human sacrifices" not wholly involuntary, since some people fought for the honor of accompanying a dead king or another important person into the afterlife. However, as the historian Robin Law points out, internalized societal expectations interfered with free will. It was usually lower-ranking people, as well as women (especially wives), who were reported to have volunteered.[36] Wives were not lower ranking as a whole—in fact, Dahomey was home to many women who outranked men in the administration and military.[37] However, the wives of the most powerful men did, in most cases, rank lower than their husbands.

HUMAN SACRIFICE AND THE
MILITARIZED WEST AFRICAN STATE

This increase in war captives helps account for why larger numbers of people were sacrificed over time in Dahomey: King Agaja's
militarized, expansion-focused leadership created larger numbers of
lower-ranking people. As Dahomey's military captured and enslaved
larger numbers of people, more were sold to Europeans into the
Atlantic slave trade. This in turn created greater wealth for the Dahomeans involved in the trade. In Dahomean society, with greater
wealth came the societal obligation to take more wives. Households
with multiple wives tended to be larger in general, which increased
the avenues of economic, political, and military connection and
success for each family.§

With this increase in wealth in Dahomey also came the expec-
tation of increased conspicuous consumption: showing off social
status by publicly displaying, using, and discarding items related to
wealth. This practice was culturally common along West Africa's
coast, and the most successful leaders engaged in it in the most
memorable ways to increase their social standing and to impress
or entice potential allies. John Conny comes to mind as an expert
in this practice as evidenced by the way he displayed his pregnant
wives, draped entirely in gold chains, and his lavish hospitality, offering visitors selections of rare European wines, American tobacco,
and various forms of animal protein and fat, like cheese and butter,
and even fishing rights in his river. Conspicuous consumption gave
access to more wives, more enslaved members of the household,
more trade relationships, and stronger military alliances. It increased the chances that one's descendants would remain wealthy.

---

§ At one point, an unnamed military captain and William Snelgrave had dinner, and Snelgrave brought out a savory pie that had been prepared and preserved by his wife for him to
take to Africa. The captain, who enjoyed this novelty dish, asked how many wives Snelgrave
had. Snelgrave wrote, "I told him we were allowed by our Laws but one, on which he fell a
laughing, saying, he had five hundred and wished fifty of them could prepare such meat for
him as mine had done" (William Snelgrave, *A New Account of Some Parts of Guinea, and the
Slave-Trade: Containing, I. The History of the Late Conquest of the Kingdom of Whidaw by
the King of Dahomè . . . II. The Manner How the Negroes Become Slaves . . . III. A Relation
of the Author's Being Taken by Pirates, and the Many Dangers He Underwent* [London: Frank
Cass, 1971], 79).

This was critical when wealthy leaders died. Wives and enslaved members of the household were often sacrificed at funerals, since only the wealthiest families could afford such a loss. Wealthy families did this because the power vacuum left by the deaths of heads of households often created political instability and uncertainty in the population. Conspicuous consumption at funerals was a means of advertising the wealth of the successors and thereby ensuring that divisive competitors from within would not take advantage of this transition in leadership to challenge the successor. In these ways, sacrifice of wives and the enslaved members of the household demonstrated to everyone who came to the funeral the level of wealth and influence the surviving members of the family still held. The increase in the scale of human sacrifice in Dahomey and other coastal West African regions is linked to the increase in wealth, much of which came directly from the increasing scale of trade with Europeans.[38]

Historians believe that the proliferation of sources that describe these sacrifices reflected the changing European attitudes toward African societies as the slave trade ramped up.[39] In other words, the increase in European feelings of racial superiority that accompanied the slave trade led European observers—most of whom were invested in the slave trade—to emphasize the aspects of African societies that seemed particularly barbarous. This served to protect the morality of the slave trade and, later, colonialism, since antiabolitionists like Snelgrave tried to argue that the African captives who came to America had the "privilege" of escaping this violence and enjoying civilization.¶

The larger scale of sacrifice in 1700s coastal West Africa coincided with the dramatic rise in the slave trade, which was the direct

---

¶ More than 150 years later in 1897, the British attacked Benin using the practice of human sacrifice as an excuse to colonize the country—Britain's rulers wanted to "civilize" the region. However, a closer look at these ritualized killings shows that Benin's priests had been sacrificing people in desperation to repel the British conquering forces. See Robin Law, "Human Sacrifice in Pre-Colonial West Africa," *African Affairs* 84, no. 334 (1985): 63–67. These attitudes suggesting that Africans who experienced the horrors of enslavement or colonialism and their descendants were somehow privileged or should be grateful for the "civilizing" experience still regularly surface among politicians in the United States and other places where culture wars often take the place of political action. It's a mindset that can be traced directly to slavery and colonialism.

result of European interventions, like the Battle of Cape Lopez, to create economic stability on the coast through the eradication of perceived threats to the trade, like piracy and African sovereigns like John Conny, who refused European rules or attempts at systematization of the trade. European communication about these events and their interference with them all point to antiabolitionist justification for a rapidly increasing trade, the cruelty and scale of which turned the stomachs of increasingly larger segments of society in Europe and in the Americas.[40]

Over time, the public sacrifice of war captives signaled to the citizens and tributaries of expansionist states like Dahomey that the rulership was politically and militarily successful. This created an obligation to continue providing more war captives for sacrifice and for sale to justify waging the wars that made expansion possible. The larger numbers of wars and war captives economically stabilized European slave traders like Snelgrave, who for the first time were profiting hand over fist.

This cycle increased the militarization of these coastal African societies. The fact that they were built on military conquest and culture made them both powerful yet also vulnerable and dependent upon European trade. It isn't exactly as Walter Rodney described in the gun-slave cycle thesis, but the principle is identical.[41] War had become an economic, political, and existential necessity for Dahomey. If they stopped, they would be swallowed and enslaved by a competing empire, most likely the Oyo, and the Europeans would fight each other to create a trading relationship with the new victors. European guns exchanged for captives also diversified and added to African military tactics and strategies and affected the way militaries were organized (not just in Dahomey, but on the Gold Coast, too, with the Elmina *asafo*, for example). During John Conny's reign Europeans and Africans alike were shocked to see African troops so well versed in European weapons and tactics, but over time this became the new standard among coastal polities. It created greater difficulty for people from the regions like Captain Tomba's Koinadugu Plateau in Sierra Leone to fight back.[42]

Therefore, in the militarized West African state of Dahomey, human sacrifice stabilized the monarchy. As the Ashanti and

Ahanta knew well, succession was a stressful and precarious time in early-eighteenth-century coastal West Africa, where the throne came through conquest as often as it did through inheritance. King Agaja, himself a usurper, knew this and realized that his own claim to the throne could be challenged easily by a stronger competitor when he grew weak unless he created a wealthy ancestor cult.

Through human sacrifice Agaja sent large numbers of enslaved people into the afterlife to serve the important deceased people in his circle.[43] This cemented his power among the living. Departing from the tradition in Ashanti and the former state of Allada, Dahomeans sacrificed to royal ancestors, not to gods. This culture of royal sacrifice reinforced the legitimacy of Agaja's bloodline and effectively prevented succession instability.

How can we be sure of this? Native West African opposition to the practice came from people who disputed Agaja's royal power and challenged the militarization of society and his close relationships with European slave traders.[44] The link between human sacrifice and the slave trade was realized through the militarization of West African values and institutions that were directly encouraged by transatlantic slave trade.[45] In other words, the slave trade itself created the conditions for the large number of Agaja's war-captive sacrifices to the ancestors. Although West Africans criticized this practice, European slavers generally accepted the human sacrifice that upheld a steady flow of captives to trade or otherwise stabilized the trade. At the same time, sacrifice that destabilized or endangered the European slave trade—such as through subversive or rebellious African spiritual practice—was derided.

OBJECTIONABLE SACRIFICE

What illustrates this point best is the introductory vignette of Snelgrave's narrative, where he described how he interrupted an act of human sacrifice at Old Calabar (in coastal Nigeria) presented for the consumption of outraged Europeans. Back in 1704, he had seen evidence of child sacrifice in the region, and when he returned in 1713, he had the "good fortune" to intervene personally.

Snelgrave wrote that "tho' 'tis a long story, and therefore may not so well suit an Introduction, yet on account of the singular Circumstances wherewith it was attended, I believe the Reader may be pleased with it."[46]

A royal named Acqua who lived at the mouth of the Calabar River was invited to hear the music of the sailors onboard Snelgrave's Humphry Morice ship, the *Anne*. The king then invited the English trader ashore and Snelgrave went, but as he "knew" Acqua's people to be "fierce brutish Cannibals," the captain brought with him eleven personnel, "all well armed with Musquets [*sic*] and Pistols, which those savage People I knew were much afraid of."[47] He and King Acqua dined together and Snelgrave wrote that he spotted a toddler tied by the leg to a stake, with two priests standing by. The king confirmed that the child was to be sacrificed, and Snelgrave called to his crew to remove the child. The king's guard advanced on the English sailor with his lance, and Snelgrave took out his pistol. King Acqua rose from his throne, and Snelgrave told the interpreter that he would not hurt anyone as long as the king's guard did not. They had a protracted discussion about morality and ownership, which Snelgrave, an enslaver and slave trader, could not win. Eventually the argument was settled when Snelgrave offered to purchase the child. Payment was exchanged, and the English men took the child to the slave ship.

The men spent another hour with the king, treating him to the European liquor and foods they had brought. Snelgrave, afraid for his life, mentioned that he "took care not to drink any of his Palm Wine (. . . which they can artfully poison) under pretense, it did not agree with me. But my people did not spare it, drinking plentifully of it with his guards."

When they returned to the ship, Snelgrave told his gunner that he should "pitch on some motherly Woman, to take care of this poor child." As there were already women captives enslaved among the three hundred below deck on the *Anne*, the gunner replied that "he already had one in his eye."

It just so happened that the day before, Snelgrave had unknowingly purchased the mother of the child. The ship's surgeon had observed that she was lactating but with no child in sight. According to Snelgrave, as soon as this poor woman saw the child handed into the ship, she ran to the sailor and snatched the child from him. He wrote, "I think there was never a more moving sight than on this occasion, between the Mother and her little Son . . . especially when the linguist told her, I have saved her child from being sacrificed."

So far, the story reads like any "exotic" colonial White savior narrative: there is a child saved from certain death among African "witch doctors," a panicked mother, and a brave White man with a gun who stands up to a "barbarous" king by calling upon his Christian god and sense of morality and, when that fails, the superiority of capital. This emotional appeal to motherhood and the innocence of a young child in the face of a despot primed eighteenth-century English readers with a trope-packed, racist, emotionally charged tale crafted to invoke gratitude that men like Snelgrave existed to sell defenseless Africans away from these dire circumstances in Africa. Snelgrave actively produced racist ideas about Africans to convince readers that African captives were best suited for slavery's confines.[48] Snelgrave concludes the tale like this:

> Having at that time above 300 Negroes on board my Ship, no sooner was the Story known amongst them, but they expressed their Thankfulness to me, by clapping their Hands, and singing a Song in my praise. This affair proved of great service to us, for it gave them a good Notion of white Mens; that we had no Mutiny in our Ship, during the whole Voyage. I went from the River of Old Callebar, to the Island of [Antigua], where our Cargoe was sold; and upon my telling one Mr. Studeley this remarkable story, he bought the Mother and her Son, and was a kind Master to them.

The antiabolitionist message of the fabricated tale is unmistakable. Snelgrave, who was hyperaware of the dangers posed by slave ship insurrections, would not have allowed the mother of the child to freely roam the deck of his ship, where she would be able to jump overboard or charge at a crew member. Like most European slave ship captains, he knew that when given opportunities to do so, enslaved Africans took them.[49] In the Humphry Morice papers and several places in his narrative, Snelgrave wrote of the securities his crew put into place to prevent enslaved captives' uprising. He was a fervent advocate of manacles and of keeping the enslaved captives crammed below deck most of the time, allowing them above deck only when chained to others for exercise and feeding, including the forced feedings that he permitted onboard his ships. The larger the slave ship, the less time on deck he permitted the captives.

African captives onboard slave ships knew why they were there and what awaited them in the Americas, and they were aware that there would be no kind arms of Mr. Studeley. First of all, the Mr. Studeleys weren't kind—all enslavers participated in systems that stripped personhood from the people whose labor and futures they stole. There was no kindness in this, and many Europeans and settlers in the Americas who lived during this time period knew it and spoke out against it.[50] By the time captives were transferred to a slave ship, they had been attacked and assaulted by an army that destroyed their homes, marched in restrictive cuffles down the coast, and imprisoned in the dungeons of a fort until they were sold. They would be poked and prodded, kept in filth, and forced to submit to examinations and assault regularly until they were rowed to a slave ship. During that time, they met with many Africans who had regular contact with Europeans and some who had even been enslaved by them and managed to return home.[51] They knew about the emerging chattel slavery and that the men with the white wigs and the invasive surgeons at their sides were going to sell them and their legal personhood, too. Needless to say, short of releasing the captives or perhaps jumping overboard himself, there is nothing Snelgrave could have done to make them burst into applause for him.

The captives who were sold to Europeans knew about the different forms of enslavement that existed in West Africa and about those that they would face in the Americas. By the 1700s, slavery had become a way of life and a way of death for West Africa. Many people held enslaved status in West Africa, serving the European companies or one of the many local families that had settled near the European trading forts to grow their fortunes. Many enslaved people were tasked with caring for the unfortunate captives who would be sold into the Atlantic trade. Although both—those enslaved in Africa and those marked for the Americas—were considered "slaves" at the time, their lives were drastically different, and the systems that claimed their labor wildly diverged during the early 1700s and would continue to do so until the era of emancipation.

While in America the chattel system had begun to take root, in West Africa, enslaved people were still found in all occupations and positions in society and possessed many relative freedoms, as enslaved people did in the Roman Empire. Europeans writing home about those enslaved in West Africa said that they did not recognize what they saw in West Africa as enslavement; they said that the enslaved there were "slaves in name only."[52] That descriptor of course makes light of their status. Enslavement in West Africa was far from "in name only."

Rather, these European descriptions highlight the drastic differences that enslaved people in West Africa and in the Americas experienced in regard to quality of life and future prospects for themselves and for their descendants. Most forms of unfree labor in West Africa were not comparable to New World slavery. Africans in West Africa did not consider the enslaved who lived there as chattel. Rather, they were perceived as subordinate family members, with a social and even legal status similar to that of children or other dependents. Enslavement in West Africa did not mean immediate social degradation, and as in ancient Rome, it was not a permanent designation. The enslaved could and did hold power and important positions, and they frequently found their way out of enslavement by taking advantage of the economic opportunities or social connections and networks prevalent on the coast. Twists of fate could render someone enslaved or free, and some people experienced it in many ways and times during their lives, moving into and out of enslavement. Perhaps most important of all, the children of the enslaved in West Africa were born free and generally were not considered property of those who had enslaved their parents. Only across the Atlantic were people born into the status of enslavement.

European traffickers, especially those who had lived or worked in the Americas, certainly tried to push back against this African notion of enslavement. For them, creating a clear distinction between who was free and who was enslaved was preferable to the messy, confusing African hierarchies and kinship networks, which Europeans percieved as sources of eternal conflict. European slavers working for the Prussian, English, and Dutch companies often expressed the desire for clarity in status; African behaviors surrounding trade allow us to infer that West Africans did not organize their worlds to please Europeans nor did they care to provide Europeans with this advantage over them. The logic of the tale William Snelgrave spun for the introduction of his narrative does not pass scrutiny. What it does, however, is set the tone for a rapid increase in trade and the ensuing cultural ramifications in Europe and the Americas.

During a time of rapid growth in the Atlantic slave trade, what Europeans said about Africa was projection honed by desire for the tremendous riches that could be extracted from the continent. This is apparent in their maps of Africa and the Americas from the time period, which often reflected projections of their desire more than geographic reality.[53] So it was with much of the documents created during this time by the likes of William Snelgrave, John Atkins, William Smith, James Houstoun, and Chaloner Ogle. Most Europeans who dirtied their hands in Africa never saw those riches, but everyone working the slave trade knew someone who knew someone who struck it wildly rich. A mix of equal parts intense coercion and greed kept Europeans working the least desirable trade in the world. As the numbers of exported Africans increased, so did narratives like those of Snelgrave, which helped to soothe his empire's conscience as he padded its coffers.

William Snelgrave was born into the vocation of enslaver: his father, also named William Snelgrave, was first mate on a slave ship, and after he died in 1704, his son worked his way to captaincy. During his life, Snelgrave piloted a total of fourteen slave ship voyages, all between the years of 1701 and 1730. This was an unusually high number, considering the average length of a voyage, the rate of mortality among captains, and the high numbers who abandoned the trade after experiencing the horror of their first voyage. Snelgrave ended up trafficking around five thousand Africans to the Americas, mostly to Virginia and Jamaica.[54] His published accounts of his voyages also earned him a tidy sum, so by the time he retired, he was a wealthy man.

King Agaja would continue to rule Dahomey, expanding the empire and warring with the Oyo Empire to the East. The Oyo wanted the tribute that they had always received from the Aja kingdoms to which Agaja belonged. Agaja's attempts to renegotiate these terms led to war. In 1730, Huffon, the deposed king of Ouidah, took advantage of a weakness created by the Oyo to join forces with the British and French and retake his throne. Agaja asked the women of his empire to dress as male soldiers and march to reclaim Ouidah. Seeing the massive force, Huffon's forces retreated, ceding the area back to Agaja. With the aid of Portuguese traders, Agaja and the Oyo worked out a treaty, with Agaja's son Tegbessou living with the Oyo as incentive for honoring it. For the remainder of his life, Agaja consolidated his expanding kingdom while trading with the European companies. After his death in 1740, Tegbessou left Oyo and took up his father's legacy.

Like the downfall of the Ahantan king John Conny of Cape Three Points, the exchange between William Snelgrave and King Agaja after the Battle of Cape Lopez is but one very small story within the larger story of the Atlantic slave trade. However, it is emblematic of the wider processes that occurred throughout the trade's entirety in every region that it touched: the destruction of forces that destabilized the trade and the increasing number of African captives forcibly taken from the continent by the British. The stories of Black Bart, John Conny, and William Snelgrave concern trade in the regions of Sierra Leone, the Gold Coast, and Benin—the regions from which most of the enslaved people in the United States and the English-speaking Caribbean hailed—because this is mainly where the British were able to obtain enslaved captives for their experiment in the most pernicious institution the world had ever seen before: the American chattel slavery system.

Chapter Ten

─────────○─────────

Consequences

As in West Africa, the 1720s marked a definitive change in the world. From the 1722 Battle of Cape Lopez to the 1727 Dahomean takeover of Ouida, the slave trade in the Atlantic increased and would not stop increasing until the era of abolition. Captain Chaloner Ogle's victory at Cape Lopez allowed the British Empire to expand its trade in African captives at a time when its primary competitor, the Dutch Republic, was struggling with John Conny's free-trade policy reducing Dutch trade. Fear for Anglo supremacy pushed the Dutch to rearrange the face of the western region of the Gold Coast to surmount Conny once and for all. At the same time, to the east, Dahomey fought its way to the coast, took over the stable trade at Ouidah, and increased it. Both the Gold Coast and Benin saw dramatic increases in slave trade activity in the 1720s and 1730s after the twin threats of Black Bart and John Conny were eliminated.

The result? Slave traders like William Snelgrave were able to bring larger, slower ships and forcibly remove larger numbers of enslaved captives to sell in the Americas. This increased demand in Africa put pressure on the population, and West Africa saw an uptick in slave raiding and politics that kept some groups of African peoples (relatively and temporarily) safe at the expense of others. Entire states like Ahanta collapsed, redirecting trade routes. What was once a thriving Ashanti trade to the Pokesu coast at Fort Great Fredericksburg became little more than a Dutch watering hole. The

geographically closest new locus of trade in the area became Dahomean trade to Ouidah's coast under the rule of King Agaja. Like
Agaja, new rulers emerged, utilizing strategies with Europeans that
created new patterns of consumption, economy, and culture. It affected every aspect of life in West Africa from economy to religion
and gender relations.[1] Ultimately these changes coerced coastal
societies to militarize, which weakened the region over time as war
captives were killed or sold, leaving West Africa with fewer fighters
to resist future colonial interference from Europe.[2]

In Europe, this newfound stability in the slave trade also generated wide-ranging commercial, cultural, and political legacies. All
European nations that took part in the slave trade profited, though
perhaps none more handsomely than the British. Like Captain
Chaloner Ogle, many Europeans who worked in proximity to the
slave trade in Africa became involved in politics, and politicians
throughout Europe often had robust connections to former enslavers and human traffickers. When Ogle sold the Black pirates from
Black Bart's crew into the slave trade and pocketed the profits and
then confiscated the gold that Black Bart had extorted from the
slave traders at Ouidah before the Battle of Cape Lopez, he justified his theft, explaining that someone of "his station" (meaning
soon to be promoted to admiral, knighted, and given a seat in Parliament) needed access to such astronomical funds.[3]

Recent efforts to calculate the immense wealth that Europeans
enjoyed at the expense of enslaved Africans are returning results
far beyond even the most liberal historians' estimates, and the vast
majority of cultural collections available to Europeans—of art,
scientific objects, books, and so forth—were amassed with funds
that came directly from plantations that functioned as forced-labor
camps for enslaved Africans.[4]

In the Americas, the systemization of the British trade specifically was the catalyst for the emergence of chattel slavery. Although
the British trade in enslaved Africans rose significantly, it still could
not keep up with demand in the British North American and Caribbean colonies. Simply put, Roman-inspired models for enslavement were not efficient in the eyes of British settlers. Planters who
had much to gain from those whom they enslaved did not want to

acknowledge the humanity of the enslaved at all. Settlers departed from the Roman-derived systems of slavery after the Battle of Cape Lopez and moved toward a legacy of total ownership and dominion over their involuntary workforce and any future descendants in what is now referred to as the chattel model.

ENSLAVEMENT BEFORE 1722

With this sustained increase in the trade came a demographic shift that would affect the culture of Atlantic enslavement, and this is where the fate of the United States comes into play. Before the eighteenth century and this dramatic shift, the Portuguese were the first and central European participants in the slave trade who set the tone for enslavement in the Atlantic world. They brought with them to the trade the Roman understanding of slavery. Under the systems of the Roman Empire, enslavement was often a temporary state of being, not a permanent identity. Enslavers could claim the labor of their enslaved, but not their full personhood. Enslaved people had a lesser status and fewer rights, yet some of their key human rights remained recognized. They could and did make use of the legal system, suing enslavers for cruel treatment, for their emancipation, or for the emancipation of their children.

The Portuguese enshrined this system of enslavement in West Central Africa and Brazil beginning in the 1500s. In the Atlantic world, enslaved people in Brazil frequently appear in court records from this earlier period all the way through abolition and emancipation, testifying against free people or enslavers and, in some cases, generating lawsuits against their enslavers or, more commonly, the enslavers of their children. Those enslaved in the worst positions were still legally guaranteed the right to nuclear familial integrity. Large swaths of the cultures in West Central Africa, Portugal, and Brazil recognized this, though many enslavers broke these laws when profit or convenience outweighed the legal consequences.[5]

Enslavement in the 1600s Dutch Atlantic world tended to follow suit. The Dutch began their forays into trafficking in West Africa by emulating their first competitors, the Portuguese, and also following their lead in the Americas, particularly in what would later become the United States.[6] On the Gold Coast, some Africans enslaved unlawfully by the Dutch were able to avail themselves of the Dutch courts to appeal for freedom.[7] In New Netherlands, in the area including parts of present-day New York and Delaware, records reflect enslaved people purchasing their freedom and formerly enslaved Africans marrying free Dutch people in the mid-1600s. Enslaved Africans and their descendants earned wages that they were permitted to keep, worshipped in the Dutch Reformed Church alongside White and free Black settlers, and some owned farmland in Manhattan. They appear with regularity in church and court records, testifying on their own behalf and insisting on their rights.[8] It is not until the English began importing Africans in its takeover of New Netherland in 1664 that more rigid race-based rules and racial designations took hold in the region.[9]

Within the Spanish Atlantic world, including Florida and what would become Texas, the situation was similar. Free Blacks held down the borderlands of empire in Spanish settlements, much like the Portuguese. In Florida, the most well-known example was Fort Mose, just north of Saint Augustine, which was composed largely of self-emancipating Afro-descended refugees formerly enslaved by settlers in the British North American territories. The Spanish Crown granted them freedom and citizenship and then armed them—if they converted to Catholicism and agreed to defend Spanish territory from the encroachment of English settlers to the north. No laws prohibiting interracial marriages existed there, and many such unions were performed right up until 1832, nine years after Florida became part of the United States. Compare this to other states in the US South, where it remained illegal until 1967.[10]

Enslavement in the French Americas also operated under the premise that the enslaved were to be treated as human beings with limited rights rather than viewed or treated as objects outright. The 1685 *Code Noir*, passed by King Louis XIV, was a treatise detailing the plethora of rights, punishments, and freedoms of the enslaved and formerly enslaved of the French Empire. As in the Dutch- and Spanish-occupied parts of North America but unlike in the British colonies, Black people in the French Empire could and did make use of the legal system for cases of torture, mutilation, or murder of the enslaved. They also were able to legally marry people of other races. The Code Noir even specified cases in which interracial marriage could be made mandatory: for example, a free man whose sexual assault of an enslaved woman resulted in pregnancy had to marry her to free the resulting child. (Less surprisingly, men could pay a heavy fine instead, ensuring that the wealthiest were not beholden to this law.) As in the Roman Empire, all those enslaved in the French Empire were granted automatic citizenship upon manumission, and formerly enslaved free persons of the French Empire were granted, in theory, the identical rights of any other French citizen. Institutionalized racism and the rapidly growing global anti-Black bias, however, often ran counter to these laws in the experience of people of African descent.[11]

By contrast, the British Empire were relative latecomers to the slave trade. They had been trading in Africa since the 1600s, but it took them longer to get a foothold in the trade. In the Atlantic world, they spent the first half of the seventeenth century battling the other European empires for Caribbean and West African territory and mercantile opportunities. Unlike their Portuguese, Spanish, Dutch, and French competition, Britain's colonies in North America were administered under a variety of companies and stakeholders, and each colony was created for its own purposes and therefore had its own regulations regarding enslavement. Each procured forced African labor in a variety of ways, often relying on the illicit inter-American market when the British Royal Africa Company (RAC) was unable to meet the voracious demand of colonists. As demand grew and supply did not keep up, colonists stripped more and more rights and freedoms from the enslaved populations to ensure maximum extraction of their labor and the labor of their children. In these ways, the aftereffects of the Battle of Cape Lopez had devastating consequences for what would become the United States.

Slave Trade Numbers

More than 12.5 million Africans were forcibly removed from West and West Central Africa throughout the Atlantic slave trade. Not nearly as many made it to the Americas. The numbers have been analyzed by every generation of scholars from the trade's inception until today. The human brain lacks the ability to comprehend horror on such an overwhelming scale, and often readers are unable to connect with the stories and the meaning they seek in extended statistical works. Rather than risk this, this section provides the briefest of background information about the numbers necessary for contextualizing the consequences of the tumultuous 1720s in West Africa.*

From Sierra Leone, the region where RAC Governor Plunkett toiled away rebuilding the burned factory at Bunce Island while Old Captain Crackers illicitly traded captured Africans like the freedom fighter Captain Tomba, a total of 388,771 people were taken. On the Gold Coast, where European forts saturated the landscape and John Conny was king in the 1710s and early 1720s, the number is around 1.2 million. From Benin, home of the Kingdom of Ouidah, Allada, and then Dahomey, nearly 2 million captives were forced onto European ships. In the Bight of Biafra, home to the River Calabar, the setting for Snelgrave's fictional story about the child he saved from sacrifice in the introduction of his antiabolitionist narrative, it was more than 1.5 million. The largest ports by far in terms of number of enslaved captives sold were in West Central Africa, the regions known as Kongo-Angola, where more than 5.5 million Africans were forced from their homes and onto ships. The regions of Senegambia, offshore Atlantic islands (such as Príncipe, where the pirate captain Howell Davis was killed by the Portuguese governor), the Windward Coast, and southeast Africa and Africa's Indian Ocean islands make up the remaining numbers. With numbers like this, it becomes easier to imagine how the violent loss of so many people decimated West African cultures.

When broken down by decade, the marked increases in the eighteenth-century slave trade can be seen more clearly. Between the 1690s (when 339,557 enslaved people were taken) and the 1740s (when the number had grown to 566,589), each decade averaged 58,000 more people sold than the previous one. The

---

* Unless otherwise noted, all numbers come from the Transatlantic Slave Voyages Database, and I encourage you to make your own investigations using the data: www.slavevoyages .org.

most profound increase during that time period was, as predicted, between the 1710s (1711–1720) and the 1720s (1721–1730): the number of enslaved captives forcibly removed from Africa rose by nearly 95,000. Some of this increase can be attributed to the surge of European slavers who came to West Africa after the British naval victory at the Battle of Cape Lopez (1722) drastically reduced the number of pirates on West Africa's coast. Another significant component of that increase came from the captives from the Dahomean takeover of the Kingdoms of Allada (1724) and Ouidah (1726). European traders, who had depended on the trade with the Ashanti until the end of John Conny's reign (1724), rushed to Ouidah to fill their ships.

In the Americas, the numbers of enslaved Africans who arrived were far more disparate; between the 1710s and the 1720s, the numbers remained steady among the Spanish and Portuguese colonies. The increases were most prevalent in British North America and the Anglo Caribbean, followed by the Dutch Americas, with far smaller increases in the French and Danish territories. Much of the large increase in captives removed from Africa during this period ended up in British and Dutch colonies, mostly traded by the British RAC, Dutch West Indies Company, the ten percenter companies that the British Crown allowed to trade, and the British and Dutch independent merchants called interlopers who engaged in trafficking without royal permit.

The way these numbers line up means that British North America, the British Caribbean, and the Dutch American colonies absorbed a comparatively large number of African captives from Sierra Leone, the Gold Coast, and Benin. In many cases, there were triple the number of new arrivals from Africa. In mainland North America, for example, the 1710s saw the arrival of 16,073 African captives. In the 1720s, that number swelled to 44,605. Most disembarked in the Chesapeake, though the Carolinas, Georgia, and the Gulf States together absorbed nearly 17,000. Of course, these numbers fail to account for the newly arrived Africans who were resold and transported to other locations.

Enslaved African Arrivals to Mainland North America

Years	Northern United States	Chesapeake	Carolinas/ Georgia	Gulf States	Unspecified (United States)
1711–1720	1,002	11,735	2,724	612	0
1721–1730	1,002	26,606	9,419	7,223	355

Note: All numbers from this table and in this section of the chapter were taken at the time of publication directly from the Transatlantic Slave Voyages Database, the largest, most complete, and up-to-date collection of information in existence from documented slave ships flying the flags of Portugal, Spain, England/Britain, France, the Dutch Republic, Sweden, Brandenburg, Denmark, and the United States. The numbers here are still on the conservative side, because many more African captives were transported in ships that were unmarked with no manifests, did not pay taxes, and therefore generated no official import records. The database is regularly updated as more evidence is found and is available at www.slavevoyages.org. I urge readers to check the database to see the most current counts.

The numbers indicate that in the 1720s, the British North American colonies that would become the United States absorbed an unusually large increase in new arrivals from Africa. As one might imagine, this created ripple effects throughout the colonies as demographics shifted. However, these numbers illustrate only a fraction of the enslaved population at the time. The British North American colonies had relatively high populations of enslaved Africans and their descendants but relied far less on new arrivals than did other colonies.[12] Still, prior to 1820, nearly three times as many enslaved Africans crossed the Atlantic as Europeans did.[13] By 1722, this demographic imbalance was cited as a source of anxiety among European settler populations who, like Snelgrave, were concerned about what could happen if the enslaved population ever got the upper hand.

ENSLAVEMENT AFTER 1722

The nature of enslavement in the British territories that were to become the United States changed after the Battle of Cape Lopez in 1722. The increase in the slave trade volume afforded by the British maritime victory allowed British settlers to reject the

Portuguese, Dutch, French, and Spanish notions of enslavement modeled after the Roman system, which had become the norm in the Atlantic world. Instead, they adopted the economically efficient chattel model in all of their American colonies. This model spread as neighboring colonies, such as French Louisiana and Spanish Florida, became part of the United States after Louisiana was admitted to the union (1812) and the ratification of the Adams-Onis treaty (1821).

Under this new model of slavery, the enslaved were described as chattel, a word that shares its root with cattle, one of the most important forms of nonhuman capital at the time and in the history of the world. The ramifications for the enslaved were dire: slavery became a permanent identity, passed along generations. Enslavers claimed not only the labor of their enslaved, but their entire beings. There was little to no legal recourse for the enslaved who experienced severe punishments nor was there any justice for the enslaved who were tortured and murdered by their enslavers. People with slave status could not testify in court, because for the first time in the Atlantic system, they were legally considered objects rather than human beings.

The development of global capitalism and chattel slavery therefore went hand in hand.[14] The economic efficiency of chattel slavery caused the widespread adoption of this British-introduced model across most of what would become the slaveholding United States and beyond. This is why, for example, other European colonies created in the Americas after this date, like Dutch Suriname, tended more toward the British chattel model.[15]

For a nation like the United States, with a history of colonial Spanish, Dutch, Swedish, French, and British occupation, this means that an incredibly complicated and diverse experience of enslavement slowly gave way to the overarching model that we know today. The formerly Dutch-, Spanish-, and French-occupied areas began navigating the chattel system for the first time. This meant that as formerly Dutch New Amsterdam, Spanish Florida, and French Louisiana became part of the British North American colonies and then the United States, opportunities for the enslaved and their descendants rapidly dwindled.

The results were catastrophic and their reverberations far reaching. The United States would not confer citizenship onto the enslaved, freedmen, or their descendants until the ratification of the Fourteenth Amendment in 1868—183 years after the French Empire granted citizenship to this population among her colonies. And although interracial marriages remained common in Dutch, Spanish, and French colonies throughout the era of slavery, many of the British North American colonies made interracial marriage illegal in the late 1600s with a series of anti-miscegenation laws designed to stifle the population of free people of African descent. These laws remained on the books in the United States until the monumental Supreme Court decision of *Loving v. Virginia* in 1967. Arguably, the United States would not grant legal equality to its Afro-descended population until the Fair Housing Act of 1968. That meant that Black people in the United States attained their full legal rights 283 years after Black free persons in the French Empire.

In 1724, just two years after the Battle of Cape Lopez, French Louisiana adopted a new *Code Noir*. Gone were many of the limited protections of the original, replaced with restrictions on the lives of both enslaved and free Black people in the territory. Though few of the original French liberties remained, these new Black Codes were the predecessors of the types of laws that southern states would implement after the Civil War. They forbade interracial marriage and ensured that children of enslaved mothers legally belonged to the enslaver. They prohibited the enslaved from suing or serving as witnesses in court, although the enslaved could be prosecuted criminally. These laws closed most avenues of freedom in order to keep the population of free Blacks from growing and punished enslavers who failed to ensure that the people they enslaved adhered to these codes. They also punished nonslaveholding Whites and free Blacks for assisting an enslaved person in the violation of these codes.[16]

It is imperative to emphasize that, despite the limited protections offered under the Roman model of enslavement in the earlier Spanish, Dutch, and French colonies, the practice was still enslavement. This section of the book is not a comparison of the horrors of slavery. Comparisons for that purpose lack usefulness or compassion. Besides, the specific hardships of Atlantic world enslavement depended on a wider variety of factors than merely empire, time period, or law. Furthermore, these differing circumstances sometimes adversely affected abolition and emancipation across the Atlantic world. Several nations with more legal rights for the enslaved, such as the formerly Portuguese Brazil and the formerly Spanish Cuba, took longer to establish emancipation than the areas in which chattel slavery was the legal precedent. Some historians argue this is in part because any amelioration of the horrors of slavery made the institution more palatable to wider swaths of the population, hampering abolitionist and independence movements, and making freedom more precarious in some ways.[17] There was no "better" in a system designed purely for exploitation. The enslaved suffered unspeakably under every system. So why then are these distinctions important?

The legal rights and protections in the Portuguese, Spanish, Dutch, and French colonies were not created for the benefit of the enslaved and formerly enslaved, but for the European empires' goals for wider society. In other words, the rulers permitting slavery in their colonies knew that the creation of a slave society would corrupt its settlers, which would have the effect of endangering the institution of slavery. In these Roman-derived laws and limited protections for the enslaved is a recognition of the harms of slavery and its abuses not on the enslaved, but on everyone else: the people doing the enslaving or bearing witness to it. Laws limiting the abuse of the enslaved existed as an ill-considered means of preventing the mostly White and European-descended enslavers from degenerating into sub-humanity. Lawmakers were concerned about what would happen to the longevity of the institution of slavery in a society that accepted and normalized the worst terrors of this racist institution if slavery were left unchecked. Slave codes were a weak attempt to curtail the worst of the horrors and to placate the proverbial Cassandras who understood that the cultural acceptance of mass dehumanization of one group left every other group vulnerable and poisoned the future of the empire and its citizens.[18]

Just as the enslaved were affected by this transition to a chattel model, so were the enslavers and the nonslaveholding colonists of European descent. This slavery transformed the cultures of the

colonists. The all-encompassing nature of chattel slavery created a
new type of identity politics: it conditioned people of European ancestry to think of themselves as White and to define themselves in
opposition to Black people. This in turn sowed poisonous divisions
that Americans still reap today.

CHATTEL AND THE FORMATION OF RACE

Slavery has existed in nearly every society in the world in some
form or another. Until British Atlantic societies developed the chattel model, no form of enslavement gave such complete and utter
dominion to enslavers on such a scale. Consequently, no society
had organized its entire social, political, religious, and economic
systems around the exploitation of a more or less permanently
enslaved underclass. Over time, the British North American territories became slave societies rather than a society with slaves.
The distinction between a society with slaves and a slave society is
important. Historian Ira Berlin first noted this in 1998. The British
North American colonies began as societies with enslaved people
with the charter generations. Race and slavery were more fluid
designations, and many free people of African descent took part in
many levels of society. Over time, as plantation systems emerged,
the colonies became slave societies, wherein every aspect of the
society hinged upon the strictures of slavery, and opportunities for
people of African descent shrank dramatically.[19]

There was no clear-cut adoption of this model and no exact
date to mark the British North American colonies' transition from
societies with slaves to slave societies, though the Battle of Cape
Lopez marks a turning point after which it became an inevitability.
Prior to the 1720s, chattel slavery was not a foregone conclusion,
as many different forms and versions of enslavement coexisted in
North America during the first two centuries of Atlantic slavery:
each of the British colonies as well as the colonies of New Netherland, New Spain, New Sweden, and French and Spanish Louisiana
had their own customs and cultures of enslavement that grew more
rigid over time. The chattel system emerged in mostly British colo-

nies before its values spread across the Atlantic world. The chattel model was never fully adopted by the French, Dutch, Spanish, and Portuguese colonies, though factions in each place pushed for more of its features as they perceived the model's economic advantages within the new system of global capitalism.[20]

To maintain generational wealth and power—or at least the dream of it—Whites had to participate and coerce the participation of other Whites in the system of White supremacy that dehumanizes the enslaved other. Virginia lawmakers made informing on self-emancipating enslaved people and slave-catching mandatory for all White people, whether they personally enslaved anyone or not, whether they supported or opposed the institution. Mandatory reporting meant that failure to inform authorities when an enslaved person was doing anything they were not permitted to do could result in punishment. Legislators in Virginia even formed groups that chased enslaved persons who dared attempt to "steal" themselves by escaping enslavement or by self-emancipating. These groups of White Virginians were expected to discipline enslaved people who were found off their plantations and to guard known escape routes.[21] They were also the genesis of modern sheriff departments.

All across the US South, people of all races were arrested for helping enslaved people escape as well as merely failing to stop them. Most colonies and nations that engaged in slavery had some form of mandatory policing of the enslaved, if not an official slave patrol, which made all people—enslaving or not—complicit in helping enslavers to maintain control. This naturally resulted in the widespread adoption of White supremacy and enforcement of the enslaving social order.

This social order mandated that the children born of an enslaved person would be born into slavery themselves. For slavery to be heritable, this type of system required a strict delineation between those with enslaved status and those without it. The ability to transfer from one status to another—as the enslaved often did in West Africa and, to lesser extents, elsewhere in the sixteenth- and seventeenth-century Atlantic world—became a liability in this system, as did racial ambiguity. To keep this system stable, enslavers tied visible Blackness to the status of enslavement.

This meant that Africans in the British North American colonies were, according to Ibram X. Kendi, citing a particularly noxious speech of Jefferson Davis, "stamped from the beginning."[22] In 1662, Virginia's legislators extended the Roman principle of *partus sequitur ventrem*, a law concerning animal husbandry, to enslaved people (this is where the chattel/cattle connection stands out). This law maintained that "among tame and domestic animals, the brood belongs to the owner of the dam or mother."[23] In other words, the enslaved became the legal equal of animals. This law incentivized White enslavers to sexually assault enslaved women, as it eliminated negative legal consequences and ensured that any resulting offspring would inherit its mother's status: the legal property of the father to use or dispose of as he wished. White women, on the other hand, faced strict penalties for birthing children of African ancestry.

The presumption that enslaved women's children would be born enslaved as the property of the mother's enslaver produced a "visceral understanding," as historian Jennifer Morgan puts it, of racial formation for Black women. The Virginia colony is often used as an example for the study of race formation because the transition to slavery was slow and free Black people had some levels of autonomy and maneuverability during the first fifty years of colonial settlement. This book also uses it because most of the five thousand enslaved people that William Snelgrave trafficked out of West Africa throughout his career as a slave ship captain were sold to enslavers in this colony.

As in most of North America, race and racial thought in Virginia were more fluid initially and then calcified over time into the rigidity that chattel slavery demanded. In tying reproduction to enslavement, the *partus* act ensured that chattel slavery became enshrined by law. The law guaranteed that everything an enslaved body was able to physically do could be rendered profitable by an enslaver.[24] It also guaranteed that children born of parents with both African and European descent would be enslaved, tying slavery to the politically, socially, and culturally constructed notion of race. Both Blackness and Whiteness became concepts that could be deployed to rearrange power in ways that benefited the White elite.

This means that race was invented *specifically* to describe Blackness, which came to be defined as being at least partially of African ancestry. The result was a razor-sharp, immediately obvious line between the group of people who could be enslaved and the group who could not. After that happened, Whiteness was created in opposition to Blackness and was defined as having no ancestry from Africa (or any people of color) at all. So Blackness as a made-up category was broad and inclusive—it encompassed any African ancestry at all. Whiteness as a made-up category, on the other hand, was narrow and exclusive, defined by lack of African (or Asian or Native American) heritage.

This concept was a radical one at the time. No other Europeans practiced it until the British introduced it. And even after that, who was "White" and who was "Black" depended on context, location, and time period.[25] For example, many people who were and are considered "White" in Latin America were and are not considered so in the United States because of the way elite lawmakers of our nation have historically chosen to create and define these arbitrary racial categories.[26] It's important to note that there is no scientific basis for these categories. Beyond differences in skin color and hair texture, there is no biological way to differentiate people who have been sorted into these groups. Race is socially constructed: American "Whiteness" and "Blackness" are concepts created by the settler descendants of Europeans to empower people of European ancestry and categorize non-Europeans as inferior.[27]

Other forms of human bondage and stolen labor that White people experienced did not negate this concept, but instead upheld it. As long as race-based enslavement of people with Black skin was the norm, White indentured servants (and their children) were safe from being categorized as chattel. Even the poorest light-skinned illegitimate descendant of Europe's dregs was guaranteed a spot in the middle of the pecking order in the colonies, socially outranking all free and enslaved descendants of both Africa and the Native populations of the Americas. Although fewer than 2 percent of people in the United States were enslavers themselves, slavery increased the quality of life for nearly all Whites in the nation.[28] The increase in status for poor Whites under the system of chattel slavery bought their complicity in the system. In other words, a portion of the wealth stolen from Africans and their descendants through labor and wage theft paid for social benefits of White people, which made them more likely to condone this theft. The result of this is both structural and institutional racism that bolsters White supremacy.

The *partus* act was a predecessor to the "one-drop rule" that would emerge in many enslaving states after emancipation during the Jim Crow period in the twentieth-century United States. This legal principle, which enshrined modern structural racism, asserted that anyone with even one ancestor of African descent was considered legally Black. Now that legalized slavery was over, legal Blackness became another arbitrary category to define who was subject to the racial segregation laws that former enslavers and their supporters created after Reconstruction. In the 1980s, the last remaining laws based on racial classifications were finally purged from America's legal system, though the divisions they created persist.

There isn't enough space in this book—or in any single book— to discuss all the ways in which Africa's descendants have been the inheritors of the worst divisions and conditions to come out of chattel slavery and its legacy. Deadly policing, mass incarceration, the Thirteenth Amendment and school-to-prison pipeline, gentrification (which has its roots in White flight, which was exacerbated by redlining, which was tied to the spatial violence of urban renewal, which resulted from the blighting of Black neighborhoods, a legacy of the "separate but equal" doctrine of Jim Crow), anti-Black bias, White terror, economic inequality and substandard public services in Black neighborhoods, public health disparity, and job discrimination are just a few of the hundreds of pernicious structural means of targeting the descendants of America's enslaved population. Black people have suffered disproportionately at the hands of policymakers who used (and continue to use) racist rhetoric to justify unethical self-interest.

The slave trader William Snelgrave, the naval Captain Chaloner Ogle, his surgeon John Atkins, as well as other agents of the slave-trading companies all shared this one commonality: they all made the decision to embark on highly profitable ventures that resulted in African enslavement and death. They all justified these ventures, after the fact, in the letters and narratives they left behind. And the people today who read their writings and say things like "well, that was normal then" or "they didn't know any better" or "that was just the way things were" are missing the point. It was *not* normal then.

They *did* know better, and that was *not* just the way things were. That was the way these men *actively created* things. If it had ever been normal, moral, and acceptable to profit from the dehumanization of millions of people and to steal their labor, personhood, and that of their descendants in perpetuity, they would not have written thousands of pages to convince the readership otherwise after the Battle of Cape Lopez, and during the birth of American slavery.

Epilogue
Reverse-Engineering the Slave Society

SINCE BEFORE THE BATTLE OF CAPE LOPEZ in 1722, laws by settlers made it legal in the American colonies and then in the United States to enact ownership over people. The nation lived with this reality and became a slave society that depended on these 410 *billion* hours of unpaid labor to build the nation.[1] In exchange for the labor of enslaved Africans and their descendants, we allowed ourselves to become a nation where significant swathes of the population fear for their safety, health, and families. Upon Emancipation, our nation's dependence on coerced labor did not end, but merely changed shape.[2] Americans do not know what it is like to live in a society in which people are fairly compensated for their labor. Americans live in a society that, for centuries, stripped people of personhood in order to extract the maximum amount of labor from them.

Wider US society remains resistant to recognizing the full humanity of Black people and, by extension, other people of color. Many Americans struggle to perceive the ways in which White supremacist thought, which went hand in hand with slavery and its legacies, continues to govern the structures of the nation in ways that make life impossible for an increasingly large percentage of people. The ability to enact ownership over Afro-descended humans and to strip personhood from them in order to extract free labor has seeped into and tainted every aspect of American life. This precedent created by the nation's settler-ancestors enabled us to trivialize the lives and personhood of any group of people for the convenience of a powerful few.

In just my lifetime I have seen women, children, undocumented immigrants, queer people (especially transgender people), Brown people, Black people, Indigenous and Aboriginal people, Asians, Muslims, Jewish people, and disabled people targeted with unjust policies designed to make them fear for their safety, health, familial integrity, property, and livelihoods. Each targeted group has had little recourse to justice. With the acceptance of chattel slavery, we ingrained this precedent of allowing people to be treated as "less than" in all of our dominant cultural, legal, political, economic, and religious/moral systems. That's why it keeps resurfacing in the daily crises that parade across our phone screens.

The rights of increasingly larger segments of our population are being targeted. People who used to not see and people who chose to not see now are seeing that the threat could come to their doors for the first time. Americans will not be free of threats to personal freedom and autonomy until Black people are free of racism. As Dr. Ibram X. Kendi wrote: "It is in the intelligent self-interest of White Americans to challenge racism." All discriminatory ideology is predicated on who is fully human and who is "less than" and deserving of unfreedom. Any single type of bigotry paves the way for other types to flourish unchecked.

The good news is that if you are reading this, know that you absolutely have the power to do something about it.

Many people erroneously assume that ignorance and hate create racist ideas that lead to discriminatory policy, but it's actually the other way around: discrimination breeds racism. Racially discriminatory policies spring from economic, political, and cultural self-interest, which is constantly changing. Capitalists who sought to increase profit margins, from slave traders like William Snelgrave to Virginia's lawmakers, created and defended discrimination out of economic self-interest, not because they were racists or held racist ideas. The racism came after the fact. Racist policies have driven the history of racist ideas in America.[3]

I wrote this book with an antiracist lens because history told in any other way is inherently racist and harmful. It prevents us from collectively facing our shared reality and honestly observing who carries a heavier load and who carries one that they have the ability to put down on occasion. It impoverishes our culture and separates us from ourselves. History is meant to be "for life," as the philosopher Friedrich Nietzsche wrote. He was just one of many who warned that ignorance about where we have come from leads to ignorance about where we are going.[4]

At its very best, history sustains life, rather than upholding cultures of death, like colonialism and White supremacy. Antiracist histories give us a moment to reflect and the courage to decide to break with harmful traditions and challenge institutions that do not serve all of us so that we may together create something that does. For me, the Battle of Cape Lopez provides a lens into how things got so bad. It's a blueprint almost, and blueprints can be helpful when reverse-engineering.

History is the world I inhabit, and that's where I can do a lot of the work that is important to me. Just as important is the work that exists in your world: your home, your family, your neighborhood, your place of worship, your workplace, and your local institutions and government. Follow the leadership of the community organizers who have been doing this work all along, and equip them to succeed.

If, like me, you were born into some type of power, don't be ashamed of it or try to give it up just because others don't have it—yet. Rather, use yours to work within your community to extend this power to the people who don't. We all deserve power and ease and goodness, and there's enough for everyone.

Remember: racism and hate don't lead to discrimination. Discrimination leads to racism and hate. And that's great news, because it's really tough to change someone whose mind is filled with racism and hate; changing discrimination is a lot easier. Discriminatory policies are dismantled every day by groups of determined people working collectively in their corners of the world, leveraging the power they already have to fight them.

In these ways, we can still change the fate of slave societies.

Notes

INTRODUCTION

1. See Angela Sutton, "The Seventeenth-Century Slave Trade in the Documents of the English, Dutch, Swedish, Danish and Prussian Royal Slave Trading Companies," in *Slavery & Abolition*, 36, no. 3 (2015): 445–59.

CHAPTER ONE

1. Treaty of Butre, 1656, NA OWIC 12. A transcription and English translation of this treaty is available at Wikisource: https://en.wikisource.org/wiki/Treaty_of_Butre_(1656).

2. "Agreements and Contracts with the Natives at Brandenburg," NA 1.05.06 1163.

3. "8 March 1684, Johan Nieman's Letter from Gross-Friedrichsburg," in Adam Jones, *Brandenburg Sources for West African History, 1680–1700* (Wiesbaden: F. Steiner Verlag, 1985), 88, and "Johann Peter Oettinger's Account of His Voyage to Guinea," in Jones, *Brandenburg Sources*, 86.

4. Untitled, GStA PK, I HA Rep. 65 N. 43.

5 "28 January 1691, Statement of Charles LePetit Concerning Dutch Interference with Brandenburg Trade on the Gold Coast," in Jones, *Brandenburg Sources*, 17.

6. Untitled, GStA PK, I. HA Rep. 65 N. 43, s.1

7. See Rebecca Shumway, *The Fante and the Transatlantic Slave Trade* (Rochester, NY: University of Rochester Press, 2011), 35–74.

8. Van Severhuijsen to the Assembly of Ten, Elmina, 15 April 1700–16 November 1701, in Kwasi Konadu, *The Akan People: A Documentary History*, vol. 1 (Princeton, NJ: Markus Wiener Publishers, 2014), 226.

9. "Tableu de Guadelopeer Isles de Antilles," undated, in RA *Handel och Sjofart*, 9 Amerika.

10. Grosvenor and Phipps to RAC, March 15, 1712, BNA T70/5/81.

11. "Journal of Fort Great Fredericksburg," GStA PK I. Ha. Rep 65, N. 167.

12. Untitled, NA 1.05.01 1166.

13. "Agreements and Contracts with the Natives at Brandenburg," in NA 1.05.06 1163.

14. "Resolution of Elmina Council, April 8, 1717," NA WIC 124.

Chapter Two

1. Phillip Gosse, *The Pirates' Who's Who: Giving Particulars of the Lives & Deaths of the Pirates & Buccaneers* (London: Dulau and Company, 1924), 94.

2. John Atkins, *Voyage to Guinea, Brazil, and the West Indies in the HMS Swallow Weymouth* (London: Frank Cass and Co., 1735), 39–42.

3. "Proclamation of King James II, 1687," BNA T70/169 f. 48.

4. "Office of King James II to Court of Assistants of the RAC, 1700," BNA T70/86 f. 97.

5. Matthew David Mitchell, *The Prince of Slavers: Humphry Morice and the Transformation of Britain's Transatlantic Slave Trade, 1698–1732* (Cham, Switzerland: Springer International, 2020), 93–129.

6. William Snelgrave, *A New Account of Some Parts of Guinea, and the Slave-Trade: Containing, I. The History of the Late Conquest of the Kingdom of Whidaw by the King of Dahomè . . . II. The Manner How the Negroes Become Slaves . . . III. A Relation of the Author's Being Taken by Pirates, and the Many Dangers He Underwent* (London: Frank Cass, 1971), 197.

7. Snelgrave, *A New Account*, 199.

8. Snelgrave, *A New Account*, 203.

9. Snelgrave, *A New Account*, 211.

10. Snelgrave, *A New Account*, 212.

11. Snelgrave, *A New Account*, 275–76.

12. Snelgrave, *A New Account*, 225–26.

13. Snelgrave, *A New Account*, 241.

14. See the work of Ruud Paesie, "Lorrendrayen op Africa: De illegale goederen-en slavenhandel op West Afrika tijdens het achttiende-eeuwse handelsmonopolie van de West-Indische Compangie, 1700-1734," (Amsterdam: Bataafsche Leeuw, 2008).

15. Missive of the WIC, 22 September 1716, KITLV H 450 MF, f. 4–6.

16. GStA I. HA Rep. 65 N. 175.

17. GStA, I. HA Rep. 65 N. 175, f. 50.

18. Henk den Heijer, *Goud, ivoor en slaven: sheepvaart en handel van de Tweede Westindische Compagnie op Afrika, 1674–1740* (Zutphen: Walburg Pers, 1997), 255–62.

19. Undated (in a box with other papers concerning the Lorrendrayers from 1690s–1700), GStA, I. HA Rep. 65 N. 175, f. 47–55.

20. See item titled "Europeese Koopmanschappen, Dienede ten Handel met de Spangiarden en Naturellen in de Zuyd-Zee," GStA, I. HA Rep. 65 N. 49.

21. "Europeese Koopmanschappen, Dienede ten Handel met de Spangiarden en Naturellen in de Zuyd-Zee," GStA, I. HA Rep. 65 N. 49.

22. Calendar of State Papers 1700, as cited in Nivel Tatersfield, *The Forgotten Trade Comprising the Log of the Daniel and Henry of 1700 and Accounts of the Slave Trade from the Minor Ports of England, 1698–1725*, ed. John Fowles (London: Jonathan Cape, 1991), 174.

23. "Borgermr. Johannes Zeneman, Her Raad det Marine Rudolph Friday, Heer Krygs Comissar Abraham Jamet answer articles from Director Sivert Hoes which they received 27 Dec 1714," GStA, I. HA Rep. 65 N. 113, f. 34–35.

24. For more information on this phenomenon, see Hermann Kellenbenz's work on Saint Thomas, "Die Brandenburger auf St. Thomas," *Jahrbuch for Geschichte von Staat, Wirtschaft und Gesellschaft Lateinamerikas*, 2 (1965): 196–217.

25. "10 October 1716, Director Sivert Hoess of St. Thomas to the King of Brandenburg," GStA, I. HA Rep. 65 f. 113.

26. "Notificatie een 'Enterlooper met slaven' voor Verkoop Ligt 'Buyten Ordre' Van de WIC De Rede Van St. Eustatius, Verbod Bij De 'Enterlooper' Te Varen En Slaven Te Kopn, Op Straffe Van Konfisskatie, Beloning Vor Het Bij der Kommandeur Brengen Van Zulke Slaven, 4 May 1700," in *West Indisch Plakaatboek, St. Maarten, St. Eusatius, Saba 1648/1681–1816*, onder Redaktie van J. A. Schiltkamp en J. Th. de Smidt (Amsterdam: S. Emmering, 1979), 272–73. See also Pedro L. V. Welch,

"Intra-American and Caribbean Destinations and Transit Points for the Slave Trade," *Journal of Caribbean History* 42 (2008): 49.

27. Christian J. Koot, "Constructing the Empire: English Governors, Imperial Policy, and Inter-imperial Trade in New York City and the Leeward Islands, 1650–1689," *Itinerario* 31 (2007): 35–60 and Luis Felipe de Alencatro, "Johann Mortiz und der Sklavenhandel," in Gerhard Brunn, et al. *Sein Feld war die Weldt: Johann Moritz von Nassau-Siegen (1604–1679) Von Siegen ueber die Niederlande und Brasilien nach Brandenburg* (Muenster: Waxman, 2008), 124.

28. For works that discuss the slave trade in the interior and the ways in which Africans from the interior understood and resisted captivity, see the book edited by Sylviane A. Diouf, *Fighting the Slave Trade: West African Strategies* (Athens: Ohio University Press, 2003).

29. See Eric Robert Taylor, *If We Must Die: Shipboard Insurrections in the Era of the Atlantic Slave Trade* (Baton Rouge: Louisiana State University Press, 2006).

30. Snelgrave, *A New Account*, 174–79.

31. Snelgrave, *A New Account*, 182–84.

32. See Ibram X. Kendi's *Stamped from the Beginning: The Definitive History of Racist Ideas in America* (New York: Nation Books, 2016).

Chapter Three

1. See W. Jeffrey Bolster, *Black Jacks: African American Seamen in the Age of Sail* (Boston: Harvard University Press, 2009) and Emma Christopher, *Slave Ship Sailors and Their Captive Cargoes 1730–1807* (Cambridge: Cambridge University Press, 2006).

2. BAC employee Joost van Colster was instructed to purchase stocks of captives when they were abundant, and they should "if you see fit, be taught all kinds of crafts, and a few shall be used as sailors." "Late 1683, Instructions for Joost van Colster, Prospective Director at Gross-Friedrichsburg," in Adam Jones, *Brandenburg Sources for West African History, 1680–1700* (Wiesbaden: F. Steiner Verlag, 1985), 76.

3. BNA HCA1/17 f. 134.

4. William Snelgrave, *A New Account of Some Parts of Guinea, and the Slave-Trade: Containing, I. The History of the Late Conquest of the Kingdom of Whidaw by the King of Dahomè . . . II. The Manner How the Negroes Become Slaves . . . III. A Relation of the Author's Being Taken by Pirates, and the Many Dangers He Underwent* (London: Frank Cass, 1971), 185.

5. Arne Bialuschewski, "Black People under the Black Flag: Piracy and the Slave Trade on the West Coast of Africa, 1718–1723," *Slavery & Abolition* 29 (2008): 4, 461–75, DOI: 10.1080/01440390802486473.

6. Joel H. Baer, ed., *British Piracy in the Golden Age: History and Interpretation, 1660–1730*, vol. 3 (London: Pickering & Chatto, 2007), 70.

7. *Weekly Journal or British Gazetteer*, October 10, 1719.

8. Morice to Captain William Snelgrave with Instructions for His Voyage and Information about Other Ships, November 27, 1719, Humphry Morice Papers from the Bank of England, London, reel 4, vol. 8. Also BNA HCA1/17, f. 134; BNA ADM68/194, 121v; and BNA CO152/19, 176.

9. Charles Johnson, *A General History of the Robberies and Murders of the Most Notorious Pyrates*, 2nd ed. (London: Ch. Rivington, J. Lacy, and J. Stone, 1724).

10. Richard Frohock, "Satire and Civil Governance in 'A General History of the Pyrates' (1724, 1726)," *The Eighteenth Century* 56, no. 4. (2015): 467–83.

11. See Arne Bialuschewski, "Daniel DeFoe, Nathaniel Mist, and 'A General History of the Pyrates,'" *Papers of the Biographical Society of America* 98 (March 2004): 26.

12. Snelgrave, *A New Account*, 260.

13. Johnson, *A General History*, 285–86.

14. Rita Martins de Sousa, "Brazilian Gold and the Lisbon Mint House (1720–1807)," *e-Journal of Portuguese History* 6, no. 1 (2008): 6.

15. *Weekly Journal or British Gazetteer*, February 13, 1720.

16. Baer, "Richard Harris," in *British Piracy in the Golden Age*, 134.

17. Bartholomew Roberts, the Pirate, to Lieutenant General Mathew, *Royall Fortune*, September 27, 1720, Calendar of State Papers, item 251v, vol. 32 (1720–1721), 165.

CHAPTER FOUR

1. Sanjeev Sanyal, *The Ocean of Churn: How the Indian Ocean Shaped Human History* (New Delhi: Penguin Random House India, 2016).

2. John Atkins, *Voyage to Guinea, Brazil, and the West Indies in the HMS Swallow Weymouth* (London: Frank Cass and Co., 1735), 26.

3. See Geraldine Heng's *The Invention of Race in the European Middle Ages* (Cambridge: Cambridge University Press, 2018), Lynn T. Ramey's *Black Legacies: Race and the European Middle Ages* (Gainesville: Univer-

sity Press of Florida, 2014), Olivette Otele's *African Europeans: An Untold History* (London: Hurst, 2020), and Mary Rambaran-Olm, M. Breann Leake, and Micah Goodrich, "Medieval Studies: The Stakes of the Field," *Postmedieval* 11 (2020): 356–70.

4. There is a rich century-long history of the differences between the Roman-influenced Iberian and the English models of enslavement and race and how these have, at least in part, shaped the racism these nations and their modern former colonies face. This conversation among historians started in Brazil with Gilberto Freyre's extensive historical and anthropological work from 1933, *Casa grande e senzala*, and became a more common point of historical exploration in the United States with Frank Tannenbaum's *Slave and Citizen: The Negro in the Americas* (New York: Vintage Books, 1947). Although several aspects of the latter's explorations have been questioned by scholars of the past seventy years who point to other sources and reasons for these differences in slave law, enslavement, and racial hierarchy, more recent scholars who have had increased access to sources concerning the enslaved and their descendants return to Tannenbaum's work repeatedly to refine its main points. Seventy years of this debate is summed up succinctly in Alejandro de la Fuente, "From Slaves to Citizens? Tannenbaum and the Debates on Slavery, Emancipation, and Race Relations in Latin America," *International Labor and Working-Class History* 77, no. 1 (2010): 154–73.

5. Atkins, *Voyage to Guinea, Brazil, and the West Indies*, 39.

6. Atkins, *Voyage to Guinea, Brazil, and the West Indies*, 40–56.

7. "Robert Plunkett to Royal Africa Company," April 30, 1719, BNA T 70/19, f. 165.

8. "Sierra Leone Letters Continued," August 31, 1719, BNA T 70/6, ff. 97–98.

9. Atkins, *Voyage to Guinea, Brazil, and the West Indies*, 42.

10. In the past, most scholarship on African resistance to the Atlantic slave trade focused on slave ship insurrections, largely because the violence of colonialism and slavery made those records some of the widest available. However, there was always a robust resistance from Africans like Captain Tomba, who stayed and fought against the practices of captive taking, village raiding, family separation, and all of the devastating effects the Atlantic slave trade had on West Africa, and many Africans and Afro-descended people availed themselves of European and American courts to seek abolition and recognition of their humanity. See Walter Rodney, *How Europe Underdeveloped Africa* (London: Bogle-L'Ouverture, 1972), Walter Rodney, "African Slavery and Other Forms of Social Oppression on the Upper Guinea Coast in the Context of the Atlantic Slave

Trade," *The Journal of African History* 7, no. 3 (1966), 431–43, Sylviane Diouf, ed., *Fighting the Slave Trade: West African Strategies* (Athens: Ohio University Press, 2003), Winston McGowan, "African Resistance to the Atlantic Slave Trade in West Africa," *Slavery & Abolition* 11, no. 1 (2008): 5–29, and John Thornton, *The Kongolese Saint Anthony: Dona Beatriz Kimpa Vita and the Antonian Movement, 1684–1706* (Cambridge: Cambridge University Press, 2012).

11. Atkins, *Voyage to Guinea, Brazil, and the West Indies*, 42.

12. Atkins, *Voyage to Guinea, Brazil, and the West Indies*, 49.

13. For more reading on the relationships between Sierra Leone and the rice-growing low country, see Daniel C. Littlefield, *Rice and Slaves: Ethnicity and the Slave Trade in Colonial South Carolina.* (Baton Rouge: Louisiana State University Press, 1981), Bruce L. Mouser, Edwin Nuijten, Florent Okry, and Paul Richards, "Red and White Rice in the Vicinity of Sierra Leone: Linked Histories of Slavery, Emancipation, and Seed Selection," in *Rice: Global Networks and New Histories*, ed. Francesca Bray, Peter A. Coclanis, Edda L. Fields-Black, and Dagmar Schäfer, 138–62 (Cambridge: Cambridge University Press, 2015), and Judith Carney, "The Role of African Rice and Slaves in the History of Rice Cultivation in the Americas," *Human Ecology* 26, no. 4 (1998): 525–45.

14. See Christopher R. DeCorse, "Fortified Towns of the Koinadugu Plateau: Northern Sierra Leone in the Pre-Atlantic and Atlantic Worlds," in *Power and Landscape in Atlantic West Africa: Archaeological Perspectives*, ed. J. Cameron Monroe and Akinwumi Ogunidiran (Cambridge: Cambridge University Press: 2012), 278–308.

15. Atkins, *Voyage to Guinea, Brazil, and the West Indies*, 38–42.

16. Atkins, *Voyage to Guinea, Brazil, and the West Indies*, 57.

17. The contracts were binding alliances between the kingdom of the Netherlands and the native polity. As the Portuguese had referred to the native rulers (the chiefs, kings, caboceers, or princes, depending on who had written the document) as knights of the Kingdom of Portugal, so the Dutch had referred to them as vassals of the Netherlands. This was due to African insistence and not European policy. See Angela Sutton, "The Seventeenth-Century Slave Trade in the Documents of the English, Dutch, Swedish, Danish, and Prussian Royal Slave Trading Companies," *Slavery & Abolition* 36, no. 3 (2015): 445–59, Mariana Candido, *An African Slaving Port and the Atlantic World: Benguela and Its Hinterland* (New York: Cambridge University Press, 2013), and Roquinaldo Ferreira, *Cross-Cultural Exchange in the Atlantic World: Angola and Brazil during the Era of the Slave Trade* (New York: Cambridge University Press, 2012) for the genesis of this practice.

18. Atkins, *Voyage to Guinea, Brazil, and the West Indies*, 68.

19. See Angela Christine Sutton, *Competition and the Mercantile Culture of the Gold Coast Slave Trade in the Atlantic World Economy, 1620–1720* (PhD diss., Vanderbilt University, 2014), 153–54. Unlicensed traders engaged in any number of piratical activities to turn their profits if they felt the risk was worth it and had no company policies which tied their hands. Von der Groeben of the BAC encountered some West Africans in the village of Druvin who had recently witnessed such action. These natives were unwilling to talk for long, but "reported briefly that a short time before, two ships with white flags had passed along the coast and abducted all the blacks who came onboard." On another occasion, von der Groeben states that French ships often arrived, lured coastal natives onboard with promises of trade (as it was usual custom for West Africans to canoe up to boats passing by to inquire of trade opportunities), and then absconded with them to the Indies. Nicholas Sweerts and William Cross of the RAC reported similar incidents. Von der Groeben also reported seeing several large fires "by which the natives of the country inform one another of the presence of foreign ships."

20. Atkins, *Voyage to Guinea, Brazil, and the West Indies*, 65–66.

21. Atkins, *Voyage to Guinea, Brazil, and the West Indies*, 66.

22. BNA HCA 49, f. 104.

23 See Elizabeth Trengrove, BNA HCA 49/104, "A Journal of the Proceedings of the Court of Admiralty, held at Cabo Corso Castle on Thursday, April the 5th, 1722," in *British Piracy in the Golden Age: History and Interpretation, 1660–1730*, vol. 3, ed. Joel H. Baer (London: Pickering & Chatto, 2007), 112, and Charles Johnson, *A General History of the Robberies and Murders of the Most Notorious Pyrates*, 2nd ed. (London: Ch. Rivington, J. Lacy, and J. Stone, 1724), 266–86.

CHAPTER FIVE

1. John Atkins, *Voyage to Guinea, Brazil, and the West Indies in the HMS Swallow Weymouth* (London: Frank Cass and Co., 1735), 72–73. See also David Richardson, *Bristol, Africa and the Eighteenth Century Slave Trade to America*, vol. 1, *The Years of Expansion, 1698–1729* (Gloucester: A. Sutton, 1986); vol. 2, *The Years of Ascendancy, 1730–1745* (Gloucester: A. Sutton, 1987); vol. 3, *The Years of Decline, 1746–1769* (Gloucester: A. Sutton, 1991); vol. 4, *The Final Years, 1770–1807* (Gloucester: A. Sutton, 1997). This voyage is also in the Trans-Atlantic Slave Voyages Database

as Voyage #16303, where more details are recorded. The voyage began in Bristol as a ten percenter, took a total of 257 days, with 102 of them in the Middle Passage, or crossing the Atlantic. It stopped first in Sierra Leone, then the Windward Coast, and made two more stops on the Gold Coast to fill up before heading to Jamaica. A total of 220 captives were forced onboard, and of these, 190 survived and were sold in Jamaica.

2. Atkins, *Voyage to Guinea, Brazil, and the West Indies*, 72.

3. Atkins, *Voyage to Guinea, Brazil, and the West Indies*, 92–94, 256.

4. Atkins, *Voyage to Guinea, Brazil, and the West Indies*, 75.

5. Atkins, *Voyage to Guinea, Brazil, and the West Indies*, 78.

6. Atkins, *Voyage to Guinea, Brazil, and the West Indies*, 77.

7. Joel H. Baer, ed., "Robert Armstrong," in *British Piracy in the Golden Age: History and Interpretation, 1660–1730*, vol. 3 (London: Pickering & Chatto, 2007), 154.

8. Jean Phillippe Chippaux and Alain Chippaux, "Yellow Fever in Africa and the Americas: A Historical and Epidemiological Perspective," *Journal of Venomous Animals and Toxins Including Tropical Diseases* 24, no. 20 (2018).

9. Atkins, *Voyage to Guinea, Brazil, and the West Indies*, 139.

10. Atkins, *Voyage to Guinea, Brazil, and the West Indies*, 87.

11. See Robin Law, *Ouidah: The Social History of a West African Slaving Port, 1727–1892* (Cambridge: Cambridge University Press, 2017).

12. Several Africans to whom this happened at this time later made their way back home, either with or without the help of their kin. Two of the most well-known examples are Little Ephraim Robin John and Ancona Robin John from modern day Nigeria, who are written about in Randy Sparks's *Two Princes of Calabar: An Eighteenth Century Atlantic Odyssey* (Boston: Harvard University Press, 2008). As the slave trade calcified, other enslaved Africans who returned at later time periods often remained enslaved in the Americas until they could free themselves and purchase a voyage back to Africa years or even decades later. In the nineteenth and early twentieth centuries, many descendants of the enslaved banded together after emancipation in movements to return to "more Auspicious shores," though not necessarily from where they or their ancestors had been taken. See Caree A. Banton's *More Auspicious Shores: Barbadian Migration to Liberia, Blackness, and the Making of an African Republic* (Cambridge: Cambridge University Press, 2019).

13. See Catharine Hall, ed., *Legacies of British Slave-Ownership: Colonial Slavery and the Formation of Victorian Britain* (Cambridge: Cambridge University Press, 2016). See also the *Database of the Centre for the Study*

60

of the *Legacies of British Slavery* at the University College of London, available at www.ucl.ac.uk/lbs/.

14. "13 January 1722" BNA T 70/7.

15. Baer, "Robert Haws," 118.

16. Chancery Records, Various Six Clerks, Series I, 1715–1758, BNA C113/262.

17. "Chaloner Ogle to J. Roberts Publishers," April 5, 1722, in Baer, *British Piracy in the Golden Age*, 76–78.

18. Baer, "A Full and Exact Account of the Tryal of all the Pyrates, Lately Taken by Captain Ogle, on Board the Swallow Man of War, on the Coast of Guinea," 115.

19. Baer, "Christopher Granger," 115–16.

20. Baer, "John Stevenson," 130.

21. Atkins, *Voyage to Guinea, Brazil, and the West Indies*, 262.

22. Baer, "Tom Withstandyenot," 147.

23. Baer, "David Littlejohn," 151.

24. Atkins, *Voyage to Guinea, Brazil, and the West Indies*, 192.

25. Baer, "Robert Armstrong," 154.

26. Baer, "James Phillips," 148.

Chapter Six

1. John Atkins, *Voyage to Guinea, Brazil, and the West Indies in the HMS Swallow Weymouth* (London: Frank Cass and Co., 1735), 193.

2. See P. Gabrielle Foreman, et al., "Writing about Slavery/Teaching about Slavery: This Might Help," community-sourced document, June 7, 2022, https://naacpculpeper.org/resources/writing-about-slavery-this-might-help/.

3. See Sowande M. Mustakeem, *Slavery at Sea: Terror, Sex, and Sickness in the Middle Passage* (Chicago: University of Illinois, 2017); Juanita DeBarros, Steven Palmer, and David Wright, eds., *Health and Medicine in the Circum-Caribbean, 1800–1968* (New York: Routledge, 2009); Joost C. A. Schokkenbroek and Leon van den Broeke, "Economics without Ethics? Medical Treatment of African Slaves aboard Dutch West India Company and Private Slave Ships," *International Journal of Maritime History* 34, no. 1 (2022); Richard B. Sheridan, "The Guinea Surgeons on the Middle Passage: The Provision of Medical Services in the British Slave Trade," *The International Journal of African Historical Studies* 14, no. 4 (1981): 601–25; and Craig Koslofsky and Roberto Zaugg, *A German Barber-Surgeon in*

the Atlantic Slave Trade: The Seventeenth-Century Journal of Johann Peter Oettinger (Charlottesville: University of Virginia Press, 2020).

4. See Benjamin Colman, Some Observations on the New Method of Receiving the Small-Pox by Ingrafting or Inoculating (Boston, 1721), 15–16; Elise A. Mitchell, "Morbid Crossings: Surviving Smallpox, Maritime Quarantine, and the Gendered Geography of the Early Eighteenth-Century Intra-Caribbean Slave Trade," The William and Mary Quarterly 79, no. 2 (2022): 177–210; Kelly Wisecup, "African Medical Knowledge, the Plain Style, and Satire in the 1721 Boston Inoculation Controversy," Early American Literature 46, no. 1 (2011): 25–50.

5. John H. Baer, ed., "Peter Scudamore," in British Piracy in the Golden Age: History and Interpretation, 1660–1730, vol. 3 (London: Pickering & Chatto, 2007), 113.

6. Baer, "Peter Scudamore," 113.

7. Baer, "Peter Scudamore," 114.

8. Atkins, Voyage to Guinea, Brazil, and the West Indies, 263.

9. See Albert Van Dantzig, Forts and Castles of Ghana (Accra: Sedco Publishing, 1980); Christopher R. DeCorse, "Landlords and Strangers: British Forts and Their Communities in West Africa," in British Forts and Their Communities: Archaeological and Historical Perspectives, ed. Christopher R. DeCorse and Zachary J. M. Beier (Gainesville: University Press of Florida, 2018), 206–30.

10. Atkins, Voyage to Guinea, Brazil, and the West Indies, 98–99.

11. Atkins, Voyage to Guinea, Brazil, and the West Indies, 99–100.

12. For more about canoes and smaller vessels that navigated the shallow estuaries of West Africa, see Filipa Ribeiro da Silva, "Dutch, English, and African Shipbuilding Craftsmanship in Precolonial West Africa: An Entangled History of Construction, Maintenance, and Repair," The International Journal of Maritime History 31, no. 3 (2019): 508–20; and Robert S. Smith, "The Canoe in West African History," Journal of African History 11, no. 4 (1970).

Chapter Seven

1. See commentary by Joel H. Baer, ed., British Piracy in the Golden Age: History and Interpretation, 1660–1730, vol. 3 (London: Pickering & Chatto, 2007), 67–72.

2. Baer, "Henry Glasby," 99.

3. Baer, "Sentence against David Simpson, William Magness, Richard Hardy, Thomas Sutton, Christopher Moody, and Valentine Ashplant," 102.

4. Baer, "George Smith," 135.

5. Baer, "William Phillips," 89–90.

6. Baer, "John Ouchterlauney," 95.

7. Baer, "Joseph Mansfield," 129.

8. Baer, "John Stevenson," 130.

9. "New York, June 17," *Boston News-Letter*, June 17–24, 1717.

10. See table 1 in Kenneth J. Kinkor, "Black Men under the Black Flag," in *Bandits at Sea: A Pirates Reader*, ed. C. R. Pennell (New York: New York University Press, 2001), 201.

11. See Pablo E. Perez-Mallaina, *Spain's Men of the Sea: Daily Life on the Indies Fleets in the Sixteenth Century* (Baltimore: Johns Hopkins University Press, 2005).

12. See Jeffrey Bolster, *Black Jacks: African American Seamen in the Age of Sail* (Boston: Harvard University Press, 1998); and Ray Costello, *Black Salt: Seafarers of African Descent on British Ships* (Liverpool: Liverpool University Press, 2014).

13. See Surekha Davies, *Renaissance Ethnography and the Invention of the Human* (Cambridge: Cambridge University Press, 2016).

14. Baer, "Thomas Diggles," 124.

15. See Pierluigi Valsecchi, *Power and State Formation in West Africa: Appolonia from the Sixteenth to the Eighteenth Century* (New York: Palgrave Macmillan, 2011); Sir Walter Rodney, *How Europe Underdeveloped Africa* (London: Bogle-L'Ouverture Publications, 1972); Kwasi Konadu, ed., *The Akan People: A Documentary History* (Princeton: Marcus Weiner, 2014); Rebecca Shumway, *The Fante and the Transatlantic Slave Trade* (Rochester, NY: University of Rochester Press, 2011); Kwame Yeboa Daaku, *Trade and Politics on the Gold Coast, 1600–1720: A Study of the African Reaction to European Trade* (Oxford: Clarendon Press, 1970); and Harvey M. Feinberg, *Africans and Europeans in West Africa: Elminans and Dutchmen on the Gold Coast during the Eighteenth Century* (Philadelphia: The American Philosophical Society, 1989).

16. See Edna Bay, *Wives of the Leopard: Gender, Politics, and Culture in the Kingdom of Dahomey* (Charlottesville: University of Virginia Press, 1998); Manuel Barcia, *West African Warfare in Bahia and Cuba: Soldier Slaves in the Atlantic World, 1807–1844* (Oxford: Oxford University Press, 2017); John Thornton, *Warfare in Atlantic Africa, 1500–1800* (London: University College of London Press, 1999); and Ray Kea, "Firearms

and Warfare on the Gold and Slave Coasts from the Sixteenth to the Nineteenth Centuries," *The Journal of African History* 21, no. 2 (1971): 185–213.

17. See Rodney, *How Europe Underdeveloped Africa*; Konadu, *The Akan People*; Shumway, *The Fante and the Transatlantic Slave Trade*; Daaku, *Trade and Politics on the Gold Coast, 1600–1720*; Feinberg, *Africans and Europeans in West Africa*; and Valsecchi, *Power and State Formation in West Africa*.

18. See Molefi Kete Asante, *Erasing Racism* (Amherst, NY: Prometheus Books, 2003); Elizabeth Kowaleski, *The British Slave Trade and Public Memory* (New York: Columbia University Press, 2006); Catherine Hall, "The Slavery Business and the Making of 'Race' in Britain and the Caribbean," *Current Anthropology* 61, no. S22 (October 2020), https://doi.org/10.1086/709845; and Ibram X. Kendi, *Stamped from the Beginning: The Definitive History of Racist Ideas in America* (New York: Nation Books, 2016).

19. Baer, "A List of the Pyrates Acquitted, a List of the Pyrates Sentenced to Death," 162–64.

20. BNA SP 36/158/1/64.

21. See Mark G. Hanna, *Pirate Nests and the Rise of the British Empire, 1570–1740* (Chapel Hill: University of North Carolina Press, 2015), 71.

22. See Hugh Amory and David D. Hall, eds., *A History of the Book in America*, vol. 1, *The Colonial Book in the Atlantic World* (Cambridge: Cambridge University Press, 1999).

23. As cited in Hanna, *Pirate Nests and the Rise of the British Empire*, 391–92.

24. See Clement Downing, *A Compendious History of the Indian Wars: With an Account of the Rise, Progress, Strength, and Forces of Angria the Pyrate. Also the Transactions of a Squadron of Men of War under Commodore Matthews, Sent to the East Indies to Suppress the Pyrates. To Which Is Annex'd, an Additional History of the Wars between the Great Mogul, Angria, and His Allies. With an Account of the Life and Actions of John Plantain, a Notorious Pyrate at Madagascar; His Wars with the Natives on That Island, Where Having Continued Eight Years, He Join'd Angria, and Was Made His Chief Admiral* (London: T. Cooper, 1737).

25. Downing, *A Compendious History of the Indian Wars*, iii.

26. Baer, "Letter from Captain Ogle to Admiralty Office," September 3, 1722, 78.

27. Baer, "The Tryal of All the Pyrates, Lately Taken by Captain Ogle," 71.

28. BNA ADM 106/759/27.

29. "London, April 3," *American Weekly Mercury*, July 1–8, 1725.

30. See BNA PROB 5.5959 and PROB 31.354.220, the documents of John Ogilvie and Boatswain Edward Burges of the *Swallow*.

31. BNA PC 1.4.34.

32. John Atkins, *Voyage to Guinea, Brazil, and the West Indies in the HMS Swallow Weymouth* (London: Frank Cass and Co., 1735), 188.

33. The gun-slave cycle hypothesis was first named and introduced to scholarship by Sir Walter Rodney's *How Europe Underdeveloped Africa*. Since then, a slew of scholars has confirmed and expanded upon this idea, showing the different ways that European traffickers of people in Africa used the arms trade to strategically forge alliances, destroy competitors or uncooperative locals, and ensure an evergreen supply of enslaved captives to transport across the Atlantic. See Nathan Nunn, "The Long Term Effects of Africa's Slave Trades," *Quarterly Journal of Economics* 123, no. 1 (2008): 139–76; Warren Whatley and Rob Gillezeau, "The Fundamental Impact of the Slave Trade on African Economies," in *Economic Evolution and Revolution in Historical Time*, ed. Paul Rhode, Joshua Rosenbloom, and David Weiman (Stanford, CA: Stanford University Press, 2011); Ivor Wilks, *Forests of Gold: Essays on the Akan and the Kingdom of Asante* (Athens: Ohio University Press, 1999); John Thornton, *Warfare in Atlantic Africa, 1500–1800* (London: University College of London Press, 1999); Kea, "Firearms and Warfare on the Gold and Slave Coasts," 185–213; and Warren Whatley, "The Gun-Slave Hypothesis and the 18th Century British Slave Trade," *Munich Personal RePEc Archive*, MPRA Paper No. 80050, posted July 8, 2017, https://mpra.ub.uni-muenchen.de/80050/.

34. See Alvin O. Thompson, *Flight to Freedom: African Runaways and Maroons in the Americas* (Kingston, Jamaica: University of the West Indies Press, 2006); Orlando Patterson, "Slavery and Slave Revolts: A Sociohistorical Analysis of the First Maroon War, 1665–1740," in *Maroon Societies: Rebel Slave Communities in the Americas*, ed. Richard Price (New York: Anchor Books, 1973); Philip Wright, "War and Peace with the Maroons, 1730–1739," *Caribbean Quarterly* 16, no. 1 (1970): 5–27; and Richard B. Sheridan, "The Maroons of Jamaica, 1730–1830: Livelihood, Demography, and Health," *Slavery & Abolition* 6, no. 3 (1985): 152–72.

35. See *A True and Genuine Copy of the Trial of Sir Chaloner Ogle Knt. Rear Admiral of the Blue, before the Chief Justice of Jamaica, for an Assault on the Person of his Excellency Edward Trelawney Esq; Captain-General, General and Commander in Chief of the Said Island. Now Published, in Order to Correct the Errors, and Supply the Defects of a Thing Lately Pub-*

lished, Called The Trial of Sir Chaloner Ogle Knt. &c. (London: M. Cooper, 1743). For a breakdown as to the events and conflicts that led to this trial, see Denver Brunsman, *The Evil Necessity: British Naval Impressment in the Eighteenth-Century Atlantic World* (Charlottesville: University of Virginia Press, 2013), chap. 3.

36. Atkins, *Voyage to Guinea, Brazil, and the West Indies*, 245.

37. Atkins, *Voyage to Guinea, Brazil, and the West Indies*, 245.

Chapter Eight

1. Pierluigi Valsecchi, *Power and State Formation in West Africa: Appolonia from the Sixteenth to the Eighteenth Century* (New York: Palgrave Macmillian, 2011), 145.

2. Roberto Zaugg, "Grossfriedrichsburg, the First German Colony in Africa? Brandenburg-Prussia, Atlantic Entanglements and National Memory," in *Shadows of Empire in West Africa: New Perspectives on European Fortifications*, ed. John Kwadwo Osei-Tutu and Victoria Ellen Smith (Cham, Switzerland: Springer International, 2017), 44.

3. Valsecchi, *Power and State Formation in West Africa*, 155–57.

4. NA WIC 105, August, 14, 1721.

5. Valsecchi, *Power and State Formation in West Africa*, 259n.65, 156–57.

6. John Atkins, *Voyage to Guinea, Brazil, and the West Indies in the HMS Swallow Weymouth* (London: Frank Cass and Co., 1735), 188.

7. R. A. Kea, "Firearms and Warfare on the Gold and Slave Coasts from the Sixteenth to the Nineteenth Centuries," *The Journal of African History* 12, no. 2 (1971): 185–213, 189.

8. Kea, "Firearms and Warfare," 192.

9. This quote is from Willem Bosman's 1704 published travel account of the Komenda Wars and Dutch holdings on the Gold Coast titled *An Accurate Description of the Guinean Gold, Ivory, and Slave Coast*, as cited in Kea, "Firearms and Warfare," 194. Bosman was sixteen years old when he arrived in Africa with the WIC in 1688. He spent fourteen years at Elmina working with the company's trade in captive Africans. To read more about Bosman's life, see chapter 1 of John Parker's *In My Time of Dying: A History of Death and the Dead in West Africa* (Princeton, NJ: Princeton University Press, 2021), 9–25.

10. Kea, "Firearms and Warfare," 196.

11. James Houstoun, *Some New and Accurate Observations Geographical, Natural and Historical. Containing a True and Impartial Account of the Situation, Product, and Natural History of the Coast of Guinea, So Far As Relates to the Improvement of That Trade, for the Advantage of Great Britain in General, and the Royal African Company in Particular. By James Houstoun, M. D. Humbly Address'd to the Honourable the Court of Assistants of the Royal African Company of Great Britain* (London: J. Peele, 1725), 16–18.

12. John Parker, *In My Time of Dying*, 107–10.

13. Houstoun, *Some New and Accurate Observations*, 44–45.

14. Houstoun, *Some New and Accurate Observations*, 61.

15. Houstoun, *Some New and Accurate Observations*, 36–37.

16. Atkins, *Voyage to Guinea, Brazil, and the West Indies*, 87.

17. Daaku, *Trade and Politics on the Gold Coast*, 139.

18. Houstoun, *Some New and Accurate Observations*, 18–19.

19. Houstoun, *Some New and Accurate Observations*, 20.

20. Daaku, *Trade and Politics on the Gold Coast*, 140.

21. Agreement between Director General Houtman and John Konny, Nov. 22, 1722, NA WIC 122.

22. Albert van Dantzig, *Forts and Castles of Ghana* (Accra, Ghana: Sedco Publishing, 1980), 52.

23. Daaku, *Trade and Politics on the Gold Coast*, 236.

24. Henk den Heijer, *Goud, ivoor en slaven: scheepvaart en handel van de Tweede Westinddische Compagnie op Afrika, 1674–1740* (Zutphen, the Netherlands: Walburg Pers, 1997), 260.

25. Valsecchi, *Power and State Formation in West Africa*, 159.

26. Daaku, *Trade and Politics on the Gold Coast*, 141.

27. William Smith, *A New Voyage to Guinea Describing the Customs, Manners, Soil, Climate, Habits, Buildings, Education, Manual Arts, Agriculture, Trade, Employments, Languages, Ranks of Distinction, Habitations, Diversions, Marriages, and Whatever Else Is Memorable among the Inhabitants, Likewise, an Account of their Animals, Minerals, &c. with Great Variety of Entertaining Incidents, Worthy of Observation, That Happen'd during the Author's Travels in That Large Country* (London: John Nourse, 1744), 118.

28. Crimpelman to the Ten Gentlemen, March 25, 1725, as cited in den Heijer, *Goud, ivoor en slaven*, 260 (my translation).

29. Valsecchi, *Power and State Formation in West Africa*, 160.

30. Den Heijer, *Goud, ivoor en slaven*, 261.

31. Edward Long, *The History of Jamaica or, General Survey of the Antient and Modern State of the Island: with Reflections on its Situation, Settlements, Inhabitants, Climate, Products, Commerce, Laws, and Government*, vol. 2 (London: T. Lowndes, 1774), 424.

32. Bethel Clement, "Junkanoo in the Bahamas," *Caribbean Quarterly* 36, no. 3/4 (1990): 1–28, 8.

33. Swithin Wilmot, "The Politics of Protest in Free Jamaica—the Kingston John Canoe Christmas Riots, 1840 and 1841," *Caribbean Quarterly* 36, no. 3/4 (1990): 65–75. For modern interpretations of this festival and others in this vein, see *Digital Junkanoo*, a collaborative curatorial and design studio by Tao Leigh Goffe dedicated to the carnival arts and ceremonies of the diaspora: www.digitaljunkanoo.com.

CHAPTER NINE

1. Robin Law, *Ouidah: The Social History of a West African Slaving Port, 1727–1892* (Athens: Ohio University Press, 2005), 31.

2. Law, *Ouidah*, 30.

3. Bullfinch Lambe, as cited in William Smith, *A New Voyage to Guinea Describing the Customs, Manners, Soil, Climate, Habits, Buildings, Education, Manual Arts, Agriculture, Trade, Employments, Languages, Ranks of Distinction, Habitations, Diversions, Marriages, and Whatever Else Is Memorable among the Inhabitants, Likewise, an Account of Their Animals, Minerals, &c. with Great Variety of Entertaining Incidents, Worthy of Observation, That Happen'd during the Author's Travels in That Large Country* (London: John Nourse, 1744), 186–87.

4. I. A. Akinjogbin, "Agaja and the Conquest of the Coastal Aja States 1724–30," *Journal of the Historical Society of Nigeria* 2, no. 4 (1963): 547.

5. Law, *Ouidah*, 44.

6. Akinjogbin, "Agaja and the Conquest of the Coastal Aja States," 545–66, 546.

7. Snelgrave, as cited in Akinjogbin, "Agaja and the Conquest of the Coastal Aja States," 549.

8. See entry for the *Katherine*, ID 75248, Slave Voyages Database, www.slavevoyages.org, accessed October 31, 2022.

9. William Snelgrave, *A New Account of Some Parts of Guinea, and the Slave-Trade: Containing, I. The History of the Late Conquest of the Kingdom of Whidaw by the King of Dahomè . . . II. The Manner How the Negroes*

*Become Slaves . . . III. A Relation of the Author's Being Taken by Pirates,
and the Many Dangers He Underwent* (London: Frank Cass, 1971), 28.

10. Snelgrave, *A New Account*, 17.

11. Snelgrave, *A New Account*, 75.

12. Snelgrave, *A New Account*, 62.

13. Neil Polhemus, "A Dialogue with King Agaja: William Snelgrave's 1727 Ardra Diary and the Contours of Dahomian-European Commercial Exchange," *History in Africa* 43 (2016): 43.

14. Polhemus, "A Dialogue with King Agaja," 43.

15. Snelgrave, *A New Account*, 62–66.

16. Smith, *A New Voyage*, 266–67.

17. Akinjogbin, "Agaja and the Conquest of the Coastal Aja States," 550.

18. Polhemus, "A Dialogue with King Agaja," 29–62.

19. Snelgrave, *A New Account*, 77.

20. Snelgrave, *A New Account*, 31, 48–49.

21. Snelgrave, *A New Account*, 46–47.

22. Robin Law, "Human Sacrifice in Pre-Colonial West Africa," *African Affairs* 84, no. 334 (1985): 53–87.

23. Snelgrave, *A New Account*, 78.

24. Snelgrave, as cited in Polhemus, "A Dialogue with King Agaja," 54.

25. See Sowande Mustakeem, "'She Must Go Overboard & Shall Go Overboard': Diseased Bodies and the Spectacle of Murder at Sea," *Atlantic Studies* 8, no. 3 (201): 201–316 and Sowande Mustakeem, "'I Never Have Such a Sickly Ship Before': Diet, Disease, and Mortality in 18th Century Atlantic Slaving Voyages," *The Journal of African American History* 93, no. 4 (2008): 474–96.

26. See Philip Boucher, *Cannibal Encounters: Europeans and Island Caribs, 1492–1763* (Baltimore: Johns Hopkins University Press, 2009); Hilary Beckles, "Kalinago (Carib) Resistance to European Colonization of the Caribbean," *Caribbean Quarterly* 38 (1992): 1–124; Surekha Davies, *Renaissance Ethnography and the Invention of the Human: New Worlds, Maps, and Monsters* (Cambridge: Cambridge University Press, 2016), 65–104; and Basil A. Reid, *Myths and Realities of Caribbean History* (Tuscaloosa: University of Alabama Press, 2009), 88–99.

27. Erin Stone, "Chasing 'Caribs': Defining Zones of Legal Indigenous Enslavement in the Circum-Caribbean, 1493–1542," in *Slaving Zones: Cultural Identities, Ideologies, and the Institutions in the Evolution of Global Slavery* (Leiden: Brill, 2017), 118–47.

28. Snelgrave, *A New Account*, preface.

29. H. M. Feinberg and William Smith, "An Eighteenth-Century Case of Plagiarism: William Smith's 'A New Voyage to Guinea,'" *History in Africa* 6 (1979): 45–50.

30. Smith, *A New Voyage*, 117.

31. Smith, *A New Voyage*, 117–18.

32. See Alexandra Ganser, *Crisis and Legitimacy in Atlantic American Narratives of Piracy, 1678–1865* (Cham: Palgrave Macmillan, 2020).

33. Angela Sutton, *Competition and the Mercantile Culture of the Gold Coast Slave Trade in the Atlantic World Economy, 1620–1720* (PhD diss., Vanderbilt University, 2014), 104–15. See also Wyatt MacGaffey, "African Objects and the Idea of Fetish," *RES: Anthropology and Aesthetics* 25 (1994): 123–31.

34. Edna Bay, *Asen, Ancestors, and Vodun: Tracing Change in African Art* (Chicago: University of Illinois Press, 2008), 15–22.

35. Law, *Human Sacrifice*, 67.

36. Law, *Human Sacrifice*, 56.

37. Edna G. Bay, *Wives of the Leopard: Gender, Politics, and Culture in the Kingdom of Dahomey* (Charlottesville: University of Virginia Press, 1998).

38. Law, *Human Sacrifice*, 73.

39. Law, *Human Sacrifice*, 63.

40. Manisha Sinha, *The Slave's Cause: A History of Abolition* (New Haven: Yale University Press, 2016).

41. Walter Rodney, *How Europe Underdeveloped Africa* (Washington: Howard University Press, 1972).

42. Kea, *Firearms and Warfare*, 185–213.

43. Law, "Human Sacrifice," 75.

44. Law, "Human Sacrifice," 87.

45. Law, "Human Sacrifice," 77.

46. The story analyzed here is in the section of Snelgrave's narrative labeled "introduction" but is not paginated.

47. Snelgrave, *A New Account*, introduction.

48. Ibram X. Kendi, *Stamped from the Beginning: The Definitive History of Racist Ideas in America* (New York: Nation Books, 2016), 10.

49. Eric Robert Taylor, *If We Must Die: Shipboard Insurrections in the Era of the Atlantic Slave Trade* (Baton Rouge: Louisiana State University Press, 2009); Bruce Chadwick, *The Creole Rebellion: The Most Successful Slave Revolt in American History* (Albuquerque: University of New Mexico Press, 2022).

50. Manisha Sinha, *The Slave's Cause: A History of Abolition* (New Haven, CT: Yale University Press, 2016), 9–33; Kendi, *Stamped from the Beginning*, 4.

51. Mahdi Adamu, "The Delivery of Slaves from the Bight of Benin in the Eighteenth and Nineteenth Centuries," in *The Uncommon Market: Essays in the Economic History of the Atlantic Slave Trade*, ed. H. A. Gemery and J. S. Hogendorn (New York: Academic Press, 1979), 163–80.

52. Andrea Weindl, *Die Kurbrandenburger im 'atlantischen System', 1650–1720* (Cologne: University of Cologne, 2001), 81.

53. Angela Sutton and Charlton W. Yingling, "Projections of Desire and Design in Early Modern Caribbean Maps," *The Historical Journal* 63, no. 4 (2020): 789–810.

54. The Atlantic Slave Trade Database, accessed October 22, 2022.

CHAPTER TEN

1. See Mariana P. Candido and Adam Jones, eds. *African Women in the Atlantic World: Property, Vulnerability & Mobility, 1660–1880* (Notre Dame, IN: University of Notre Dame, 2019).

2. Babacar M'baye, "The Economic, Political, and Social Impact of the Atlantic Slave Trade on Africa," *The European Legacy* 11, no. 6 (2006): 607–22.

3. "Chaloner Ogle to the Admiralty Office," September 3, 1722, in Joel H. Baer, ed., *British Piracy in the Golden Age: History and Interpretation, 1660–1730*, vol. 3 (London: Pickering & Chatto, 2007), 76–78.

4. To explore the vast legacy of slavery in Great Britain alone, see the work being done by the Centre for the Study of the Legacies of British Slavery. Its website, www.ucl.c.uk/lbs/legacies/, contains multiple databases, inventories, estates, and publications to browse.

5. See Joseph Miller, *Way of Death: Merchant Capitalism and the Angolan Slave Trade, 1730–1830* (Madison: University of Wisconsin Press, 1988); Mariana Candido, *An African Slaving Port and the Atlantic World: Benguela and Its Hinterland* (Cambridge: Cambridge University Press, 2013); Mariana Armond Dias Paes, "Shared Atlantic Legal Culture: The Case of a Freedom Suit in Benguela," *Global Currents* 17, no. 3 (2020): 419–40; Keila Grinberg, "Re-enslavement, Rights, and Justice in Nineteenth-Century Brazil," in *Direitos e justiças: ensaios de história social*, ed. Silvia Lara and Joseli Mendonça (Campinas, Brazil: Editora da Unicamp, 2006): 101–28; and Celso Thomas Castilho, *Slave Emancipa-*

tion and Transformations in Brazilian Political Citizenship (Pittsburgh, PA: University of Pittsburgh Press, 2016).

6. Jeroen Dewulf, "Emulating a Portuguese Model: The Slave Policy of the West India Company and the Dutch Reformed Church in Dutch Brazil (1630–1654) and New Netherland (1614–1664) in Comparative Perspective," *Journal of Early American History* 4, no. 1 (2014): 3–36.

7. Gerhard de Kok and Harvey M. Feinberg, "Captured on the Gold Coast: 'Illegal' Enslavement, Freedom, and the Pursuit of Justice in Dutch Courts, 1746–1750," *Journal of Global Slavery* 1, no. 2–3 (2016): 274–95.

8. Jaap Jacobs, *The Colony of New Netherland: A Dutch Settlement in Seventeenth-Century America* (Ithaca, NY: Cornell University Press, 2009); Ellis L. Raesly, *Portrait of New Netherland* (New York: Columbia University Press, 1945), 162.

9. Thelma Wills Foote, *Black and White Manhattan: The History of Racial Formation in Colonial New York City* (Oxford: Oxford University Press, 2004).

10. Jane Landers, *Black Society in Spanish Florida* (Chicago: University of Illinois Press, 1999); Kathleen Deagan and Darcie MacMahon, *Fort Mose: Colonial America's Black Fortress of Freedom* (Gainesville: University Press of Florida, 1995). For those able to go to northern Florida, Fort Mose Historic State Park hosts the remains of the site, as well as a visitor center with exhibits and living history displays that are well worth a visit. There are also online exhibits at the Florida Museum's website: www .floridamuseum.ufl.edu/exhibits/online/fort-mose/.

11. "The 'Code Noir' (1685)," in *Le Code Noir ou recueil des reglements rendus jusq'a present* (Paris: Prault, 1767; Societé, d'Histoire de la Guadeloupe, 1980), trans. John Garrigus.

12. To read more about the population growth among the enslaved population of British North America, see David J. Hacker, "From '20 and Odd' to 10 Million: The Growth of the Slave Population in the United States," *Slavery & Abolition* 41, no. 4 (2020): 840–55. Hacker calculates a total of ten million enslaved people of African descent existed in what would become the United States throughout the centuries in which enslavement was legal. Enslavers forcibly extracted an estimated 410 billion hours of unpaid labor from them.

13. David Eltis, "'Methodology,' Trans-Atlantic Slave Trade—Understanding the Database," The Atlantic Slave Trade Database, 2018, www.slavevoyages.org/voyage/about#methodology/introduction/0/en/.

14. See the entire school of thought generated from Eric Williams, *Capitalism and Slavery* (Chapel Hill: University of North Carolina Press,

1944). The ways in which capitalism and slavery are intimately and iteratively linked are a perennial topic among economic historians and historians of slavery, and Williams's thesis is at the heart of most of the advances that have been made on the topic.

15. See Kwame Nimako, Amy Abdou, and Glenn Willemsen, "Chattel Slavery and Racism: A Reflection on the Dutch Experience," in *Dutch Racism*, ed. Philomena Essed and Isabel Hoving (Leiden: Brill, 2014), 31–51.

16. Herbert C. Covey and Dwight Eisnach, eds., "Louisiana's Code Noir (Black Code) (1724)," in *Daily Life of African Americans in Primary Documents*, vol 1 (Santa Barbara, CA: Greenwood, 2021), 229–35.

17. Sidney Chalhoub, "The Precariousness of Freedom in a Slave Society (Brazil in the Nineteenth Century)," *International Review of Social History* 56, no. 3 (2011): 405–39.

18. Guillaume Aubert, "'To Establish One Law and Definite Rules': Race, Religion, and the Transatlantic Origins of the Louisiana Code Noir," in *Louisiana: Crossroads of the Atlantic World*, ed. Cécile Vidal (Philadelphia: University of Pennsylvania Press, 2014), 21–43.

19. See Ira Berlin, *Many Thousands Gone: The First Two Centuries of Slavery in North America* (Cambridge, MA: Harvard University Press, 1998).

20. Matthew Desmond, "Capitalism," in *The 1619 Project: A New Origin Story*, ed. Nikole Hannah-Jones, Caitlin Roper, Ilena Silverman, and Jake Silverstein (New York: Random House, 2021), 195–226.

21. Betty L. Wilson, "Under the Brutal Watch: A Historical Examination of Slave Patrols in the United States and Brazil during the 18th and 19th Centuries," *Journal of Black Studies* 53, no. 1 (2022): 3–18.

22. Ibram X. Kendi, *Stamped from the Beginning: The Definitive History of Racist Ideas in America* (New York: Nation Books, 2016), 2–3.

23. Kendi, *Stamped from the Beginning*, 41–42.

24. Jennifer L. Morgan, "Partus Sequitur Ventrem: Law, Race, and Reproduction in Colonial Slavery," *Small Axe: A Journal of Criticism* 22, no. 1 (2018): 1–17.

25. W. E. B. Du Bois, "The Souls of White Folk," in *Writings*, ed. W. E. B. Du Bois (New York: Library of America, 1987); Theodore W. Allen, *The Invention of the White Race: The Origin of Racial Oppression* (London: Verso, 2022); David R. Roediger, *How Race Survived US History: From Settlement and Slavery to the Eclipse of Post-Racialism* (London: Verso, 2019).

26. Jennifer Roth-Gordon, *Race and the Brazilian Body: Blackness, Whiteness, and Everyday Language in Rio de Janeiro* (Oakland: University of California Press, 2017).

27. James C. King, *The Biology of Race* (Berkeley: University of California Press, 2022).

28. Robert L. Reece, "Whitewashing Slavery: Legacy of Slavery and White Social Outcomes," *Social Problems* 67, no. 2 (2020): 304–23.

EPILOGUE

1. David J. Hacker "From '20. and Odd' to 10 Million: The Growth of the Slave Population in the United States," *Slavery & Abolition* 41, no. 4 (2020): 840–55.

2. See Douglas A. Blackmon, *Slavery by Another Name: The Reenslavement of Black People in America from the Civil War to World War II* (New York: Anchor Books, 2008); and Michelle Alexander, *The New Jim Crow: Mass Incarceration in the Age of Colorblindness* (New York: The New Press, 2012).

3. Ibram X. Kendi, *Stamped from the Beginning: The Definitive History of Racist Ideas in America* (New York: Nation Books, 2016), 9–10.

4. Friedrich Nietzsche, *On the Advantages and Disadvantages of History for Life* (Indianapolis: Hackett, 1980).

Index

Acqua, 212
Adjoba, 19–20
Adom people, 8, 178, 187
Agaja, king, 195f, 196–202, 208,
  211, 217
Ahanta people, xxi, 3, 6–8, 16, 20,
  171, 178, 186, 204
Akinjogbin, Isaac Adeagbo, 197
Allada kingdom, 194, 196
Americas: Black Bart and, 72;
  enslavement before 1722, 221–
  23; models of slavery in, xxii–
  xxiii, 144–45, 215–16, 220–35;
  number of enslaved persons in,
  225, 226t; printing presses in,
  166–67
Angola, 164
Angre, Kanhoji, 82, 168
Anomabo, 61–62
Anta, 7
Anthony, Mary and Thomas,
  169–70
Aowin people, 176–77, 179, 187,
  191
Apani, ambassador, 5

Apollonia, kingdom of, 191
Appre, 19, 22
arms trading, 176–81, 187
Armstrong, Robert, 114–15, 136
Asameni, 177
Ashanti people, xx, 7–8, 21, 23,
  121, 170–71, 191, 207; and
  arms trading, 176–79; and
  battle of Cape Lopez, 144;
  Cabes and, 14–15; Conny and,
  25; term, xv
Ashplant, Valentine, 77, 149, 160
Atkins, John: on African rulers,
  92–93, 121; on Ashanti, 179;
  on battle of Cape Lopez, 133,
  135; on Black people, 146,
  152; on Cape Coast Castle,
  154; on Conny, 112, 119–20,
  170–71; on defeat of Conny,
  175–92; on famine, 105;
  and historiography, 107; on
  insurrection, 104, 146, 151;
  and Jamaica, 172–73; on
  pirate damage, 88; on Pokesu,
  110–12; on race, 85–87; on

265

Wasa, 21, 23, 25, 176–80, 187,
190
water issues: Conny and, 107,
114; freshwater con, 47–48;
seawater poisoning, 106
West Africa, iii*f*, 11*f*, 164–66;
arms trading in, 176–81, 187;
changes in, 7–8, 176–77, 200,
209–10, 219–21; historiography
of, 199; military forces in,
21–22, 26, 180, 186–87, 200,
208–11; number of enslaved
persons taken from, 224; piracy
in, 82; power struggle in, 1–29

West India Company (WIC). *See*
Dutch/Netherlands
White supremacy: development of,
57, 230–35; effects of, 237
Wilson, captain, 39
Wilson, George, 164–65
Withstandyenot, Thomas "Bright
Tom," 134
Wood, Richard, 127

yellow fever, 117–19

Zeneman, Johannes, 50
Zunglar, 200